Process-Tracing Methods: Foundations and Guidelines

Derek Beach and Rasmus Brun Pedersen have written the first practical guide for using process-tracing in social science research. They begin by introducing a more refined definition of process-tracing, differentiating it into three distinct variants, and explaining the applications for and limitations of each. The authors develop the underlying logic of process-tracing, including how one should understand causal mechanisms and how Bayesian logic enables strong within-case inferences. They provide instructions for identifying the variant of process-tracing most appropriate for the research question at hand and a set of guidelines for each stage of the research process (i.e., working with theories, developing empirical tests, working with evidence, selecting case studies, and nesting case studies in mixed-method designs).

This book makes three major contributions to the methodological literature on case studies. First, it develops the underlying logic of process-tracing methods in a level of detail that has not been presented previously and thus establishes a standard for their use. Second, by explaining the application of Bayesian logic to process-tracing methods, it provides a coherent framework for drawing strong inferences within cases. Finally, it offers the first coherent set of tools and standards for graduate students as well as scholars eager to use process-tracing methods in their research.

Derek Beach is Associate Professor of Political Science at the University of Aarhus, Denmark.

Rasmus Brun Pedersen is Associate Professor of Political Science at the University of Aarhus, Denmark.

Process-Tracing Methods

Foundations and Guidelines

Derek Beach *and* Rasmus Brun Pedersen

The University of Michigan Press
Ann Arbor

Published in the United States of America by
The University of Michigan Press
Manufactured in the United States of America
♾ Printed on acid-free paper

2016   2015   2014   2013   4   3   2   1

A CIP catalog record for this book is available from the British Library.

Library of Congress Cataloging-in-Publication Data

Beach, Derek.
    Process-tracing methods : foundations and guidelines / Derek Beach and
Rasmus Brun Pedersen.
        p.   cm.
    Includes bibliographical references and index.
    ISBN 978-0-472-07189-0 (cloth : alk. paper) —
    ISBN 978-0-472-05189-2 (pbk. : alk. paper) —
    ISBN 978-0-472-02885-6 (e-book)
    1. Social sciences—Methodology.   2. Social sciences—Research—
Methodology.   3. Social sciences—Case studies.   I. Pedersen, Rasmus
Brun, 1978–   II. Title.
    H61.B37   2013
    300.1'15—dc23
                                                    2012042617

Contents

Acknowledgments

This book is dedicated to the memory of our colleague, the late Professor Lise Togeby, and her intellectual curiosity. Six years ago, she asked us two innocuous questions: "What is process-tracing, and how is it different from historical methods or traditional case study methodology?" We were unable to provide her with a satisfactory answer at the time. Six years and one book later, we feel reasonably confident that we can answer the question.

We are in debt to the growing volume of work from the qualitative, post-KKV methodological community, especially John Gerring's *Case Study Research* and Alexander George and Andrew Bennett's *Case Studies and Theory Development in the Social Sciences*. We would have been unable to build up the foundations of process-tracing methodology without the pioneering work of these scholars.

We are also thankful for the opportunity to present our work at conferences and workshops; in particular, we thank the participants on panels on process-tracing and qualitative case study methods at the APSA 2010 and 2011 annual meetings as well as the participants in a research seminar at the University of Oldenburg in November 2010. We also thank the external reviewers for the detailed and perceptive comments that significantly improved the manuscript.

Finally, we thank the doctoral students who have attended our courses on process-tracing and case study methods both at the Department of Political Science, University of Aarhus, and at the ECPR Summer School in Slovenia. Teaching such bright students is a privilege and a challenge. Many of the points in this book developed out of classroom discussions about the strengths, weaknesses, and applicability of techniques in different research situations. We hope that the resulting book will prove useful for a new generation of qualitative scholars.

Derek Beach and Rasmus Brun Pedersen
Aarhus, Denmark
December 2011

CHAPTER I

Process-Tracing in the Social Sciences

You know a conjurer gets no credit when once he has explained his
trick; and if I show you too much of my method of working, you will
come to the conclusion that I am a very ordinary individual after all.
—Sherlock Holmes (A. C. Doyle 2010: 33)

The essence of process-tracing research is that scholars want to go beyond
merely identifying correlations between independent variables (Xs) and outcomes (Ys). For example, a strong statistical correlation has been found between democracy and peace (Oneal, Russett, and Berbaum 2004). Yet how
do we know that mutual democracy was the cause of peace between two
nations? How does democracy produce more peaceful relations? Answering these questions requires that we unpack the causal relationship between
mutual democracy and peace to study the causal mechanism linking the two
concepts.

Process-tracing in social science is commonly defined by its ambition to
trace causal mechanisms (Bennett 2008a, 2008b; Checkel 2008; George and
Bennett 2005). A causal mechanism can be defined as "a complex system,
which produces an outcome by the interaction of a number of parts" (Glennan 1996: 52). Process-tracing involves "attempts to identify the intervening
causal process—the causal chain and causal mechanism—between an independent variable (or variables) and the outcome of the dependent variable"
(George and Bennett 2005: 206–7).

Investigating causal mechanisms enables us to go a step further when
studying causal relationships, allowing us to "peer into the box of causality
to locate the intermediate factors lying between some structural cause and its
purported effect" (Gerring 2007a: 45). Yet process-tracing methods are argu-

ably the only method that allows us to study causal mechanisms. Studying causal mechanisms with process-tracing methods enables the researcher to make strong within-case inferences about the causal process whereby outcomes are produced, enabling us to update the degree of confidence we hold in the validity of a theorized causal mechanism. Process-tracing therefore represents "an invaluable method that should be included in every researcher's repertoire" (George and Bennett 2005: 224).

Process-tracing methods have recently experienced a surge in popularity within qualitative social science, with numerous doctoral students and established scholars attempting to use process-tracing methods in their research (e.g., Bennett and Elman 2006a, 2006b; Elman 2004; Hall 2008; Jacobs 2004; Khong 1992; Lehtonen 2008; Owen 1994). Yet despite the widespread use of process-tracing in empirical research and an increasing body of methodological literature on process-tracing and causal mechanisms, we still do not possess a clear and coherent framework for how and when valid inferences can be made using process-tracing. We also lack a set of concrete guidelines for using the methods in practice. This deficiency has prevented process-tracing from fulfilling its potential of enabling us to open up the black box of causality using in-depth case study methods to make strong within-case inferences about causal mechanisms.

In this book, we seek to reveal how the trick is performed. In so doing, we show readers that process-tracing is an "ordinary" social science method, like many others, with comparative strengths and weaknesses. It is not a panacea, but when applied in appropriate research situations, it can enable us to make strong within-case causal inferences about causal mechanisms based on in-depth single-case studies that are arguably not possible with other social science methods.

1.1. Defining Process-Tracing

Process-tracing methods are tools to study causal mechanisms in a single-case research design. While scholars generally agree that process-tracing methods can be defined by their ambition to trace causal mechanisms, the existing literature retains considerable confusion about both the ontological and epistemological foundations of process-tracing methods and guidelines for what good process-tracing entails in practice. Basic questions such as what types of causal mechanisms are being traced and to what degree process-tracing case studies can be nested in broader, mixed-method research designs have been left relatively unanswered. The resulting lack of coherent foundations and concrete guidelines has prevented the method from fulfilling its potential.

This confusion results partly from the literature's definition of process-tracing as a single research method. A lot of the murkiness about what process-tracing is and how it should be used in practice can be cleared up by differentiating process-tracing into three variants within social science: theory-testing, theory-building, and explaining-outcome. The three differ along several dimensions, including whether they are theory- or case-centric, the types of inferences being made, how they understand causal mechanisms, and whether and how they can be nested in mixed-method designs.

Theory-testing process-tracing deduces a theory from the existing literature and then tests whether evidence shows that each part of a hypothesized causal mechanism is present in a given case, enabling within-case inferences about whether the mechanism functioned as expected in the case and whether the mechanism as a whole was present. No claims can be made, however, about whether the mechanism was the only cause of the outcome.

Theory-building process-tracing seeks to build a generalizable theoretical explanation from empirical evidence, inferring that a more general causal mechanism exists from the facts of a particular case. Although this type of process-tracing is analytically useful, to our knowledge, the literature offers no guidelines about how to proceed with this approach.

Finally, explaining-outcome process-tracing attempts to craft a minimally sufficient explanation of a puzzling outcome in a specific historical case. Here the aim is not to build or test more general theories but to craft a (minimally) sufficient explanation of the outcome of the case where the ambitions are more case-centric than theory-oriented. This distinction reflects the case-centric ambitions of many qualitative scholars and echoes arguments found in the burgeoning literature on topics such as eclectic theorization (where the case is front and center) (Sil and Katzenstein 2010) and pragmatism as a research strategy (Friedrichs and Kratochwill 2009). Accounting for the outcome of a case usually requires an eclectic combination of different mechanisms, some of them case-specific/nonsystematic (see chapters 2 and 4).

We do not suggest this differentiation for its own sake. Instead, by identifying three variants, we can bring alignment between what we practice and what we preach, as these differences have important methodological implications for research design that are masked when we treat process-tracing as a single method.

1.2. How Process-Tracing Differs from Other Case Study Methods

Taken together, process-tracing methods can be distinguished from most other small-n case study methods by the types of inferences being made. Process-tracing seeks to make within-case inferences about the presence/absence of causal mechanisms in single case studies, whereas most small-n methods attempt cross-case inferences about causal relationships. These different inferential ambitions require different logics of inference, resulting in fundamentally different methodologies (see chapter 5).

Few case study methods enable within-case inference, and the most prominent alternative to process-tracing is what George and Bennett term the *congruence method* (2005: chapter 9). In the congruence method, based on the value of the independent variable (X), researchers test whether the prediction about the outcome that should follow from the theory is congruent with what is found in the case, investigated either temporally or other across aspects of the outcome(s) (181–204; Büthe 2002).

The congruence method is often used as a way of structuring a narrative of a historical process, testing predicted values of X and Y at different times during an empirical process (t_0, t_1, ... t_n) (Büthe 2002). "In addition to presenting information about correlations at every step of the causal process," this type of narrative case study "can contextualize these steps in ways that make the entire process visible rather than leaving it fragmented into analytical stages" (486). For example, Tannenwald's (1999) study of the nuclear taboo involves congruence case studies where she investigates whether the observable implications of X (norms against using atomic weapons) measured as "taboo talk" or Z (material factors) measured as "materialist arguments" are present in decision-making processes within the U.S. government. She uses a historical narrative of four cases of nuclear use and nonuse and finds a strong correlation between the presence of taboo talk (X) and nonuse of nuclear weapons (Y) in three cases where nuclear weapons could conceivably have been used.

What marks the difference between the congruence method and process-tracing methods is the explicit focus on investigating causal mechanisms. Congruence investigates correlations between X and Y, whereas process-tracing investigates the workings of the mechanism(s) that contribute to producing an outcome. Process-tracing methods go beyond correlations by attempting to trace the theoretical causal mechanism(s) linking X and Y.

Process-tracing case studies usually cannot be presented in narrative form, in contrast to what Rubach (2010) and others have argued. While evidence in the form of events or temporal sequences can be relevant in testing the presence of one part of a causal mechanism, depending on the type of observable implications that are predicted (see chapter 6), other types of evidence such as pattern evidence (e.g., the number of documents produced by different agencies) can be relevant for testing other parts of the mechanism. Process-tracing case studies should therefore usually be presented as a stepwise test of each part of a causal mechanism, especially in the theory-testing variant. For example, Owen's (1994) study of the democratic peace mechanism is presented as a step-by-step test of each part of his theorized mechanism instead of a narrative of events in the case (see chapter 5).

1.3. Themes of the Book

Process-tracing methods are used when we want to gain a greater understanding of the nature of causal relationships than can be provided by other social science case study methods, such as comparative cross-case methods. However, a key deficiency in the existing methodological literature on process-tracing is the absence of sufficient exposition of the logical foundations of the method or research design, especially with regard to how process-tracing differs from other qualitative case study methods.

This book rectifies this omission by exploring in detail how the ontological and epistemological foundations of process-tracing differ from those of other case study methods, such as congruence methods or structured, focused comparisons (for more on these two methods, see George and Bennett 2005). *Ontology* refers to our understanding of the nature of the social world—specifically, here, the nature of causality. *Epistemology* refers to arguments regarding how we should best study causal relationships in the social world. The argument that we present builds on Hall's (2003: 374) assertion that research methodologies and ontology need to be aligned: "Ontology is ultimately crucial to methodology because the appropriateness of a particular set of methods for a given problem turns on the assumptions about the nature of the causal relations they are meant to discover." As chapter 3 establishes, adopting the mechanismic and deterministic ontology of causality of process-tracing implies using quite different methodological tools for empirical analysis than if a regularity understanding of causality forms the basis for theorization. Further, the goal of making within-case inferences about causal mechanisms also implies that a different logic of inference is adopted than if we are using other small-n methods such as congruence (see chapter 5).

Chapter 2 explains the three distinct variants of process-tracing, elaborating on what elements they share as well as their crucial differences, which have important methodological implications.

Chapter 3 introduces the reader to the ontological debates within the philosophy of science that deal with the nature of causality to understand how the mechanismic and deterministic understanding of causality used in process-tracing methods differs from other social science methods—in particular, large-n statistical analysis and comparative case study research. We then explore different ways of investigating causal mechanisms, including tracing empirical processes, studying them as intervening variables between X and Y, and using mechanismic, system-oriented understandings. We contend that to take seriously the study of causal mechanisms, we should adopt the mechanismic understanding in process-tracing, conceptualizing causal mechanisms as a series of parts composed of entities engaging in activities. In so doing, we focus our analytical attention on the transmission of causal forces through the mechanism. The chapter concludes with a discussion of the different theoretical levels of mechanisms along with the question of whether mechanisms can be directly observed in empirical research.

Chapter 4 deals with questions relating to the theorization of causal mechanisms. How can causal mechanisms best be conceptualized in a manner that enables empirical analysis to capture the workings of mechanisms in a case study? How can causal theories of X→Y be translated into causal mechanisms composed of a set of parts that describe the theorized process whereby an explanatory factor (variable or condition) produces an outcome? Further, how can we work backward from an outcome to build a sufficient explanation that details the causal mechanisms that produced that outcome? We discuss how theoretical concepts and causal theories should be conceptualized in process-tracing before turning to discussion of the specific challenges in working with each of the three variants of process-tracing.

In chapter 5, we discuss why mainstream inferential tools used in both classical statistical analysis and comparative methods cannot be used to make within-case inferences. Here we continue the argument that methodology must be brought in line with ontology. In particular, we illustrate that the inferential tools used in other social science methods are not applicable in process-tracing, given that we are interested in making within-case inferences about the presence/absence of causal mechanisms. We then present the Bayesian logic of inference and how it can be adapted for use as a tool for making within-case inferences in process-tracing. The chapter concludes by discussing in more detail the types of inferences that can be made using different variants of process-tracing methods and, equally important, what types of inferences cannot be made.

Chapter 6 turns to the question of developing strong empirical tests that investigate whether a hypothesized causal mechanism is present in a single case. Based on the Bayesian logic of inference, our goal in process-tracing is to update our confidence in the presence of a mechanism in light of our empirical tests. To enable updating to take place, our empirical tests need to be designed in a manner that maximizes their inferential power. Each test details the case-specific predictions for what we should expect to see in the empirical record if each part of the hypothesized causal mechanism is present in the case.

Empirical material is then gathered to see whether the predicted evidence is present. However, "raw" empirical observations need to be evaluated for their content, accuracy, and probability before they can be used as evidence that enables us to update our confidence. We discuss the evaluation process in chapter 7, introducing Bayesian-compatible tools for evaluating empirical material. If there is a strong match between the predicted and found evidence for each part of the mechanism, we can infer with a certain degree of confidence that the hypothesized causal mechanism is present in the case based on the Bayesian logic of inference (Bennett 2008a).

Finally, chapter 8 broadens the picture, looking at questions of case selection and whether, when, and how the three variants of process-tracing can be embedded in mixed-method research designs. We discuss case selection for each of the variants, showing why existing prescriptions do not always apply. The chapter argues that the theory-building and -testing variants of process-tracing can be combined with other methods in mixed-method designs, whereas explaining-outcome designs cannot be meaningfully combined with other research methods. The key difference is that the former variants focus on systematic mechanisms, enabling their theories to communicate with those used in other methods, whereas the latter includes nonsystematic, case-specific parts, the inclusion of which limits the generalizability of results.

Finally, the appendix presents a practical checklist for the use of the three different variants of process-tracing, walking through each step of the research process to offer guidelines and questions that can be used to structure a process-tracing analysis.

CHAPTER 2

The Three Different Variants of Process-Tracing and Their Uses

This chapter develops the argument that there are three different research situations in which process-tracing methods can be used, resulting in three distinct variants of process-tracing. In contrast, the state of the art treats process-tracing as a singular method, resulting in murky methodological guidelines. Whereas most case studies that use process-tracing employ a case-centric variant that we term the explaining-outcome process-tracing, most methodological works prescribe a theory-centric version of process-tracing that involves the deductive testing of whether a generalizable mechanism is present in a single case. The dissonance between what we practice and what we preach has resulted in considerable confusion about what good process-tracing is. We contend that clearer prescriptions can be developed when we differentiate process-tracing into three distinct variants.

We do not suggest this differentiation for its own sake. These differences have important methodological implications for research design that are masked when we treat process-tracing as a single method. We explore these implications throughout the rest of this book. For example, the three variants differ on key questions such as how causal mechanisms are understood, whether the purpose is to make inferences about whether a mechanism is present in a case or to account for a particular outcome, and whether they can be nested into mixed-method designs.

We first summarize the state of the art, showing that existing work on process-tracing treats it as a singular method. We then illustrate that there are three distinct research situations that call for different methodological tools, implying the need to differentiate the method into three distinct variants that reflect these different purposes. We conclude by briefly illustrating each of the three variants, showing what we are tracing in each of them and how analysis proceeds.

2.1. The State of the Art—One Method

In their chapter-length presentation of process-tracing, George and Bennett (2005) mention the range of different forms of process-tracing as they have been used in practice. The authors argue that process-tracing has been used in a variety of ways, including both detailed narratives and case studies, where "at least parts of the narrative are accompanied with explicit causal hypotheses highly specific to the case without, however, employing theoretical variables for this purpose or attempting to extrapolate the case's explanation into a generalization" (210–11). In other varieties of process-tracing, "the investigator constructs a general explanation rather than a detailed tracing of a causal process" (211). Yet in the rest of their chapter, George and Bennett treat process-tracing as a singular method, masking the differences that relate to the different uses.

More recent accounts also treat process-tracing as a single method, often defining it as a deductive tool to test whether causal mechanisms are present and function as theorized. For example Gerring (2007a: 172–85) describes a two-stage deductive research process where the analyst first clarifies the theoretical argument and then empirically verifies each stage of this model. Checkel describes process-tracing as the attempt to "trace the process in a very specific, theoretically informed way. The researcher looks for a series of theoretically predicted intermediate steps" (2008: 363). The end result is a middle-range theory. Bennett describes process-tracing as a method that involves "the examination of 'diagnostic' pieces of evidence within a case that contribute to supporting or overturning alternative explanatory hypotheses. A central concern is with sequences and mechanisms in the unfolding of hypothesized causal processes. The research looks for the observable implications of hypothesized explanations. . . . The goal is to establish whether the events or processes within the case fit those predicted by alternative explanations" (2010: 208).

Yet treating process-tracing as a singular method results in a large discrepancy between our prescriptions for good process-tracing (which rely on a relatively deductive variant of process-tracing) and what we do in practice (where many scholars want to use the method either to build theories or to account for particularly puzzling outcomes). The result of treating process-tracing as one method is a set of murky methodological guidelines, along with confused students and practitioners.

2.2. The Three Different Uses of Process-Tracing Methods

Process-tracing methods have three distinct research purposes. As illustrated in figure 2.1, distinctions exist among having the research goal of testing whether a causal mechanism is present in a case, building a theoretical mechanism, and crafting an explanation that accounts for a particular outcome. There is a clear bifurcation overall between theory-centric and case-centric process-tracing, reflecting a choice between building/testing (relatively) parsimonious causal mechanisms that can be generalized across a bounded context of cases and focusing on explaining particular outcomes through the pragmatic use of mechanismic explanations to account for the important aspects of the case.

In theory-testing process-tracing, a causal mechanism is hypothesized to be present in a population of cases of a phenomenon. The researcher selects a single case where both X and Y are present, and the context allows the mechanism to operate. Here the goal is to evaluate whether evidence shows that the hypothesized causal mechanism linking X and Y was present and that it functioned as theorized. The ambition is to go beyond correlations and associations between X and Y, opening up the black box of causality to study more directly the causal mechanism whereby X contributes to producing Y (see section 3.3).

Theory-building process-tracing involves building a theory about a causal mechanism between X and Y that can be generalized to a population of a given phenomenon, starting from a situation where we are in the dark regarding the mechanism.

Third, and most common in practice, is the situation where we want to explain a particularly puzzling historical outcome. Here the ambition is not the theory-centric one of building or testing a generalizable theorized mechanism; instead, the aim is to craft a sufficient explanation of the outcome. Instead of studying mechanisms that cause war (Y), the analysis would focus on explaining a particular outcome such as World War I.

The bifurcation into case- and theory-centric variants of process-tracing captures a core ontological and epistemological divide within the social sciences. On the theory-centric side are both neopositivist and critical realist positions, where the understanding is that the social world can be split

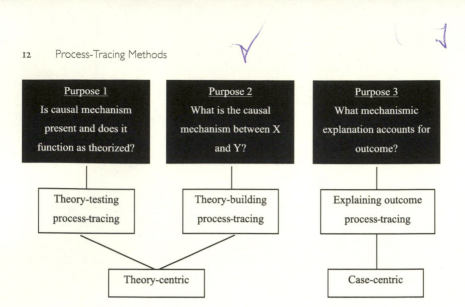

Fig. 2.1. Three different uses of process-tracing methods

into manageable parts that can be studied empirically (Jackson 2011). The ambition here is to build generalizable theories, irrespective of whether we have the more narrow ambition of working with midrange theories that are bound within specific contexts or the (perhaps unattainable) ambition to find law-like generalizations. As chapter 3 discusses, causal mechanisms in theory-centric studies are understood to be systematic factors, meaning that they can be generalized across cases that are within the context in which they are expected to operate (Falleti and Lynch 2009). Here, causal mechanisms are understood as relatively simple, parsimonious pathways whereby X contributes to producing Y, but they are not theorized as sufficient causes of Y by themselves.

Case-centric process-tracing methods operate with a different ontological understanding of the world. The philosophy of science offers many different paths to the case-centric position. One path is described by Jackson, who illustrates the difference between what he terms a dualistic ontology of mind-world relations where the world exists independent of its human observers and a monist ontology where "the objects of scientific investigation are not inert and meaningless entities that impress themselves on our (natural or augmented) senses or on our theory-informed awareness" (2011: 114). The monist ontology implies that instead of attempting what is perceived to be the mission impossible of building and testing law-like generalizations (theory-centric research), we should instead adopt a form of instrumentalism aimed at accounting for outcomes in particular cases.

Irrespective of the philosophical path to this position, case-centric researchers agree that the social world is very complex, multifactored, and extremely context-specific. This complexity makes the ambition of producing knowledge that can be generalized across many cases difficult, if not impossible. Instead, the ambition is to account for particularly puzzling outcomes.

Theories are used here in a much more pragmatic fashion—that is, as heuristic instruments that have analytical utility in providing the best possible explanation of a given phenomenon (Peirce 1955). Case-centric research scholars contend that it makes little sense to distinguish between systematic and case-specific parts, given the impossibility of generalization in the complex social world. Further, theories that are developed are much more eclectic, often including conglomerates of different mechanisms along with more case-specific mechanisms.

The ambition is not to prove that a theory is correct but instead to prove that it has utility in providing the best possible explanation. Explanations are case-specific and cannot be detached from the particular case (Humphreys 2010: 269–70) (see chapter 5).

2.3. The Three Variants of Process-Tracing

What are the core elements of each of the three variants of process-tracing? A number of commonalities exist across the three variants. For example, all variants share the goal of studying causal mechanisms. Ontological assumptions about the nature of causal relationships are also shared. These include the use of deterministic theorization and a mechanismic understanding of causation that focuses on the process whereby causal forces are transmitted through a series of interlocking parts of a mechanism to produce an outcome (see chapter 3). The three variants of process-tracing share a theoretical understanding of mechanisms as invariant; they are either present or not (see chapter 4). In addition, all three methods draw on a Bayesian logic of inference to make within-case inferences about the presence/absence of causal mechanisms (see chapter 5).

What differentiates the three variants is

- whether they are *theory-centric* or *case-centric* designs
- aim to *test* or *build* theorized causal mechanisms
- their understanding of the *generality of causal mechanisms* (from systematic mechanisms expected to be present in a set of cases [population] to case-specific mechanisms)

- the types of inferences being made, where theory-testing
  or -building variants make inferences about the *presence/absence* of
  a mechanism, whereas explaining-outcome process-tracing enables
  inferences about the *sufficiency* of the explanation to be made.

We now turn to a presentation of what each variant is actually tracing, illustrating a typical research process for each variant.

Theory-Testing Process-Tracing

In theory-testing process-tracing, we know both X and Y and we either have existing conjectures about a plausible mechanism or are able to use logical reasoning to formulate a causal mechanism from existing theorization.

Figure 2.2 illustrates a simple abstract example of a theory-testing case study. The first step in testing whether a hypothesized causal mechanism was present in the case is to conceptualize a causal mechanism between X and Y based on existing theorization along with making explicit the context within which it functions. In this example, a two-part mechanism between X and Y is deduced, with each part composed of entities engaging in activities. This theorized causal mechanism then needs to be operationalized (step 2), translating theoretical expectations into case-specific predictions of what observable manifestations each of the parts of the mechanism should have if the mechanism is present in the case. In practice, theory-testing has inductive elements, especially regarding the operationalization of empirical tests, where we draw on existing empirical work to make case-specific empirical predictions about what evidence we should see if the theory is valid (see chapter 6).

Once the mechanism and context are conceptualized and operationalized, the analyst proceeds to step 3, where she collects empirical evidence that can be used to make causal inferences, updating our confidence in (1) whether the hypothesized mechanism was present in the case and (2) whether the mechanism functioned as predicted or only some parts of the mechanism were present. The bold lines in figure 2.2 illustrate the inferences made in theory-testing process-tracing, where we infer from the empirical evidence collected that a causal mechanism was present in the case.

The empirical analysis in step 3 proceeds stepwise, testing whether evidence indicates that each part of the mechanism was present. Most important, the evidence necessary to test whether the different parts are present can be very different, making evidence for the parts noncomparable with each other. Therefore, a case study usually does not read like an analytical

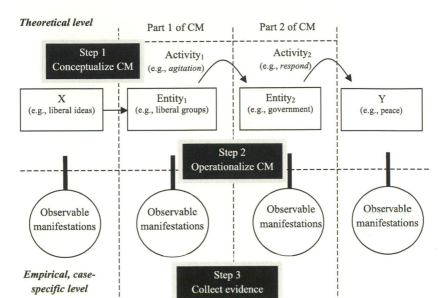

Fig. 2.2. Theory-testing process-tracing

narrative, in that while evidence in the form of events can be an observable manifestation of one part of a causal mechanism (depending on the type of observable implications that are predicted), other types of evidence, such as pattern evidence (e.g., the number of documents produced by different agencies) can be equally relevant (see section 3.3.).

What, then, are we actually tracing when we engage in theory-testing process-tracing? What is being traced is not a series of empirical events or narratives but instead the underlying theorized causal mechanism itself, by observing whether the expected case-specific implications of its existence are present in a case (see chapter 3).

Theory-testing process-tracing enables inferences to be made about whether a causal mechanism was present in a single case along with whether the mechanism functioned as expected. However, theory-testing process-tracing does not enable us to test the relative explanatory power of competing mechanisms against each other except in the rare situation where two competing mechanisms can be conceptualized so that they are composed of the same number of diametrically opposite parts with observable implications that rule each other out (see chapter 5). Further, given that we can make inferences only about whether a mechanism was present in the single case, no claims about the necessity of the mechanism can be logically made. To do so requires cross-case analysis (see chapter 8).

Theory-Building Process-Tracing

The second identifiable variant of process-tracing also has theoretical ambitions beyond the confines of the single case. In its purest form, theory-building process-tracing starts with empirical material and uses a structured analysis of this material to detect a plausible hypothetical causal mechanism whereby X is linked with Y. While it is mentioned as a possibility in the literature, this inductive, theory-building variant of process-tracing is surprisingly neglected. To our knowledge, the literature contains no attempts to show how it is done in practice.

Theory-building process-tracing is utilized in two different research situations: (1) when we know that a correlation exists between X and Y but we are in the dark regarding potential mechanisms linking the two (X-Y-centric theory building) as we have no theory to guide us; or (2) when we know an outcome (Y) but are unsure about the causes (Y-centric theory building). In the second instance, the analysis first traces backward from Y to undercover a plausible X, turning the study into an X-Y-centric analysis.

What is also being traced here is a theoretical causal mechanism that is expected to be present across a population of cases (i.e., it is a systematic mechanism). The core difference between theory-testing and -building process-tracing involves theory before fact versus fact before theory. In theory-building process-tracing, empirical material is used to build a hypothesized theory, inferring first that what is found reflects the observable implications of an underlying causal mechanism. A second leap is then made by inferring from these observable implications that they reflected an underlying causal mechanism. However, both variants share a focus on tracing a generalizable causal mechanism by detecting its empirical manifestations.

While theory-building process-tracing as an inductive method has some elements that overlap with explaining-outcome process-tracing, the key difference between the two is that theory-building process-tracing seeks to build a midrange theory describing a causal mechanism that is generalizable outside of the individual case to a bounded context (e.g., spatially or temporally bounded), whereas explaining-outcome process-tracing focuses on building a minimally sufficient explanation of the outcome in an individual case. Theory-building process-tracing studies do not claim that the detected causal mechanism is sufficient to explain the outcome.

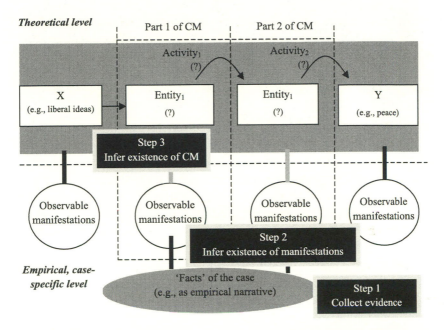

Fig. 2.3. Theory-building process-tracing. (Bold lines = direct inferences; shaded lines = indirect (secondary) inferences; shaded area = what is being traced.)

Figure 2.3 illustrates the basic framework of a theory-building process-tracing case study. After the key theoretical concepts (X and Y) are defined, theory-building proceeds to investigate the empirical material in the case (step 1), using evidence as clues about the possible empirical manifestations of an underlying causal mechanism between X and Y that fulfills the guidelines for a properly conceptualized causal mechanism (see chapters 3 and 5). This process involves an intensive and wide-ranging search of the empirical record.

Step 2 involves inferring from the observable empirical evidence that these manifestations reflect an underlying causal mechanism that was present in the case. Evidence does not speak for itself. Theory-building often has a deductive element in that scholars seek inspiration from existing theoretical work and previous observations. For example, an analyst investigating socialization of administrative officials within international organizations could seek inspiration in theories of domestic public administration or in psychological theories of small group dynamics while also reading more descriptive accounts of the workings of international organizations for plausible causal mechanisms. Here, existing theory can be conceived as a form of grid to detect systematic patterns in empirical material, enabling inferences about observable manifestations. In other situations, the search for mechanisms is based on hunches drawn from puzzles that are unresolved by existing work. In step 3, the secondary leap is made from observable manifestations to infer that they reflect an underlying causal mechanism.

Figure 2.3 illustrates that theory-building process-tracing is examining an underlying theoretical causal mechanism, depicted as the shaded area that forms the backdrop of the theoretical level (X, causal mechanism, Y). In contrast to theory-testing process building, the empirical analysis itself, understood as the collection of the "facts" of the case, is two inferential leaps removed from the theorized causal mechanism (i.e., the inferences are indirect). This is illustrated by the bold lines linking the "facts" with observable manifestations (direct inferences) and the subsequent secondary inferential leap from these observable implications to the inference that parts of an underlying causal mechanism existed.

In reality, theory-building process-tracing is usually an iterative and creative process. Hunches about what to look for that are inspired by existing theoretical and empirical work are investigated systematically, with the results of this search forming the background for further searches. This means that steps 1 and 2 are often repeated before step 3 is reached.

Explaining-Outcome Process-Tracing

The goal of many (if not most) process-tracing studies is to explain a particular interesting and puzzling outcome. While existing prescriptions for process-tracing speak almost exclusively about what we understand as the theory-centric variants, what most scholars are actually using is explaining-outcome process-tracing.

This type of process-tracing can be thought of as a single-outcome study, defined as seeking the causes of a specific outcome in a single case (Gerring 2006).[1] Here the ambition is to craft a minimally sufficient explanation of a particular outcome, with sufficiency defined as an explanation that accounts for all of the important aspects of an outcome with no redundant parts being present (Mackie 1965). This approach marks a significant departure from the two theory-centric variants. For example, in theory-testing process-tracing, no claims are made about whether the mechanism is sufficient; rather, inferences are made only about whether the postulated mechanism is present or absent in the single case.

While explaining-outcome process-tracing studies sometimes more closely resemble historical scholarship, this type of process-tracing is in our opinion still social science research, as the ultimate explanation usually involves more generalized theoretical claims than historians feel comfortable with. In addition, explaining-outcome studies often have theoretical ambitions that reach beyond the single case.

It is vital to note that the term *causal mechanism* is used in a much broader sense in explaining-outcome process-tracing than in the two theory-centric variants. First, whereas theory-testing and -building variants of process-tracing aim to test/build mechanisms that are applicable across a range of cases, crafting a minimally sufficient explanation almost always requires combining mechanisms into an eclectic conglomerate mechanism to account for a historical outcome (see chapter 3). Second, given that the ambition is case-centric and seeks to craft a minimally sufficient explanation of a particular outcome, it is usually necessary to include nonsystematic parts in the causal mechanism, defined as a mechanism that is case-specific.

Explaining-outcome process-tracing is an iterative research strategy that aims to trace the complex conglomerate of systematic and case-specific causal mechanisms that produced the outcome in question. The explanation cannot be detached from the particular case. Theorized mechanisms are therefore seen as heuristic instruments whose function is to help build the best possible explanation of a particular outcome (Humphreys 2010; Jackson 2011).

While explaining-outcome process-tracing as an iterative strategy most closely resembles abduction, which is a dialectic combination of deduction and induction (Peirce 1955), for our purposes it is more helpful to disaggregate two alternative paths that can be chosen when building the best possible explanation of an outcome—deductive and inductive paths, as shown in figure 2.4. This figure does not split the mechanism into parts, as the previous figures do, because of the complexity of a pictorial depiction of the parts of an overlapping, conglomerate mechanism.

The deductive path follows the steps described previously under theory-testing, where an existing mechanism is tested to see whether it can account for the outcome. This process is illustrated using black arrows for each of the three steps. The first arrow is where a theory is conceptualized as a mechanism. In the second step, empirical tests are developed that are then evaluated against the empirical record. Finally, the third arrow illustrates the stage where the analyst assesses whether a sufficient explanation has been crafted.

However, in most explaining-outcome studies, existing theorization cannot provide a sufficient explanation, resulting in a second stage of research

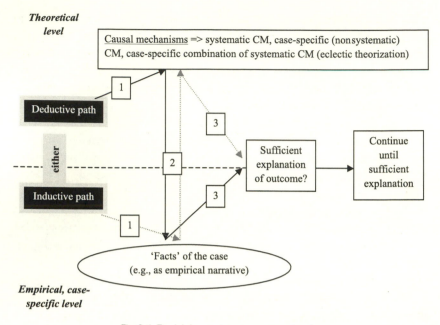

Fig. 2.4. Explaining-outcome process-tracing

where either a deductive or inductive path can be chosen, informed by the results of the first empirical analysis. If the deductive path is chosen again, alternative theories must be tested to see whether they provide a sufficient explanation. Alternatively, the inductive path can be chosen in the second iteration, using empirical evidence to build a better explanation.

The inductive path is often used when we are examining a little-studied outcome. This path is depicted in figure 2.4 as gray arrows, starting from the empirical level. Here, the analyst can proceed in a manner more analogous with historical methodology or classic detective work (Roberts 1996)—for example, working backward from the outcome by sifting through the evidence in an attempt to uncover a plausible sufficient causal mechanism that produced the outcome. This is a bottom-up type of analysis, using empirical material as the basis for building a plausible explanation of causal mechanisms whereby X (or multiple Xs) produced the outcome.

The important question is then when should we stop this process—that is, How do we know a minimally sufficient explanation when we see it? There is no foolproof answer to this question; instead, the decision that we have a minimally sufficient explanation is based on an assessment of whether all of the relevant facets of the outcome have been accounted for adequately while ensuring that the evidence is best explained by the developed explanation instead of plausible alternative explanations. This is an iterative process where we update the model until it provides what can be thought of as the best possible explanation (Day and Kincaid 1994). We can never confirm a theory with 100 percent certainty; instead, we stop when we are satisfied that the found explanation accounts for the most important aspects of the outcome (see chapter 5).

2.4. Conclusions: A New Understanding of Process-Tracing

We need to differentiate process-tracing methods into three distinct variants to bring alignment between what we practice and what we preach. Common to all three variants is the ambition to trace causal mechanisms, although

TABLE 2.1.   Summary of the Main Differences between the Three Variants of Process-Tracing

	Theory-Testing	Theory-Building	Explaining-Outcome
Purpose of analysis— research situation	*Situation one* Correlation has been found between X and Y, but is there evidence that there exists a causal mechanism linking X and Y?	*Situation two* Build a plausible causal mechanism linking X:Y based on evidence in case	*Situation three* Explain particularly puzzling historical outcome by building minimally sufficient explanation in case study
Ambitions of study	Theory-centric	Theory-centric	Case-centric
Understanding of causal mechanisms	Systematic (generalizable within context)	Systematic (generalizable within context)	Systematic, nonsystematic (case-specific) mechanisms and case-specific conglomerates
What are we actually tracing?	Single, generalizable mechanism	Single, generalizable mechanism	Case-specific, composite mechanism that explains the case
Types of inferences made	(1) Parts of causal mechanism present/absent (2) Causal mechanism is present/absent in case	Observable manifestations reflect underlying mechanism	Minimal sufficiency of explanation

the term *causal mechanism* as used in theory-testing and theory-building variants refers to relatively parsimonious mechanisms that are generalizable to a bounded population of cases, whereas in explaining-outcome process-tracing, mechanisms refer to systematic mechanisms, case-specific, non-systematic mechanisms (events leading to an outcome), and eclectic case-specific conglomerates of different mechanisms.

Table 2.1 summarizes the main points of difference across the three variants of process-tracing. There are three different purposes of process-tracing methods: (1) testing whether a generalizable causal mechanism exists in a case and functions as expected; (2) building a generalizable mechanism from evidence in a case; and (3) explaining a particular outcome. The methods differ regarding whether they are theory- or case-centric, along with what they are actually tracing and the types of inferences they enable.

The rest of this book addresses the commonalities and differences across the three variants of process-tracing with regard to their ontological and epistemological foundations (chapter 3), the practical guidelines for each stage of the research process from working with theories (chapter 4), and the types of inferences being made (chapter 5). The book also explores developing empirical tests (chapter 6), working with evidence (chapter 7), and answering questions of case selection and nesting case studies in broader, mixed-method research designs (chapter 8).

How can we judge this from a single case?

CHAPTER 3

What Are Causal Mechanisms?

This chapter focuses on debates about the nature of causality and the under-standing of causal mechanisms that form the ontological and epistemological underpinnings of all three process-tracing variants. This chapter introduces the reader to the ontological debates within the philosophy of science that deal with the nature of causality itself to understand how the mechanismic understanding of causality used in process-tracing analysis differs from the other understandings of causality that are prevalent in social science, partic-ularly large-n statistical analysis and comparative case study research. As this book is not a treatise on the lengthy philosophical debates on causality—a topic that has been the subject of heated exchanges since ancient Greece—the chapter only briefly reviews two key debates about the ontology (nature of) causality that are necessary to grasp how causal mechanisms are under-stood within theory-centric and case-centric process-tracing variants. The first debate relates to whether we should understand a causal relationship in a skeptical, neo-Humean fashion, where causality is seen purely in terms of patterns of regular association (regularity), or whether causality refers to a deeper connection between a cause and effect (e.g., a mechanism). The second debate deals with whether causal relations should be understood in a deterministic or probabilistic fashion.

The chapter then discusses the nature of causal mechanisms. After de-fining causal mechanisms in the mechanismic understanding, we identify a common core regarding how causal mechanisms are understood within process-tracing methods and how they differ from an understanding where mechanisms are seen as either empirical events or intervening variables. However, significant differences exist within process-tracing depending on the variant chosen. In case-centric analyses, a mechanism is often considered a loose conglomerate of systematic and nonsystematic parts that together account for a particular outcome. In contrast, theory-centric analyses operate with relatively simple causal mechanisms that include only systematic parts that can be generalized beyond the confines of the single case.

The chapter concludes with an in-depth discussion of several key points of contention about the nature of causal mechanisms. These points include the ontological debate about whether mechanisms should be understood as operating solely at the micro/actor level or whether macro/structural mechanisms also have a reality of their own as well as more epistemological debates about whether we can directly observe causal mechanisms or whether we can only observe the implications of their existence.

3.1. The Ontology of Causality in the Social Sciences

This section provides a brief overview of the main lines of debate in the philosophy of science regarding the nature of causality itself (mechanisms or regular association) and whether causality should be understood in a probabilistic or deterministic fashion.

Causality as Regular Association versus Causal Mechanisms

When we speak of a causal relationship between X and Y, what is the nature of causality in the relationship? Social science takes two main ontological positions on the nature of causal relations.[1] First, the skeptical, neo-Humean understanding of causality as patterns of regular empirical association has traditionally been the most prevalent in social science (Brady 2008; Kurki 2008). David Hume, in a reaction to the then-prevalent theory that saw causality as a necessary connection in the form of a "hook" or "force" between X and Y, contended that we cannot measure the "secret connection" that links causes and effects. We can observe that an object falls to the ground, but we cannot observe the gravitational forces that caused the object to fall. Given this inability to empirically verify that X caused Y, Hume argued that we should define causes merely in terms of constant conjunction (correlations) between factors; any theorization of "undetectable" mechanisms would quickly, in his opinion, degenerate into metaphysics (Brady 2008; Hume 1975). Causation is therefore taken to mean nothing but the regular association between X and Y, controlled for other relevant possible causes (Chalmers 1999: 214; Marini and Singer 1988).

Causation in the regularity approach is therefore understood in terms of regular patterns of X:Y association, and the actual causal process whereby X produces Y is black-boxed. Regularity can be analyzed by examining patterns of correlation between X and Y. For causality to be established, Hume argued that three criteria for the relationship between X and Y need to be fulfilled: (1) X and Y must be contiguous in space and time; (2) X occurs before Y (temporal succession); and (3) a regular conjunction exists between X and Y (Holland 1986). For example, a regular association between governments that impose austerity measures to cut deficits (X) and their inability to win the subsequent election (Y) would in this understanding suggest the existence of a causal relationship between X and Y, assuming that the three criteria are fulfilled.

The second ontological position in social science is a mechanismic understanding of causality, a position that underlies process-tracing methods (Bennett 2008b). Scientific realists such as Bhaskar (1978), Bunge (1997), and Glennan (1996) have contended that Descartes's mechanismic understanding of causal mechanisms, which was prevalent prior to Hume's treatise, should be reintroduced in a modified fashion. The defining feature of a mechanismic ontology of causation is that we are interested in the theoretical process whereby X produces Y and in particular in the transmission of what can be termed causal forces from X to Y. A mechanismic understanding of causality does not necessarily imply regular association. Indeed, a mechanism can be infrequent. What is necessary is that X actually produces Y through a causal mechanism linking the two (Bogen 2005).

The focus in mechanismic understandings of causality is the dynamic, interactive influence of causes on outcomes and in particular how causal forces are transmitted through the series of interlocking parts of a causal mechanism to contribute to producing an outcome. Philosopher Stuart Glennan, for example, defines a mechanism as "a complex system, which produces an outcome by the interaction of a number of parts" (1996: 52; Glennan 2002). Within social science research, Andrew Bennett has defined causal mechanisms as "processes through which agents with causal capacities operate in specific contexts to transfer energy, information or matter to other entities (2008b: 207). David Waldner has defined a mechanism as "an agent or entity that has the capacity to alter its environment because it possesses an invariant property that, in specific contexts, transmits either a physical force or information that influences the behavior of other agents or entities" (2012: 18).

In contrast to the regularity understanding, causality is therefore understood in more complex terms as the causal mechanism linking X to Y, depicted as X → mechanism → Y. By studying mechanisms, scholars gain what Salmon (1998) terms deeper explanatory knowledge.

Probabilistic versus Deterministic Understandings of Causality

Another key ontological distinction is between probabilistic and deterministic understandings of causality. Probabilistic causality means that the researcher believes that we are dealing with a world in which there are random (stochastic) properties, often modeled using error terms (see, e.g., King, Keohane, and Verba 1994: 89 n. 11). This randomness can be the product either of an inherent randomness, where the social world is understood in terms analogous to quantum mechanics, or of complexity. In the latter case, while we might assume that the world is inherently deterministic, the social world contains nonlinear associations, feedback, and other complex features that make it appear as if there are stochastic elements. At the end of the day, whether the stochastic elements of the social world are inherent or the product of complexity is irrelevant, as their implications for probabilistic theorization are the same (Marini and Singer 1988).

Probabilistic theories therefore assume that there are both systematic and nonsystematic (i.e., random) features of reality. For example, in the study of genetics, many scholars contend that a large portion of any individual's cognitive abilities is inherited from his/her parents (e.g., Bouchard 2004; Haworth et al. 2010; Herrnstein and Murray 1994). However, geneticists do not expect that children will always have the same IQ as their parents; instead, heredity has an inherent degree of randomness that results in a relationship best expressed as a probability distribution in the form of a bell curve, where on average higher-IQ parents have higher-IQ children, and vice versa. This causal relationship is understood as probabilistic, where even precise knowledge of the parents' IQ would not enable us to make exact predictions of the IQ of any individual child, only a probable range of outcomes. Hypotheses in probabilistic causal models therefore take the form of "Y tends to increase when X increases."

A probabilistic ontology has methodological implications in that it only makes sense to investigate probabilistic causal relationships with cross-case methods, investigating mean causal effects of systematic parts across the population or a sample of the population of the phenomenon. A single case study comparing the IQ of a child and her parents tells us nothing about the strength of the relationship between IQ and heredity in the population, as we have no way of knowing whether the correlation in the single case is the product of pure chance or is close to the predicted mean causal effects of heredity.

For statisticians, the term *deterministic causality* means a theoretical model where there is no error term (i.e., no random component), which basically means that, if properly specified, a deterministic model should explain 100 percent of the variance of a given dependent variable. Qualitative social scientists have a more pragmatic understanding of determinism. Mahoney succinctly summarizes this understanding: "The assumption of an ontologically deterministic world in no way implies that researchers will successfully analyze causal processes in this world. But it does mean that randomness and chance appear only because of limitations in theories, models, measurement and data. The only alternative to ontological determinism is to assume that, at least in part, 'things just happen'; that is, to assume truly stochastic factors . . . randomly produce outcomes" (2008: 420).

Deterministic causal relationships can be studied at the population level but are more often associated with small-*n* case study research (Mahoney 2008). For qualitative scholars, the term *deterministic* is used primarily to refer to discussions of necessary and sufficient causes in individual cases or combinations of these types of conditions (417). This means that what we are examining is not whether a given X tends to covary with Y in a population but whether X is either a necessary and/or sufficient cause of Y in an individual case (Collier, Brady, and Seawright 2010a: 145; Mahoney 2008: 417). A condition is necessary if the absence of it prevents an outcome, regardless of the values of other variables, whereas if a sufficient condition is present, the outcome will always take place.[2]

The Ontologies of Causality Adopted in Different Social Science Methods

Table 3.1 illustrates the four different logical combinations and the social science methods that have utilized them. Cell 1 illustrates the most widely used ontological position in social science methods, where regularity is coupled with a probabilistic understanding. X is theorized to increase the probability that outcome Y occurs in a population, and if we find that the three criteria for assuming causality are fulfilled (contiguity, temporal succession, and regular association), we can infer that X is a cause of Y. Methods that utilize this position include large-*n,* quantitative statistics and the adaption of them by King, Keohane, and Verba (KKV) to qualitative case study research (1994).

In contrast to KKV's pronouncements regarding probabilistic causality and case studies, most qualitative methodologists counter that this is unfaithful to the tenets of qualitative case-oriented methodology and that we instead should adopt deterministic understandings of causality (Blatter and Blume 2008; Mahoney 2008). Mahoney (2008) argues that it makes no sense to use a probabilistic understanding of causality when we are investigating single cases and their causes: "At the individual case level, the ex post (objective) probability of a specific outcome occurring is either 1 or 0; that is, either the outcome will occur or it will not. . . . [S]ingle-case probabilities are meaningless" (415–16). This makes cell 3 a logical impossibility in a single-case research design, whereas studying mechanisms is not feasible for larger-n studies (see chapter 5).

Instead, Mahoney (2008) contends that we should utilize a deterministic understanding in small-n case research. In cross-case studies, this can involve comparative case study methods (cell 2) where patterns of regular association between conditions are investigated. Congruence methods are within-case studies where the similarities between the relative strength and duration of the hypothesized causes and observed effects are assessed (George and Bennett 2005: 181–204; Blatter and Haverland 2012).

Process-tracing involves studying causal mechanisms in single-case studies. The basic point is that if we take mechanisms seriously, this implies that evidence from individual process-tracing studies cannot be compared with that gathered in other studies given that the evidence is case-specific. What is relevant evidence in one case cannot be meaningfully compared with evidence in another case, making cross-case comparisons more or less impossible. Therefore, if we are interested in studying causal mechanisms, we need to adopt the deterministic ontology of causality (Mahoney 2008). This is depicted as cell 4 in table 3.1.

TABLE 3.1. The Ontological Assumptions regarding Causality of Different Social Science Methodologies

	Probabilistic	Deterministic
Regularity	(1) Large-n quantitative statistical methods, KKV's qualitative case study methods	(2) Congruence case studies (within case), comparative cross-case study methods (small-n), and qualitative comparative analysis (QCA) (medium-n)
Mechanisms	(3) Not logically possible in single case studies, not feasible to examine mechanisms in larger-n study	(4) Process-tracing methods (single case)

3.2. Causal Mechanism—A Mechanismic Definition

In the mechanismic understanding introduced earlier, a causal mechanism is defined as a theory of a system of interlocking parts that transmits causal forces from X to Y (Bhaskar 1979; Bunge 1997, 2004; Glennan 1996, 2002). Bunge defines a theoretical causal mechanism as "a process in a concrete system, such that it is capable of bringing about or preventing some change in the system as a whole or in some of its subsystems" (1997: 414). Another good definition that summarizes this position is that "a mechanism is a set of interacting parts—an assembly of elements producing an effect not inherent in any one of them. A mechanism is not so much about 'nuts and bolts' as about 'cogs and wheels'—the wheelwork or agency by which an effect is produced" (Hernes 1998: 78).

The mechanism linking a cause and outcome can be understood using a machine analogy. Each part of the theoretical mechanism can be thought of as a toothed wheel that transmits the dynamic causal energy of the causal mechanism to the next toothed wheel, ultimately contributing to producing outcome Y. We use the machine analogy merely as a heuristic aid in the conceptualization and operationalization of a given causal mechanism. We by no means imply that all social causal mechanisms exhibit machine-like qualities; indeed, many social causal mechanisms are more dynamic (Bunge 1997; Pierson 2004). They are not necessarily neutral transmission belts. A small trigger can have a disproportional effect, as the forces are amplified through a causal mechanism. A strong cause also can have its effect muted through a causal mechanism. Moreover, the transmission of causal forces can be nonlinear through a mechanism, or the workings of the mechanisms can result in the alteration of the causal forces in another direction. This implies that causal mechanisms can have effects that cannot merely be reduced to the effect of X, making it vital to study causal mechanisms together with causes instead of causes by themselves.

Each of the parts of the causal mechanism can be conceptualized as composed of entities that undertake activities (Machamer 2004; Machamer, Darden, and Craver 2000). Entities are the factors engaging in activities (the parts of the mechanism—i.e., toothed wheels), where the activities are the producers of change, or what transmits causal forces through a mechanism (the movement of the wheels).

What is the logical relationship between the parts of a mechanism and the whole in the mechanismic understanding? We adapt the terminology of necessary and sufficient conditions to this relationship. In comparative methods, explanatory conditions are viewed as necessary, sufficient, or some combination of the two, such as being INUS conditions (Braumoeller and Goertz 2000; Mahoney 2000; Ragin 1988). Mackie defines INUS conditions as an insufficient but necessary part of an unnecessary but sufficient condition (1965). Necessary conditions are conditions that have to be present for an outcome to occur and where the absence of X results in an absence of the outcome. In contrast, sufficiency describes a situation where a condition (or set of conditions) is able to produce an outcome. If X, then always outcome Y.

While the cross-case comparative literature usually describes causes (Xs) as conditions, there is no logical reason why we cannot adapt the logic of necessary and sufficient conditions to the present purposes of analyzing the mechanisms that produce an outcome. The difference is that while a comparativist thinks of a condition as X, we argue that we can also adapt the language to the analysis of the parts of a mechanism and the whole.

Each part of a mechanism can be illustrated as $(n_n \rightarrow)$, where the n_n refers to the entity (n) and the arrow to the activity transmitting causal energy through the mechanism to produce an outcome. * is used to refer to logical *and*. As a whole, a causal mechanism can therefore be portrayed as

$$X \rightarrow [(n_1 \rightarrow) * (n_2 \rightarrow)] Y$$

This should be read as X transmits causal forces through the mechanism composed of part 1 (entity 1 and an activity) and part 2 (entity 2 and an activity) that together contribute to producing outcome Y. This is a "context-free" mechanism, and a proper study would also detail the contextual conditions that enable the mechanism to become activated (Falleti and Lynch 2009).

An analogy can be made to a car, where X could be the motor and Y is the movement of the car. However, without a driveshaft and wheels, the motor by itself cannot produce forward movement. Here the driveshaft and wheels can be thought of as the causal mechanism that transmits forces from X (motor) to produce Y (movement).

We contend that all three variants of process-tracing research strategies share an understanding of the parts of a causal mechanism, where they should be conceptualized as insufficient but necessary parts of an overall mechanism. Each part of the mechanism is by itself insufficient to produce an outcome Y, as it only functions together with the rest of the "machine." Second, explicit in a mechanismic ontology is a view that the parts that we include in our conceptualization of a given causal mechanism are absolutely vital (necessary) for the "machine" to work, and in the absence of one part, the mechanism itself cannot be said to exist. This is denoted by the logical *and*. If we have conceptualized a three-part causal mechanism as $(n_1 \rightarrow) * (n_2 \rightarrow) * (n_3 \rightarrow) = Y$, and $(n_2 \rightarrow)$ is either empirically or theoretically superfluous, then the mechanism should be reconceptualized as $(n_1 \rightarrow) * (n_3 \rightarrow) = Y$. This introduces a disciplining effect when we attempt to model a given theory as a causal mechanism. Basically, if a logical, theory-based argument cannot be formulated for why the particular part is a vital (necessary) part of a causal mechanism and in particular describes how the specific entity or entities engage in activities that transmit causal forces from X to Y, then the part should be eliminated from the theoretical model as being redundant. In addition, if our empirical analysis has found that a part is not necessary, then the mechanism should also be reconceptualized to exclude it.

This disciplining effect means that when we engage in the theoretical modeling of mechanisms, we do not suffer from the problem of infinite digression into a plethora of parts at an ever more microlevel of explanation (for a particularly good discussion of this problem, see Roberts 1996); instead, we model only the parts of a mechanism that are theorized as absolutely essential (necessary) to produce a given outcome. This approach also helps us remedy some of the problems of adding various ad hoc explanations for why a theory or hypothesis might eventually hold in a specific case when we are engaging in theory-centric process-tracing, as we need to be able to argue that all of the parts of the mechanism can hypothetically exist in other cases.

The understanding of the parts of a causal mechanism as individually necessary requires that a deterministic ontology of causality is adopted, enabling causal inferences about the existence of the individual parts of a causal mechanism. Using a probabilistic ontology, if we empirically investigate whether a specific part of a causal mechanism exists in a case and find no confirming evidence, we are left in the dark as to whether we should disconfirm its existence or merely ascribe it to the randomness of any individual case in circumstances where there is otherwise a strong mean causal effect across the population. The methodological prescription here would be to increase the number of cases (increase the *n*), as KKV suggest, but doing so is inappropriate for process-tracing given that the aim is to test the presence/absence of mechanisms within single-case studies.

In contrast, in process-tracing methods, each part of a mechanism is conceptualized as an individually necessary element of a whole. Yet although these examples are single-case studies, we contend that we can make inferences about the presence of the parts of a mechanism using the Bayesian logic of inference (see chapter 5).

Further, if we find strong disconfirming evidence for one part of a multipart mechanism, we disconfirm the existence of the whole hypothesized causal mechanism. In this situation, there are two ways forward: One can either completely discard the hypothesized mechanism or engage in theoretical revision using more inductive tools in an attempt to detect an underlying mechanism (theory-building). If we find strong confirming evidence of the existence of each part of the mechanism, we can infer that the mechanism actually exists (with a certain degree of confidence).

3.3. Debates about the Nature of Causal Mechanisms

While it is relatively easy to differentiate the mechanismic and deterministic understanding of causality used in process-tracing from the regularity and probability understandings that underlie methods such as large-*n* statistical analysis, a considerable degree of ambiguity exists about what causal mechanisms actually are (Gerring 2010; Mahoney 2001).

Many social science scholars contend that they are studying causal mechanisms with a variety of research methods: Some scholars believe that causal mechanisms should be understood as systems that transmit causal forces from X to Y, while others see them as series of empirical events between the occurrence of X and Y. Still others have considered causal mechanisms in terms of intervening variables between X and Y. We illustrate how taking mechanisms seriously implies instead a certain understanding of mechanisms as systems whereby X contributes to producing an outcome.

Within process-tracing methods, disagreements have arisen about the exact nature of these mechanismic systems. As introduced in chapter 2, there is disagreement across the theory/case-centric divide regarding whether they should be seen as relatively parsimonious and singular or as case-specific conglomerates. Additional disagreements that do not span this divide include whether causal mechanisms operate solely at the micro/actor level or whether there are also macro/structural-level mechanisms that cannot be reduced to the microlevel? Finally, can we observe causal mechanisms in action or only indirectly observe the implications of their existence? On these two points, we suggest that there are no logically imperative reasons for choosing one or the other position, suggesting that we should remain agnostic about levels or whether mechanisms are observable.

Causal Mechanisms Are More Than Just Empirical Events

Many scholars contend that they are studying causal mechanisms but are in reality only tracing an empirical process, understood as a series of empirical events that are temporally and spatially located between the occurrence of X and the outcome Y (an empirical narrative).

Figure 3.1 depicts how some scholars misuse the term *process-tracing* to refer to scholarship that traces an empirical process (sequence of events) occurring between X and Y but where the causal mechanism linking them is in effect black-boxed (Bunge 1997). This type of research takes the form of an empirical narrative: "Actor A did X to actor B, who then changed his position on issue Y, and so forth." This type of scholarship is a valuable form of descriptive inference that describes a series of empirical events and provides valuable historical knowledge regarding what happened but tells us little about the underlying how and why an outcome occurred. The focus is on events instead of a theory-guided analysis of whether evidence suggests that a hypothesized causal mechanism was present.

In process-tracing, the research focuses on the causal mechanism through which X contributes to producing an outcome Y. This is most evident in what we termed the theory-centric variants of process-tracing (figure 3.2), where a relatively simple causal mechanism is front and center in the analysis. In the theory-testing variant, the mechanism is explicitly theorized along with the empirical manifestations of each part of the mechanism. The case study then assesses whether we find the predicted empirical evidence. For each part of the hypothesized causal mechanism, we investigate whether the predicted empirical manifestations of the mechanism were present or absent. Different types of evidence are gathered, depending on what is best suited to enable us to update our confidence in the presence/absence of the mechanism.

For example, a theorized rational decision-making mechanism could be theorized as having the four parts: decision makers would (1) gather all relevant information; (2) identify all possible courses of action, (3) assess the alternatives based on the decision makers' utility function, and finally (4) choose the alternative that maximizes the expected utility (Oneal 1988). The empirical manifestations of these four parts would be very different, and different types of evidence would be used to assess whether part 1 or part 4 was present. Determining whether part 1 took place before part 2 could be a manifestation of the presence of part 1 measured by investigating the temporal sequence of events. However, the sequence of events would not be enough to establish whether parts 1 or 2 were present. Instead, for example,

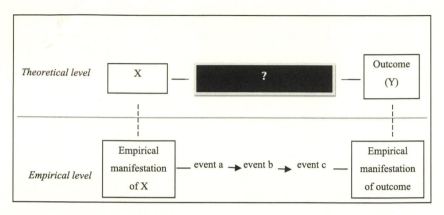

Fig. 3.1. Empirical narratives are the black-boxing of mechanisms.

to assess part 2, we would test whether other predicted manifestations were also present, including evidence that showed whether or not all possible courses of action were assessed. Although we are testing the empirical manifestations of each part of the mechanism, we are in effect tracing the underlying theoretical causal mechanism, illustrated in figure 3.2. Our analysis is structured as focused empirical tests of each part of a mechanism instead of a narrative empirical presentation of the story of events of the case. Theory is guiding our process-tracing analysis irrespective of whether or not we have a theory-centric or case-centric ambition. In contrast, by tracing events, we gain no knowledge of the underlying causal mechanism.

Complicating the picture slightly is the difference in how causal mechanisms are understood in theory-centric and case-centric process-tracing variants. In the theory-centric variant, mechanisms are understood as mid-range theories of mechanisms that transmit causal forces from X to Y and are expected to be present in a population of cases, assuming that the context that allows them to operate is present. Analysis seeks to determine whether a single mechanism such as learning or policy drift is present in a particular case, but given that most social outcomes are the product of multiple mechanisms, no claims of sufficiency are made. This means that we are studying singular mechanisms instead of complex conglomerates.

In contrast, when the purpose of analysis is to craft a sufficient explanation of a particular outcome, we almost always need to combine mechanisms into an eclectic conglomerate mechanism to account for a particular outcome. Evans, for example, writes, "Cases are always too complicated to vindicate a single theory, so scholars who work in this tradition are likely

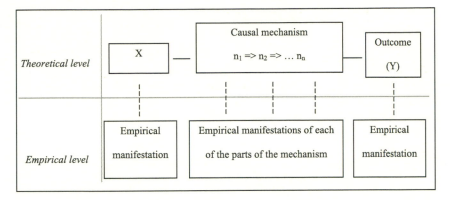

Fig. 3.2. Theory-centric process-tracing methods

to draw on a mélange of theoretical traditions in hopes of gaining greater purchase on the cases they care about" (1995: 4). Schimmelfenning notes that "eclecticism is the unintended result of research that seeks to explain specific events as well as possible" (cited in Sil and Katzenstein 2010: 191). The result is more complicated, case-specific combinations of mechanisms (see chapter 4).

Further, given that the ambition is to craft a minimally sufficient explanation of a particular outcome, it is usually necessary to include nonsystematic parts in the causal mechanism, defined as a mechanism that is case-specific. While Elster contends that mechanisms have to be at a level of generality that transcends the particular spatiotemporal context (i.e., they are systematic mechanisms) (1998: 45), thereby excluding the use of nonsystematic mechanisms in explaining outcomes, other scholars have more pragmatically argued that mechanisms that are unique to a particular time and place also can be defined as mechanisms. Wight, for example, has defined mechanisms as the "sequence of events and processes (the causal complex) that lead to the event" (2004: 290). Nonsystematic mechanisms can be distinguished from systematic ones by asking whether we should expect the mechanism to play any role in other cases.

The importance of nonsystematic mechanisms in explaining a particular outcome makes explaining-outcome process-tracing sometimes more analogous to the historical interpretation of events (Roberts 1996). However, these nonsystematic parts will almost never stand alone, given that social reality is not just a random hodgepodge of events but includes mechanisms that operate more generally across a range of cases within a bounded population.

Further, the inclusion of nonsystematic mechanisms that are sometimes depicted as events has an important advantage in that it enables us to capture actor choice and the contingency that pervades historical events, immunizing our research from the criticisms of social science from historical scholars (Gaddis 1992–93; Roberts 1996; Rueschemeyer 2003; Schroeder 1994). In the words of Lebow, "Underlying causes, no matter how numerous or deepseated, do not make an event inevitable. Their consequences may depend on fortuitous coincidences in timing and on the presence of catalysts that are independent of any of the underlying causes" (2000–2001: 591–92).

The admission of case-specific mechanisms does not mean that they are preferable (Gerring 2006). "To clarify, single-outcome research designs are open to case-centric explanation in a way that case study research is not. But single-outcome researchers should not assume, *ex ante,* that the truth about their case is contained in factors that are specific to that case" (717). What differentiates explaining-outcome process-tracing from historical research is both the causal-explanatory focus—where the analysis is theory-guided—and the ambition to go beyond the single case (Gerring 2006; Hall 2003). With regard to the ambition to go beyond the single case, this involves attempts to identify what mechanisms are systematic and nonsystematic in the specific case study. This is best seen in book-length works, where lessons for other cases are developed in the conclusions. For example, what parts of the conglomerate mechanism do we believe can be systematic based on the findings of our study and in light of what we know from other research? What findings can be exported to other cases, and to what extent are they unique to a particular case? Individual causal mechanisms can be exported, but the case-specific conglomerate (usually) cannot be exported.

Figure 3.3 illustrates the more complex nature of the causal mechanisms that are being traced in explaining-outcome process-tracing. The analysis still focuses on the theoretical level of causal mechanisms, although these are understood in a broader and more pragmatic fashion.

Causal Mechanisms Are More Than Just Intervening Variables

Another common misunderstanding about mechanisms is made by those who conceptualize mechanisms as a series of intervening variables. The most widely used definition of causal mechanism sees them as a series of intervening variables through which an explanatory variable exerts a causal effect on an outcome variable (e.g., Falleti and Lynch 2009: 1146; George and Bennett 2005: 6; Gerring 2007b, 2010; Hedström and Ylikoski 2010; King, Keohane,

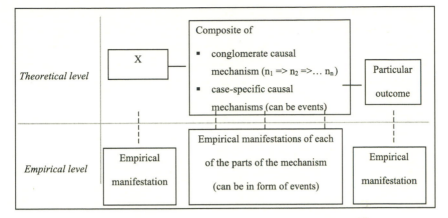

Fig. 3.3. Mechanisms in explaining-outcome process-tracing

and Verba 1994; Waldner 2011). This understanding is best exemplified in the definition of causal mechanisms given in KKV's book, *Designing Social Inquiry*: "This definition would also require us to identify a series of causal linkages, to define causality for each pair of consecutive variables in the sequence, and to identify the linkages between any two of these variables and the connections between each pair of variables" (1994: 86). For KKV, mechanisms are simply chains of intervening variables that connect the original posited cause and the effect on Y (87). These intervening variables are usually expressed as nouns.

The causal linkages are viewed as variables in this definition. This means that the values they can take vary and that they have an existence independent of each other, as each variable is in effect a self-contained analytical unit. Variance implies that a probabilistic understanding of causality is utilized—something that makes little sense when we are engaging in single-case studies.

Second, the use of intervening variables usually has the practical consequence that the linkages between the variables are neglected. The neglect of the causal linkages between variables results from the simple fact that when a causal mechanism is conceptualized as being composed of a series of intervening variables, it is far easier to measure the presence/absence of an intervening variable than the linkages between them. The analytical focus on variables instead of linkages is strengthened by the regularity understanding of causality that is used by King, Keohane, and Verba (1994), among others.[3]

The result is that the intervening variable understanding ends up gray-

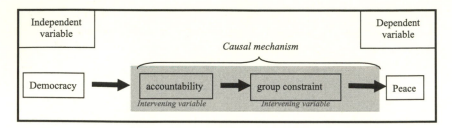

Fig. 3.4. Causal mechanism defined as a series of intervening variables. (Drawn from Rosato 2003.)

boxing the causal mechanism itself (Bunge 1997; Mahoney 2001; Waldner, 2012). While the mechanism is slightly unpacked, the actual transmission of causal forces from X that produce Y is not explicitly studied (Bunge 1997). Waldner goes as far to say that "mechanisms explain the relationship between variables because they are not variables" (2012: 18). Furthermore, causal mechanisms themselves can affect how causal forces are transmitted from X to Y—for example, by magnifying the effects of X through a mechanism. Mechanisms are therefore more than just sets of intervening variables.

An example of the prevalent intervening variable understanding of causal mechanisms can be seen in an article by Rosato (2003) that critically examines democratic peace theory. He contends that he is conceptualizing the mechanisms linking democracy and peace but then describes one mechanism as being composed of two intervening variables, accountability and group constraints. Accountability means that political elites will be voted out of office if they adopt unpopular policies. In the model, leaders are theorized to be especially responsive to the wishes of domestic antiwar groups, creating a constraint emerging from groups that affects the ability of leaders to engage in war (585). This theory is depicted in figure 3.4.

However, the actual causal forces that are transmitted through a mechanism to produce the outcome (peace) are left out of the analysis; they are, in effect, gray-boxed. Both accountability and group constraints are theorized to be linked with peace, but the conceptualization prevents us from analyzing *how* democracy produces peace, as the causal linkages between the intervening variables are not explicitly theorized. Instead, the analyst would measure only the presence/absence of the intervening variables as well as potentially the covariance between each intervening variable and the outcome (Y). If strong evidence exists, the analyst can first infer that the intervening variable is present. If each of the intervening variables was found to be present, a further leap can be made by inferring that the theorized mechanism was present. But it is important to underline that we are not studying how democracy produced peace but only measuring a series of covariants.

We agree with social scientists such as Bennett (2008a) and Waldner (2012) who contend that we should take seriously the distinct ontological nature of the mechanismic understanding of causality in process-tracing. This understanding has important methodological benefits, as conceptualizing mechanisms as systems results in an empirical analysis that has a more explicit focus on the causal linkages between X and Y that produce the outcome, enabling stronger within-case inferences to be made.

The mechanismic understanding involves opening up the black box of causality as much as possible (Bennett 2008a; Bhaskar 1978; Bunge 1997; Glennan 1996). Mechanisms are more than just a series of intervening variables. Instead, mechanisms are invariant with regard to both the whole mechanism and each individual part. Either all of the parts of a mechanism are present, or the mechanism itself is not present (Glennan 2005: 446).

The difference between a theoretical conceptualization of a mechanism as a system and one composed of intervening variables is illustrated in figure 3.5, where the same mechanism described in the example of the democratic peace thesis is conceptualized in terms of a system that produces an outcome through the interaction of a series of parts of the mechanism. Each part is composed of entities that engage in activities. In the example, instead of conceptualizing the mechanism as two intervening variables (accountability and group constraints), the mechanism is unpacked further by focusing on the two entities (liberal groups and governments) and their activities ("agitate" and "respond") that make up the two parts of this simple mechanism. Each of the entities can be thought of as a wheel, where the activities are the movement that transmits causal forces to the next part of the mechanism.

Part 1 of the mechanism is liberal groups agitating against war before the government, and part 2 is the government responding to this agitation by adopting conciliatory foreign policies that result in peaceful relations. Together, the two parts comprise the simple theorized causal mechanism. In figure 3.5, we see that the entities that undertake the activities transmit causal forces through the mechanism are first "liberal groups" and then "governments." A subsequent process-tracing study of this mechanism would involve testing whether the hypothesized parts of the mechanism were present in a given appropriately chosen case.

By explicitly conceptualizing the activities that produce change, the mechanismic approach to causal mechanisms draws our attention to the actions and activities that transmit causal forces from X to Y—that is, how the mechanism produces an outcome and the context within which the

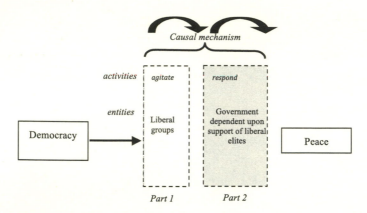

Fig. 3.5. A democratic peace example of a causal mechanism

mechanism functions. If we then can confirm the existence of a hypothesized causal mechanism in a theory test, we have produced strong evidence that shows how the theorized parts of the causal mechanism produce Y and how X and Y are causally connected by the mechanism (Bunge 1997, 2004). Understanding mechanisms in these terms enables us to capture the process whereby causal forces are transmitted through a causal mechanism to produce an outcome, forces that are black-boxed or gray-boxed when they are understood as events or intervening variables.

Are Mechanisms Only at the Micro/Actor Level?

Philosophers of social science have engaged in considerable debate about whether mechanisms always have to be reducible to the microlevel (Hedström and Swedberg 1998) or whether there are also macrolevel mechanisms that cannot be reduced to the microlevel (Bunge 2004; Mayntz 2004; McAdam, Tarrow, and Tilly 2001). Should we reduce every causal mechanism to the microlevel, investigating the actions of individuals, or are there causal mechanisms that have macrolevel properties?

To introduce the level of causal mechanism debate, Hedström and Swedberg have a helpful figure that illustrates how the level debate relates to the study of causal mechanisms (1998: 22) (figure 3.6). However, they take an extreme position that there are no purely macrolevel mechanisms. George and Bennett take a similar position when they state that mechanisms are "processes through which agents with causal capacities operate" (2005: 137).

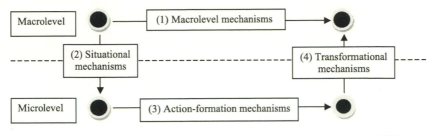

Fig. 3.6. Levels of causal mechanisms. (Based on Hedström and Swedberg 1998: 22.)

They go on to define mechanisms as the microfoundations of a causal relationship that involve the "irreducibly smallest link between one entity and another" (142).

In our view, this viewpoint unnecessarily restricts the uses of process-tracing methods to purely microlevel examination, usually at the level of individual actors and their behavior in specific decision-making processes. Yet many of the most interesting social phenomena we want to study, such as democratization, cannot meaningfully be reduced solely to the actor level but in certain situations can be better analyzed empirically at the macrolevel (McAdam, Tarrow, and Tilly 2001). Given that this conundrum is in essence the classic debate between agent and structure, we argue for an agnostic and pragmatic middle-ground position, where the choice of level that is theorized is related to the level at which the implications of the existence of a theorized causal mechanism are best studied. Mechanism may occur or operate at different levels of analysis, and we should not see one level as more fundamental than another (Falleti and Lynch 2009: 1149; George and Bennett 2005: 142–44; Mahoney and Rueschemeyer 2003: 5; McAdam, Tarrow, and Tilly 2001: 25–26).

Macrolevel mechanisms are structural theories that cannot be reduced to the actions of individuals (Type 1). Many sociologists claim that the search for the microlevel foundations of behavior is futile and that much of the capacity of human agents derives from their position in society (structure) (Mahoney 2001; McAdam, Tarrow, and Tilly 2001; Wight 2004). Many of the important causal mechanisms in the social world are arguably macrolevel phenomena that are "collaboratively created by individuals yet are not reducible to individual" action (Sawyer 2004: 266). Sawyer terms this the concept of "emergence," which means that macrolevel mechanisms have their own existence and have properties that cannot be reduced to the microlevel.

Institutional roles, norms, and relational structures can play a significant role for actor behavior, and mechanisms can have structural properties that cannot be defined solely by reference to the atomistic attributes of individual agents (266). For example, system-level theories in international relations include neorealism, where Waltz (1979) theorizes the balancing mechanism as solely the product of macrolevel factors.

Three different types of mechanisms are related to the microlevel actions of agents, and two of them combine macrolevel properties with microlevel actions. At the microlevel are action-formation mechanisms (Type 3), or what Hedström and Ylikoski term "structural individualism," where all social facts, their structure and change, are in principle explicable in terms of individuals, their properties, actions, and relations to one another (2010: 59). Purely microlevel theories relate to how individuals' interests and beliefs affect their actions and how individuals interact with each other (Type 3). However, this does not mean that actors are necessarily individual humans. Social science operates with many forms of collective actors that are treated as if they were individuals, most bravely captured by Wendt's contention that "states are people too" (1999: 194). One example of a purely microlevel theory is Coleman's (1990) rational-choice-based theory of social action, where even actions such as altruism are reduced solely to individual self-interested motivations (desire for reciprocity in a long-term iterated game).

Situational mechanisms link the macro- to the microlevel (Type 2). Situational mechanisms describe how social structures constrain individuals' action and how cultural environments shape individuals' desires and beliefs (Hedström and Swedberg 1998). Examples of a macro-micro-level mechanisms include constructivist theories of actor compliance with norms that are embedded at the macrolevel (structural).

Transformational mechanisms describe processes whereby individuals, through their actions and interactions, generate various intended and unintended social outcomes at the macrolevel (Type 4) (Hedström and Swedberg 1998). An example of this type of micro-macro-level mechanism could be socialization processes, whereby actors through their interaction create new norms at the macrolevel. Another example is from game theory, where individual actions in situations like the prisoner's dilemma create macrolevel phenomena such as the tragedy of the commons.

There is no single correct answer to the question of at which level a causal mechanism should be theorized. Here we argue for a pragmatic approach. There are social mechanisms whose observable implications can best be theorized and measured at the macrolevel. Therefore, we agree with Stinchcombe's conclusions that

Where there is rich information on variations at the collective or structural level, while individual-level reasoning (a) has no substantial independent empirical support and (b) adds no new predictions at the structural level that can be independently verified, theorizing at the level of [individual-level] mechanisms is a waste of time. (1991: 380)

Further, by disaggregating macrolevel mechanisms from their microlevel components, we risk the problem of infinite regress. Kincaid puts it well when he states that if we want to study the mechanism linking two macrolevel factors, "Do we need it at the small-group level or the individual level? If the latter, why stop there? We can, for example, always ask what mechanism brings about individual behavior. So we are off to find neurological mechanisms, then biochemical, and so on" (1996: 179). If we go down this path, the result is that no causal claims can be established without absurd amounts of information (Steel 2004).

The pragmatic middle ground advocated in this book states that mechanisms can hypothetically exist at both the macro- and microlevels, along with mechanisms spanning the two levels (situational and transformative mechanisms). The choice of level for our theorization of causal mechanisms in process-tracing depends on the pragmatic concern of the level at which the empirical manifestations of a given causal mechanism are best studied. If the strongest tests of a given mechanism are possible at the macrolevel, then it should be theorized and studied empirically at this level, whereas if the empirical manifestations are better observed at the microlevel, then we should conceptualize and operationalize our study at this level.

Can We Observe Causal Mechanisms?

Can we directly measure mechanisms or only infer their existence through their observable implications? Many scholars hold the view that causal mechanisms are unobservable. For example, George and Bennett posit that mechanisms are "ultimately unobservable physical, social, or psychological processes through which agents with causal capacities operate" (2005: 137). Hedström and Swedberg (1998) argue that causal mechanisms are merely analytical constructs that do not have a real-world existence.

In contrast, other scholars contend that the parts of a mechanism should be understood as having a "kind of robustness and reality apart from their place within that mechanism" (Glennan 1996: 53). In the words of Bunge,

"Mechanisms are not pieces of reasoning but pieces of the furniture of the real world" (1997: 414). Reskin (2003) suggests that we can answer the question of how an outcome was produced only by investigating observable causal mechanisms, thereby excluding many cognitive and macrolevel mechanisms.

As with the question of the level of analysis of mechanisms, a full answer to this question would involve a lengthy philosophical discussion that is outside the scope of this book. Our position here is pragmatic: We agree with scientific realist scholars such as Bunge and Glennan that our ambition should be to attempt to get as close as possible to measuring the underlying causal mechanism but that this ideal may not be achievable for theoretical and empirical reasons.

Some types of causal mechanisms can be conceptualized and operationalized in a manner that permits quite close observation of actual mechanisms and where plentiful evidence exists that enables us to measure the mechanism quite closely. For example, Owen (1994, 1997) conceptualizes and operationalizes a democratic peace mechanism that results in empirical tests that come quite close to measuring the mechanism directly (see chapter 5). Other types of causal mechanisms, such as groupthink mechanisms that deal with conformity pressures in small-group decision making, are so complex and involve such difficult measurement issues relating to access to confidential documents and problems relating to measurement of sociopsychological factors that we can measure the mechanism only in an indirect fashion through proxies (indicators) of the observable implications (see Janis 1983).

What are the methodological implications of the choice between adopting an understanding of causal mechanisms as observable or unobservable? If we believe that mechanisms can be observed quite directly, when we operationalize a mechanism, we are aiming to examine the fingerprints that the mechanism should have left in the empirical record. In contrast, if we believe that mechanisms are ultimately unobservable, we should instead think in terms of the observable implications that a mechanism should leave. In practice, the two positions result in similar forms of operationalization (see chapter 6).

The next chapter turns to the more practical question of working with theories of causal mechanisms.

CHAPTER 4

Working with Theories of Causal Mechanisms

Theoretical concepts are not self-explanatory. Nor are causal mechanisms self-evident from causal theorization of relationships between X and Y. Instead, causal theories need to be transformed so they offer a clear hypothesized mechanism describing how a type of outcome is produced. Therefore, theoretical concepts and causal mechanisms need to be carefully defined before they can be employed in process-tracing analysis. While there are numerous methodological texts relating to conceptualization techniques in political science, existing guidelines are not always applicable when we are using process-tracing methods.[1] This chapter adapts existing guidelines to each of the three variants of process-tracing.

We start by discussing some of the common challenges shared by the three variants of process-tracing methods. First, we discuss how concepts should be conceptualized, arguing that defining key concepts in set-theoretical terms is more compatible with process-tracing than viewing concepts as variables. We then elaborate on the common theoretical elements that causal mechanisms share in the three variants—in particular, the need to elaborate the content of each of the parts of the mechanism that are composed of entities that engage in activities. Activities are explicitly conceptualized in process-tracing to capture how causal forces are transmitted through a causal mechanism to produce an outcome. We then discuss how causal mechanisms differ across four types of theoretical explanation, the analytical level at which they operate, the degree of contextual specificity, and the time span in which they are theorized to operate.

The second section illustrates the specific challenge in working with theories in each of the three variants of process-tracing: theory-testing, theory-building, and explaining-outcome. We show that the conceptualization phase of theory-testing process-tracing involves the mostly deductive task of using existing theorization to flesh out the causal mechanism between X and Y, whereas theory-building derives theories from a more inductive analysis of empirical material. In contrast, conceptualization is an ongoing and iterative process in explaining-outcome process-tracing, involving multiple stages of analysis of evidence and theoretical reformulation (see chapter 2).

4.1. Common Challenges Shared by All Three Variants

Defining Key Concepts

Key to any research design is the definition of the central concepts that form the basis for theoretical propositions. Adcock and Collier (2001) refer to this as the translation of abstract theoretical concepts into what they term *systematized concepts*. Most important theoretical concepts are contested, with multiple plausible meanings, and they are often quite ambiguous and vague at the abstract level. We therefore need clear systematized definitions that distinguish between what is included and not included in the concept that allow us to know it when we see it.

Defining systematized concepts is not an "anything goes" process. For most concepts, a considerable amount of theoretical work describes what the concept should include and not include, and our systematized concepts should be faithful to this work (Adcock and Collier 2001: 532). Conceptualization involves defining the constitutive dimensions of a concept and how they relate to each other (Goertz 2006). For example, a systematized definition of democracy could include the two characteristics of civil rights and competitive elections. These secondary characteristics obviously should not rule each other out. It is also important to note that concept formation in qualitative case study research such as process-tracing is attentive to the details of cases, resulting in more context-specific conceptual definitions that have a narrower scope than are commonly used in large-*n* analysis (Ragin 2008: 78–81).

There are important differences in how concepts are defined depending on whether they are considered to be variables or conditions. In the understanding put forth by King, Keohane, and Verba (KKV), theoretical concepts are variables. Causal relationships are then formulated in terms of an independent variable (X) (or set of variables) that are theorized to cause variation in the dependent variable (Y) (King, Keohane, and Verba 1994). This type of theory usually describes a probabilistic causal relationship, where an increase in X raises the probability of Y occurring in a given case (Gerring 2005: 167). The term *variables* means that they must be able to vary. If we are conceptualizing democracy as a variable, then we also need to take into consideration whether democracy is a dichotomous variable (democracy—autocracy) or an interval scale variable (for example, from 0 to 7 as in the Polity measure of democracy [Marshall and Jaggers 2002]). This means that when viewing concepts as variables, we need to define the positive pole (full democracy), the negative pole (autocracy), and the scale of the intervening continuum (e.g., dichotomous, ordinal, interval, or continuous) (Goertz 2006: 35). In the Polity measure, the characteristics that compose the positive pole (democracy) are juxtaposed against another set of characteristics that define the negative pole (autocracy).

We argue that process-tracing methods are more closely aligned with the conceptualization of conditions as used in set theory than when they are understood as variables. Set-theoretical causal relationships describe a causal condition (or set of conditions) that is necessary and/or sufficient for the occurrence of an outcome.[2] Set-theoretical causal relationships are usually studied with comparative methods. For example, after comparing all of the cases that compose the set of social revolutions, Skocpol concludes that peasant village autonomy is a necessary causal condition for the occurrence of social revolutions (1979: 112–54).

When analyzing set-theoretical relationships, the focus is not on defining the full variation of the concept (differences in degree) but instead is on defining the concept itself and its negation (i.e., the concept is present or not present—differences in kind). For example, if we are conceptualizing democracy as a necessary condition, we need to have a full definition of the positive pole (democracy), but the negative pole (autocracy) would not have to be defined in the same manner, as only the presence or absence of democracy is under investigation. If we are studying a democratic peace mechanism, we are interested in studying democracy and its effects on peace (outcome). The negative pole (autocracy) is analytically irrelevant, since studying autocracy does not tell us anything about how democracy produces peace. Here, we would conceptualize democracy as having two poles: the characteristics associated with democracy, and a second pole where absence is defined as anything but democracy. Outcomes are conceptualized in the same manner, with the focus on the concept and its presence or absence and the negative pole defined as the absence of the outcome. In explaining-outcome process-tracing, in contrast, the outcome is not defined as a theoretical concept (a case of . . .), but as the historical event to be explained (e.g., the Cuban Missile Crisis or the French Revolution).

When we engage in process-tracing, we need to define carefully the concept and its absence, but we do not need to include both the positive (democracy) and negative (autocracy) poles along with the nature of the continuum in-between. The definition of concepts in process-tracing is therefore usually closer to how concepts are defined in set theories, where we are interested in whether or not a concept is present. Defining concepts as variables, however, introduces superfluous elements.

For the purpose of case selection, in some research situations, information regarding varying degrees to which a cause or outcome is part of the set of a concept can be relevant (see chapter 8). Recently developed set-theoretical methods such as fuzzy-set QCA have opened the possibility of studying both differences in kind, defined as membership or nonmembership in a concept, and differences in degree of membership or nonmembership, ranging from full membership to more in than out (Ragin 2000, 2008). When we are, for example, selecting a most-likely case, it can be relevant to find a case where the theorized cause and outcome are present (differences in kind) as well as where the cause and outcome have high degrees of membership of the sets of the concepts. In contrast, a least-likely case will involve a cause and/or outcome that are merely more in than out, meaning that they are only marginally within the set of the concepts.

Concepts are not divorced from theory but are instead an intrinsic part of it (Goertz 2006). This view has implications for process-tracing in that the initial cause (e.g., democracy) should be conceptualized in a manner that includes the attributes that are causally relevant for the causal mechanism. If we want to study the democratic peace thesis, our definition of democracy (X) should include characteristics that lead to the mechanism that contributes to producing Y. For example, Owen defines democracy (liberal democracy) as "states that are dominated by liberal ideology, and that feature, in both law and practice, free discussion and regular competitive elections" (1994: 102). All of these characteristics are related to his theorized mechanism (chapter 5). In other words, conceptualizing democracy in this manner captures how causal forces are transmitted from X into the causal mechanism itself.

At the same time, it is important to be as conscious as possible about the causal hypotheses that are embedded within definitions of key concepts (Goertz 2006: 65–66). Goertz suggests that when conceptualizing in process-tracing, one should "think hard before hardwiring hypotheses into concepts.

Often hardwiring makes it difficult to test hypotheses down the road and often will raise problems when gathering data. . . . Avoid in particular hypotheses that come into play when using the concept on the dependent variable side. . . . Potential causes of the phenomenon should almost always be left out of the concept itself" (66). If one defines the outcome in this manner, a theoretical proposition can become a self-fulfilling prophesy.

The Implications of Taking Causal Mechanisms Seriously— Conceptualizing Causal Forces

In process-tracing, we theorize more than just X and Y; we also theorize the mechanism between them. Doing so involves defining a more encompassing number of theoretical concepts for all of the parts between X and Y. Conceptualizing in these terms enables us to capture the theorized process whereby causal forces are transmitted through a causal mechanism to produce an outcome; forces that are black-boxed in both frequentist and set-theoretical causal theorization. For example, Casillas, Enns, and Wohlfarth (2009) put forward a causal theory on the impact that public opinion (X) has on the decisions made by the U.S. Supreme Court (Y). They then collect data that enables them to test whether changes of public opinion in a more liberal direction are followed by changes in judicial decisions in a more liberal direction, however the causal mechanism linking X and Y is black-boxed in the analysis. In contrast, studying the causal mechanism(s) would require describing both the causal condition that starts the causal mechanism and the outcome as well as the theoretical mechanism between X and Y that produces the outcome. A process-tracing analysis of the theorized relationship between public opinion and Supreme Court decisions would analyze a causal mechanism that theorizes about the process whereby public opinion becomes salient for judges and how and when judges are theorized to respond to perceived shifts in public opinion.

Each of the parts of the causal mechanism should be conceptualized as composed of entities that undertake activities, as illustrated in figure 4.1. Entities engage in activities (the parts of the mechanism—i.e., toothed wheels), while activities are the producers of change, or what transmits causal forces through a mechanism (the movement of the wheels). Entities can be individual persons, groups, states, classes, or structural phenomena depending on the level of the theory. The theoretical conceptualization of the entities uses nouns, whereas activities should include verbs that define the transmitters of causal forces through the mechanism. In social science terms, social

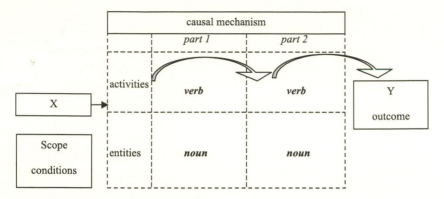

Fig. 4.1. A mechanismic conceptualization of a causal mechanism

entities have causal powers that can be understood as a "a capacity to produce a certain kind of outcome in the presence of appropriate antecedent
conditions" (Little 1996: 37).

When conceptualizing the mechanism, each part should be seen as an individually insufficient but necessary part of the whole (see chapter 3). Parts have
no independent existence in relation to producing Y; instead, they are integral
parts of a "machine" that produces Y. Understood as one part of a causal mechanism, the engine of a car by itself has little utility in producing forward movement without a drivetrain or wheels. Understood in this manner, the necessity
of parts of a mechanism has an important disciplining effect in our theoretical
development, as redundant parts should be eliminated from the model.

By explicitly conceptualizing the activities that produce change, the
mechanismic approach to causal mechanisms draws our attention to the
actions and activities that transmit causal forces from X to Y—that is, how
the mechanism produces an outcome. If we then can confirm the existence
of a hypothesized causal mechanism with process-tracing with a reasonable
degree of certainty, we have produced strong evidence that shows how the
theorized parts of the causal mechanism produce Y and shows that X and Y
are causally connected by the mechanism (Bunge 1997, 2004).

The clear elaboration of mechanisms into parts composed of entities engaging in activities should be thought of as an ideal typical conceptualization
that sometimes is not attainable in practice. For example, we cannot always
capture the activities of entities for each part of a mechanism in our conceptualizations, especially when theorizing at the macrolevel, where structural
"activities" can be difficult to conceptualize. (For a good discussion of some
of the challenges relating to studying structure, see Wight 2006.)

Theory-testing and theory-building process-tracing seek to generalize, aiming at developing and testing theories beyond the context in which they were developed, whereas explaining-outcome process-tracing focuses on crafting a minimally sufficient explanation of a particular case. This distinction is important to note when we are conceptualizing a causal mechanism, as it determines the types of parts that we include in our theories. In a theory-centric study, only systematic parts that have causal effects beyond a particular case for the whole population of the phenomenon are included in the theoretical model.[3] For example, in Owen's study of the democratic peace mechanism, the phenomenon under investigation was the impact of democracy on the war-proneness of states (see chapter 5). The theoretical proposition (democratic peace) is taken by many scholars to be close to universal, being applicable to almost all times and places. Theory-building process-tracing attempts to trace the mechanism whereby X (or a set of Xs) contributed to producing an outcome. For example, what are the mechanisms whereby economic development contributes to producing democratic change? Here both concepts would need to be carefully defined, involving careful thinking about the scope of the theoretical proposition. Is the ambition to uncover a broad theoretical mechanism or a more bounded proposition that applies for example to East Asia in the past fifty years?

In contrast, explaining-outcome process-tracing starts with defining the particular outcome of interest. The focus here is less upon testing or building theoretical propositions and more on the outcome for its own sake. The French Revolution is an important outcome in and of itself as a consequence of its substantive historical importance. However, even here it is important to think carefully about a case's outcome to enable the use of existing theories as starting points for crafting a sufficient explanation of the outcome. For example, the French Revolution can be considered a case of either the theoretical concept of "social revolutions" or "political revolution," enabling us to draw on a series of existing theoretical tools that are then supplemented by new hypotheses after the analytical first cut (see below for more on explaining-outcome process-tracing).

In explaining-outcome process-tracing, nonsystematic, case-specific mechanisms would be included. An example could be a case-specific mechanism that describes how inclement weather impeded voter turnout in a specific election—a mechanism that could be vital to understanding the particular outcome but that probably does not have systematic, cross-case effects. Usually in explaining-outcome process-tracing studies, we cannot build a minimally sufficient explanation without including certain nonsystematic, case-specific parts that are particularly significant in the case. For example, we cannot fully account for Indian democratization without capturing the role played by the Congress Party (Mahoney 2008: 416). Yet the role played by the party in Indian politics is unique: a mass-incorporating party in all other contexts has other effects. Therefore the role played by the Congress Party is a case-specific, nonsystematic part of the explanation.

4.2. Different Types of Causal Mechanisms

While the conceptualization of theoretical propositions as causal mechanisms should contain certain common elements, they will also differ in terms of the type of theoretical explanation, analytical level, the extent of the scope conditions of the mechanism (from "universal" mechanisms that are applicable across space and time to mechanisms explaining particular outcomes), and the temporal dimension.

Different Types of Theoretical Explanations

There are differences in what elements a typical causal mechanism contains depending on the type of theoretical explanation. Parsons (2007) helpfully distinguishes between four types of explanation within the social sciences: structural, institutional, ideational, and psychological. In this chapter, we focus on the conceptual commonalities of the different types of explanation, thought of in terms of building blocks that they share. For example, institutional mechanisms share different common building blocks than do ideational mechanisms. Chapter 6 discusses the challenges these different types of explanations encounter when we test them empirically.

Structural causal mechanisms focus on the exogenous constraints and opportunities for political action created by the material surroundings of actors (Parsons 2007: 49–52). Common building blocks for structural mechanisms include how certain preferences and a given material structure dictate observed behavior (or in a looser sense, create a pattern of structural constraints and incentives) (65). Another building block of structural mechanisms is that action is theorized to be a rational process (52). For structure to have any impact, actors have to react in predictable (rational) ways to their structural positions (52).

An example of a structural mechanism is found in the theorization on electoral realignment in the U.S. context, where realignments at the congressional and local level are theorized to be the product of changes in demographic factors and other slow-moving structural mechanisms (Miller and Schofield 2008).

Institutional mechanisms are distinct from structural ones in that institutions are man-made and thereby can be manipulated. Institutions can be defined as "formal or informal rules, conventions or practices, together with the organizational manifestations these patterns of group behavior sometimes take on" (Parsons 2007: 70). Typical institutional mechanisms deal with how certain intersubjectively present institutions channel actors unintentionally in a certain direction. The exact content of institutional mechanisms is determined by which of the different subtypes of institutional theory is being utilized—sociological institutionalist mechanisms that have norms and institutional cultures as common building blocks, rationalists who share a focus on institution-induced equilibria, historical institutionalists who conceptualize mechanisms in ways that capture the unforeseen consequences of earlier institutional choices, prioritizing the building blocks of path-dependency and temporal effects. An example of an institutional mechanism is Streek and Thelen's layering mechanism, where progressive amendments and revisions slowly change existing political institutions (2005: 22–23).

Ideational mechanisms share the argument that outcomes are (at least partially) the product of how actors interpret their world through certain ideational elements (Parsons 2007: 96). Here, the focus is not on how structures or institutions constrain behavior but instead on how ideas matter in ways that cannot be reduced to the objective position of an actor. Common theoretical building blocks include the view that actions reflect certain elements of ideas and that elements arose with a degree of autonomy from preexisting objective conditions (i.e., ideas are not just manifestations of structures). An example is Khong's (1992) mechanism that theorizes how historical analogies impact how actors interpret the world, making certain foreign policy choices more likely than would otherwise have been the case.

Finally, *psychological mechanisms* deal with mental rules that are hardwired into the human brain, resulting in behavioral regularities. Common building blocks include theorization about how and how much internal psychological dispositions interacted with other factors to produce action. An example is Janis's groupthink mechanism, where the innate social needs of individuals are theorized to produce a mechanism that results in poor decision-making processes that are dominated by premature consensus.

Determined how?

Different Analytical Levels, Contextual Specificity, and Temporal Conditions

Another key difference between mechanisms is whether they are theorized to be at the microlevel, macrolevel, or linking the two. In chapter 3, we introduced the debate about analytical levels in theorizing causal mechanisms, distinguishing between purely macrolevel, purely microlevel (action-formation mechanisms), and micro-macro mechanisms (transformational) and macro-micro (situational) mechanisms. The pragmatic middle ground that we espouse in this book states that mechanisms can hypothetically exist at the macro- or microlevels or can span the two levels (situational and transformative mechanisms). The choice of level at which to analyze a causal mechanism depends pragmatically on at which level the empirical manifestations of a theorized mechanism are best studied.

Another dimension of difference regards the degree of contextual specificity of mechanisms, defined as the scope conditions that are necessary for a given mechanism to function (Falleti and Lynch 2009; Walker and Cohen 1985). Context can be defined as the relevant aspects of a setting where the initial conditions contribute to produce an outcome of a defined scope and meaning through the operation of a causal mechanism (Falletti and Lynch 2009: 1152).[4]

When defining context, it is first important to make clear what phenomenon is under investigation. In other words, what is the phenomenon a case of, and what is the population of cases to which a theoretical proposition refers (Gerring 2007a)? Theoretical mechanisms can range from very broad, law-like propositions to bounded propositions applicable only to a small population of cases delimited in time and space or even case-specific mechanisms explaining the causes of a particular outcome. The bounds of applicability of the causal mechanism need to be explicitly theorized by defining the context within which the mechanism is expected to operate (Abbott 1997; Falletti and Lynch 2009). Is it theorized to be a causal mechanism that is broadly applicable across space and time or applicable within a narrow context, or is it case-specific? Defining the context in which a mechanism is expected to function is vital, as the same causal mechanism placed in two different contexts can hypothetically contribute to producing two very different outcomes (Falleti and Lynch 2009: 1160).

Finally, causal mechanisms also vary on the temporal dimension according to both the time horizon of the causal forces that produce an outcome and the time horizon of the outcome. We adapt Pierson's (2003, 2004) theorization on the temporal dimension in causal theory to theorization of causal mechanisms in process-tracing.

Many scholars traditionally have theorized causal relationships
of short time horizons with regard to the cause, the mechanism,
outcome. Khong's (1992) process-tracing analysis of the impact c
gous reasoning in U.S. government decision making in the escalation of the
Vietnam War is an example of a short-term mechanism in terms of both
mechanism and outcome.

Yet theories can vary depending on the length of the time within which
the mechanism is theorized to be acting and the time horizon of the outcome
(Pierson 2004). Incremental causal mechanisms have causal impacts that first
become significant only after they have been in action over a long time period. In threshold-type causal mechanisms, after an incremental mechanism
has been in play for a long period, a cusp is reached, after which the outcome
becomes immediately apparent. For example, many analyses of treaty reform
in the EU take a relatively short-term view, focusing on the grand bargains
between governments on more integration (e.g., Dyson and Featherstone
1999; Moravcsik 1998). Other scholars working with historical institutionalist types of explanations have contended that this snapshot-type analysis
misses the important long-term effects of an institutional mechanism of "informal constitutionalization," which is theorized as an incremental process of
small decisions by actors that over time accumulate, resulting in the creation
of a structure that forms a pro-integrative context for governmental decisions
(Christiansen and Jørgensen 1999; Christiansen and Reh 2009).

In addition, one can theorize that the outcome of a causal mechanism
can first become apparent over a longer time period (Pierson 2004: 90–92).
An example is seen in the work of Campbell (2005), who contends in an
analysis of globalization (X) and institutional change (Y) that institutional
change is not always self-evident. Different forms of institutional change
are theorized to vary depending on their time span, including evolutionary
change composed of small incremental steps along a single path; punctuated
equilibrium, where nothing happens for long periods followed by a period
of relatively rapid and profound institutional change; and punctuated evolu-

TABLE 4.1. The Temporal Dimension of Causal Mechanisms

		Time Horizon of Outcome	
		Short	Long
Time horizon of mechanism producing an outcome	Short	Normal "Tornado-like"	Cumulative effects "Meteorite/extinction"
	Long	Thresholds "Earthquake-like"	Cumulative causes "Global warming"

Source: Adapted from Pierson 2003: 179, 192.

tion, where the two forms of change are combined (long periods of evolutionary change followed by a rapid alteration) (33–35).

It is therefore important to theorize explicitly about the time dimension involved in the workings of a mechanism along with how an outcome manifests itself. A longer-term mechanism will look very different from a short-term mechanism; in particular, these differences manifest themselves in the types of observable implications that an incremental, long-term mechanism will be expected to have in comparison to a short-term mechanism (see chapter 6). In an incremental mechanism, we should expect small, almost unnoticeable empirical traces that will be apparent only if one knows what one is looking for.

Threshold mechanisms are also challenging to study empirically. In this type of mechanism, there is very little observable evidence available until the mechanism has reached a cusp, after which a very sudden development (outcome) occurs. This type of mechanism could be mistaken for a short-term mechanism, but incorrectly theorizing that the outcome resulted from a short-term mechanism would cause us to miss the longer-term incremental process that was most important for producing the outcome.

We now turn to the challenges relating to the conceptualization phase for each of the three variants of process-tracing research strategies.

4.3. Theory-Testing Process-Tracing

In theory-testing process-tracing, we know both X and Y, and we either have existing conjectures about a plausible mechanism or are able to deduce one relatively easily from existing theorization. If a causal mechanism is theorized to require both X and Z to function, both should be included when conceptualizing. This can take the form of (X + Z) → mechanism → Y. In the rest of this section, we discuss the simpler situation where a causal mechanism has a monocausal start (only X).

Conceptualization in theory-testing process-tracing starts as a deductive exercise. Using logical reasoning, we formulate a plausible causal mechanism whereby X contributes to producing Y, along with the context within which we expect it to operate. In practice, theory-testing has many inductive elements—for example, when we review existing empirical work for ideas about how we can flesh out the logical steps in a mechanism to transform a causal theory (X → Y) into a causal mechanism.

The amount of logical work necessary to flesh out a causal mechanism depends on whether existing theories are formulated in terms of mere correlations (X:Y), as plausible causal links between X and Y (e.g., intervening variables), or as full-fledged causal mechanisms. Most common is the situation where we know X and Y but where the process (i.e., causal mechanism) whereby X causes Y has not been explicitly conceptualized. For example, in the three political science journals with the highest impact factor, in the period from 2005 to 2010, fewer than 10 percent of articles even mentioned mechanisms in their theorization of causal propositions.[5]

Even if causal mechanisms have been formulated in prior research, we need to ensure that they are conceptualized in a manner that explicitly captures the transmission of causal forces through a mechanism. Despite using the term *mechanism*, most studies are conceptualized as a series of intervening variables where the transmission of causal forces is not explicitly theorized (see also section 3.3.). For example, Finkel, Pérez-Líñan, and Seligson (2007) conceptualize what they term a causal mechanism linking democratic promotion by external powers through foreign assistance (X) with democratic change in a receipt country (Y). They then describe both an indirect mechanism and a direct effect mechanism of foreign assistance. For illustrative purposes, we focus only on the direct effect mechanism, noting that the indirect effect mechanism suffers from the same conceptual problem. The direct effect mechanism is formulated in the following manner:

> Targeted democracy assistance, by contrast, works to educate and empower voters, support political parties, labor unions, and women's advocacy networks, strengthen human rights groups, and otherwise build "constituencies for reform"; it thus attempts to influence democratic outcomes in both the short term and the medium term. (410)

While this conceptualization describes the first part of the mechanism (from assistance to constituencies for reform), it does not explicitly theorize how the constituency for reform produces democratic change. Instead, it merely posits that a condition (existence of a constituency for reform) potentially acts as an intervening variable that can produce democratic change. The analytical result of this lack of conceptualization of the causal forces whereby X contributes to producing Y is that their empirical analysis only investigates inputs (foreign assistance) and outputs (democratic change), with no investigation of the theoretical process linking X and Y.

We argue that if scholars want to take seriously the study of causal mechanisms, they need to conceptualize mechanisms in a manner that enables us to study what happens between X and Y. For Finkel, Pérez-Líñan, and Seligson, the mechanism could be reconceptualized by logically gaming through the theoretical process whereby foreign democracy assistance can plausibly influence democratic outcomes, with more explicit theorization of how democracy assistance builds constituencies for reform (part 1) and then how these constituencies pressure the government to engage in democratic reform (part 2). Conceptualizing the mechanism in this manner would force us to investigate empirically the process within the black box of the mechanism that is theorized to link X with part 1, part 2, and the outcome.

A good starting point for conceptualizing a plausible causal mechanism for a given theorized causal relationship is to start with a thorough reading of the existing theorization on the phenomenon. Review articles are often particularly useful, as are descriptions of the state of the art in peer-reviewed journal articles and books. It is important to note that this reading should be as encompassing as possible. In theorizing about the mechanisms whereby nonstate supranational actors such as the EU Commission can wield political power in EU negotiations, Moravcsik (1999) not only incorporates theoretical scholarship on the phenomenon itself but also casts his net wider by finding inspiration from general bargaining theory, international relations theory, and theories of American and comparative politics.

The next step is to game through the different steps of a hypothesized mechanism, filling in the dots between X and Y to detail the nuts, bolts, wheels, and cogs between them. One way to start is to draw a mind map of plausible links between X (or a set of Xs) and Y, using boxes to illustrate each part of the mechanism. Each of the parts is insufficient to produce the outcome on its own, but all are necessary. In particular, we must focus on conceptualizing the entities and their activities. In practice, we cannot always do this, especially with regard to macrolevel mechanisms, where the activities of structural entities are not always self-evident.

Examples—Moravcsik's Study of EU Negotiations and Ghiecu's Study of Norms

An example of how the conceptualization of mechanisms can look in theory-testing process-tracing can be seen in Moravcsik (1999). While Moravcsik uses the term *variables* for the parts of his institutional mechanism (independent, intervening, and dependent), given that the intervening variables have no independent existence but only make sense as part of the theorized mechanism, it makes more theoretical sense to think of them as parts of a causal mechanism, each of them necessary to produce supranational influence over negotiation outcomes (Y) (275). Here, the parts of the mechanism

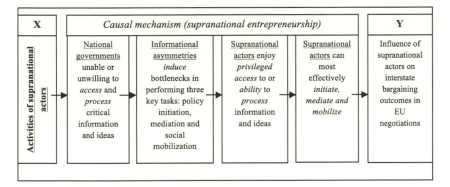

Fig. 4.2. A causal mechanism of how supranational actors can influence EU negotiations. (Based on Moravcsik 1999: 275.)

are depicted in terms of the entities engaging in activities, although activities can also take the form of nonactivity (see part 1 in figure 4.2). X is the activities of supranational actors (EU Commission), which produces supranational influence through the supranational entrepreneurship causal mechanism that is conceptualized as composed of four parts, each of which can be thought of as individually insufficient but necessary parts of the mechanism.

It is important to consider how many parts of the mechanism are logically necessary. A given mechanism should be kept as parsimonious as possible when we are engaging in theory-testing process-tracing. But at the same time, the process whereby X produces Y needs to avoid large logical gaps. In the case of Finkel, Pérez-Líñan, and Seligson, a substantial gap exists between the constituencies for reform and the outcome (democratic reforms), and additional parts of the mechanism should be theorized to fill in the gap.

Another example of a causal mechanism is found in Gheciu (2005), where she develops two ideational causal mechanisms that theorize the impact that the activities of international institutions such as NATO as an institution (X) have on the socialization of state actors to the norms of the institution (Y). Drawing on existing theorization in several different fields, Gheciu develops two different theoretical mechanisms that can result in socialization: persuasion and teaching. Gheciu fleshes out the causal relationship by developing the scope conditions under which the persuasion mechanism is theorized to work, thereafter detailing a simple two-part ideational mechanism where (1) actors engaged in persuasion use arguments to get other actors to rethink their conclusions, and (2) actors try to present a given course of action as the "right thing to do" (981–82).

In theorizing a mechanism, it is important to keep in mind that the theory should be internally consistent, meaning that two parts cannot contradict one another. Further, the outcome must be an outcome, not a potential cause. In addition, one should choose to include observable concepts whenever possible.

4.4. Theory-Building Process-Tracing

It is of the highest importance in the art of detection to be able to recognize out of a number of facts which are incidental and which vital. Otherwise your energy and attention must be dissipated instead of being concentrated.

—Sherlock Holmes (A. C. Doyle 1975: 138)

In its purest form, theory-building process-tracing starts with empirical material and uses a structured analysis of this material to detect a plausible hypothetical causal mechanism whereby X is linked with Y. While this is at heart an inductive exercise, existing theorization is usually used to inspire us in collecting evidence on which we can build theories.[6]

Theory-building process-tracing is utilized in two different types of research situations.[7] The first situation is when we know that a correlation exists between X and Y but are in the dark regarding potential mechanisms linking the two. In this form of X-Y-centric theory-building, the analyst examines a typical case to uncover a plausible causal mechanism that can be tested empirically in subsequent research. The second variant of theory-building process-tracing is when we know an outcome (Y) but are unsure what caused it to happen (i.e., X is unknown).

While theory-building process-tracing has some significant overlap with the explaining-outcome variant, a number of key differences exist (see also chapter 2). Of relevance here is the difference in the type of causal mechanisms being traced. Theory-building seeks to detect a systematic and relatively simple mechanism that contributes to producing an outcome across a bounded context of cases, whereas explaining-outcome uses eclectic conglomerates of systematic and nonsystematic mechanisms instrumentally to craft a minimally sufficient explanation for a particular outcome.

Conceptualization prior to empirical analysis is necessary in theory-building process-tracing only with regard to X and Y in X-Y-centric or Y in Y-centric theory-building. The actual mechanism between X and Y is naturally not conceptualized at the start.

Theory-building then proceeds to investigate the empirical material in the case, using evidence as clues about the possible empirical manifestations of an underlying causal mechanism between X and Y that fulfills the guidelines for a properly conceptualized causal mechanism. This process involves an intensive and wide-ranging search of the empirical record: In the words of Sherlock Holmes, "'Data! Data! Data!' he cried impatiently. 'I can't make bricks without clay'" (A. C. Doyle 1892: 343).

Theory-building process-tracing seeks to uncover middle-range theories formulated as a causal mechanism that works within a bounded context—for example, spatially (by region, such as Southeast Asia) or temporally (such as post–World War II). According to Evans, to "be useful, these configurations had to be conceptualized in ways that were potentially separable from the settings in which they were originally derived" (1995: 6).

As chapter 8 develops further, theory-building process-tracing is usually part of a larger mixed-method research design, where the theory that is developed is then tested using either process-tracing or another form of theory test (e.g., a fsQCA analysis).

Observable evidence does not speak for itself. Theory-building often has a deductive element in that scholars seek inspiration from existing theoretical work and previous observations. For example, an analyst investigating socialization of international administrative officials within international organizations could seek inspiration in theories of domestic public administration or in psychological theories of small-group dynamics while reading more descriptive accounts of the workings of international organizations as sources for plausible causal mechanisms. In other situations, the search for mechanisms is based on hunches drawn from puzzles for which existing work cannot account.

An Example—Janis on Groupthink

Janis (1983) attempts to build a causal mechanism that details how conformity pressures in small groups can have an adverse impact on foreign policy decision making, using a selection of case studies of policy fiascoes (Y) that were the result of poor decision-making practices by small cohesive groups of policymakers (X). He uses the term *groupthink* to describe the causal mechanism that details how conformity pressures in small groups produce premature consensus.

The first exploratory case he uses is the Bay of Pigs fiasco. He notes that the groupthink mechanism is not expected to be the sole cause of fiasco (Janis 1983: 32), but he also notes a puzzle for which existing explanations cannot account: Why did the "best and the brightest" policymaking group in the Kennedy administration not pick to pieces the faulty assumptions underlying the decision to support the intervention. "Because of a sense of incompleteness about the explanation," Janis "looked for other causal factors in the sphere of group dynamics" (32–33).

For each case study, Janis starts by drawing on psychological theories of group dynamics; relevant political science theories, such as Allison's (1971) organizational model; and Janis's own previous research for clues about potential systematic mechanisms. His search for parts of the mechanism is also informed by accounts of the Bay of Pigs decision. For example, when Janis "reread Schlesinger's account, I was struck by some observations that earlier had escaped my notice. These observations began to fit a specific pattern of concurrence-seeking behavior that had impressed me time and again in my research on other kinds of face-to-face groups. . . . Additional accounts of the Bay of Pigs yielded more such observations, leading me to conclude that group processes had been subtly at work" (1983: vii). Here we see the importance that imagination and intuition play in devising a theory from empirical evidence, although the search is also informed by existing empirical research.

Step 1 involves collecting empirical material to detect potential observable manifestations of underlying causal mechanisms. Empirical evidence is then used to infer that observable manifestations existed (step 2), resulting in the secondary inference that an underlying mechanism was present in step 3. Janis writes, "For purposes of *hypothesis construction*—which is the stage of inquiry with which this book is concerned—we must be willing to make some inferential leaps from whatever historical clues we can pick up. But I have tried to start off on solid ground by selecting the best available historical writings and to use as my springboard those specific observations that appear to be solid facts in the light of what is now known about the deliberations of the policy-making groups" (1983: ix). Further, "What I try to do is to show how the evidence at hand can be viewed as forming a consistent psychological pattern, in the light of what is known about group dynamics" (viii).

Janis's presentation of the empirical evidence is not in the form of an analytical narrative describing events or causal steps between X and Y. Instead, he writes, "Since my purpose is to describe and explain the psychological processes at work, rather than to establish historical continuities, I do not present the case studies in chronological order. The sequence I use was chosen to convey step-by-step the implications of group dynamics hypotheses" (1983: viii–ix). He describes four different "symptoms" of groupthink that can be understood as observable manifestations of a groupthink mechanism, including the illusion of invulnerability held in the group, the illusion of unanimity within the group, the suppression of personal doubts, and the presence of self-appointed mind guards in the group. For example, the shared illusions of invulnerability and unanimity helped members of the group maintain a sense of group solidarity, resulting in a lack of critical appraisal and debate that produced a dangerous level of complacent overconfidence.

Janis concludes, "The failure of Kennedy's inner circle to detect any of the false assumptions behind the Bay of Pigs invasion plan can be at least partially accounted for by the group's tendency to seek concurrence at the expense of seeking information, critical appraisal, and debate" (47).

4.5. Explaining-Outcome Process-Tracing

Explaining-outcome process-tracing refers to case studies whose primary ambition is to explain particular historical outcomes, although the findings of the case can also speak to other potential cases of the phenomenon. Examples of explaining-outcome process-tracing include Allison's (1971) classic study of the Cuban Missile Crisis, Wood's (2003) study that attempted to explain the puzzle of insurgent collective action in the high-risk circumstances of the Salvadoran civil war, and Schimmelfenning's (2001) study of why countries that were skeptics about EU enlargement decided to support it.

Explaining-outcome process-tracing is an iterative research process where theories are tested to see whether they can provide a minimally sufficient explanation of the outcome. Minimal sufficiency is defined as an explanation that accounts for an outcome, with no redundant parts. In chapter 2, we described the inductive and deductive paths in explaining-outcome process-tracing.

The first stage of conceptualization in explaining-outcome process-tracing involves examining existing scholarship for potential mechanisms that can explain the particular outcome. Here, one suggestion is to discuss what Y is a potential case of, although historical outcomes typically contain multiple theoretical phenomena. Wood's (2003) study, for example, views the Salvadoran civil war as a case of insurgent mobilization.

In most explaining-outcome studies, existing theorization cannot provide a sufficient explanation, resulting in a second stage in which existing theories are reconceptualized in light of the evidence gathered in the preceding empirical analysis. The conceptualization phase in explaining-outcome process-tracing is therefore an iterative research process, with initial mechanisms reconceptualized and tested until the result is a theorized mechanism that provides a minimally sufficient explanation of the particular outcome. The revised theoretical mechanism is then tested on its own terms on new evidence gathered from the same case.

In developing sufficient explanations, the following strategies can be utilized: combining existing mechanisms (eclectic theorization), developing new theories (or parts thereof), or incorporating nonsystematic parts into an explanation to account for the outcome. Here we discuss eclectic theorization and the incorporation of nonsystematic parts; the question of developing new theories using inductive research was discussed in section 4.4.

Eclectic theorization can be conceived as the combination of different mechanisms in a complex composite to craft a minimally sufficient explanation of a particular outcome (Sil and Katzenstein 2010). It "offers complex causal stories that incorporate different types of mechanisms as defined and used in diverse research traditions [and] seeks to trace the problem-specific interactions among a wide range of mechanisms operating within or across different domains and levels of social reality" (419). According to Hirschman, "Ordinarily, social scientists are happy enough when they have gotten hold of one paradigm or line of causation. As a result, their guesses are often farther off the mark than those of the experienced politician whose intuition is more likely to take a variety of forces into account" (quoted in Sil and Katzenstein 2010: 413–14).

Eclectic theorization does not seek to create synthetic grand theories; rather, it is a more pragmatic strategy aimed at capturing the multiplicity of mechanisms that produce particular historical outcomes. For this reason, eclectic theorization is also termed *problem-oriented research*. According to Evans, "Cases are always too complicated to vindicate a single theory, so scholars who work in this tradition are likely to draw on a mélange of theoretical traditions in hopes of gaining greater purchase on the cases they care about" (1995: 4).

However, while mechanisms from different research traditions can be combined, it is also important to make sure that key concepts and theoretical assumptions are compatible with one another to explain a concrete problem (Sil and Katzenstein 2010: 414–15). For example, one cannot combine a theorized ideational mechanism that contends that subjective beliefs drive actor behavior with an institutionalist mechanism where behavior is driven purely by the rational maximization of material interests. Here, one would have to reconceptualize the two mechanisms by, for example, developing a form of bridging theory that explains interaction between the two mechanisms and develops scope conditions for when one or the other mechanism is expected to dominate.

Given the ambition to craft a minimally sufficient explanation of a particular outcome, it is usually necessary to include nonsystematic mechanisms or parts of mechanisms in the explanation. An illustrative example of how a nonsystematic mechanism can be added to an explanation is found in Layne (2006), which employs explaining-outcome process-tracing to explain why U.S. grand foreign policy strategy after the early 1940s was dominated by an extraregional hegemony strategy, an outcome that cannot be explained using other theories. The outcome being explained is not great power behavior in general but rather a particular historical case (U.S. grand strategy after the early 1940s vis-à-vis Western Europe).

Layne (2006) undertakes an analytical first cut that uses Mearsheimer's (2001) offensive realist theory to test whether a structural causal mechanism based solely on relative power and geography can explain the aggressive U.S. hegemonic strategy. Mearsheimer's structural mechanism contends that based on the strong relative power of the United States, we should expect that the system pushes the United States towards a global hegemonic strategy, but that the stopping power of water prevents the United States from attaining that goal. The United States cannot project enough power outside of the North American region to dominate powers in other regions such as China or Russia. However, Layne finds that Mearsheimer's theory can explain only a more limited version of hegemony—what he terms offshore balancing—and cannot account for the outcome (U.S. extraregional hegemony in Western Europe after World War II).

Layne (2006) then draws on existing historical scholarship to build a case-specific ideational mechanism that can be termed the "Open Door" mechanism, illustrated in figure 4.3.[8] This ideational mechanism links strong U.S. relative power with the particular outcome. As the figure shows, the parts of the causal mechanism are case-specific, relating to factors that are based on U.S. domestic beliefs and ideas that are unique to the United States, temporally specific to the post-World War II period, and geographically restricted to Western Europe. They therefore cannot be used to account for the grand strategy of other great powers in other cases, making the mechanism nonsystematic, or what we term case-specific.

Layne (2006) contends that without this case-specific Open Door mechanism, we cannot explain U.S. extraregional hegemony strategy vis-à-vis Western Europe. Further, he notes that the mechanism explains puzzles relating to the case for which other theories cannot account, such as why

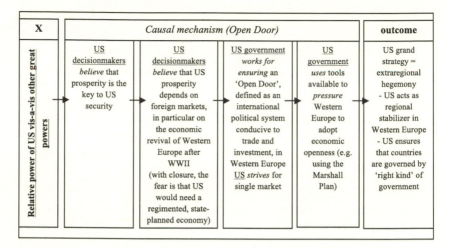

X	Causal mechanism (Open Door)				outcome
Relative power of US vis-a-vis other great powers	US decisionmakers *believe* that prosperity is the key to US security	US decisionmakers *believe* that US prosperity depends on foreign markets, in particular on the economic revival of Western Europe after WWII (with closure, the fear is that US would need a regimented, state-planned economy)	US government *works for* ensuring an 'Open Door', defined as an international political system conducive to trade and investment, in Western Europe US *strives for* single market	US government *uses* tools available to *pressure* Western Europe to adopt economic openness (e.g. using the Marshall Plan)	US grand strategy = extraregional hegemony - US acts as regional stabilizer in Western Europe - US ensures that countries are governed by 'right kind' of government

Fig. 4.3. Layne's case-specific Open Door mechanism. (Based on Layne 2006.)

the United States has remained in Western Europe after the Soviet Union's collapse (38).

Scholars choose explaining-outcome process-tracing precisely because they prioritize accounting for cases about which they care more than they prioritize theoretical parsimony. Here, claims about what makes a good theoretical explanation are based primarily on an explanation's ability to account for particular outcomes. Therefore, both eclectic theorization and the inclusion of nonsystematic mechanisms are prevalent.

An Example—Schimmelfennig's Study of Eastern Enlargement

A good example of how theories of causal mechanisms are developed in explaining-outcome process-tracing can be seen in Schimmelfennig (2001). The article attempts to explain a particular empirical puzzle—why France and other countries that initially opposed eastern enlargement of the EU eventually supported it (49).

Schimmelfennig's case study uses three iterations of the deductive path (see figure 2.4). He takes as his point of departure two competing theorized causal mechanisms from rationalist and sociological theories of international cooperation to explain the existing EU member states' positions regarding eastern enlargement. He finds that a rationalist mechanism can account for initial national preferences but not for the final decision to enlarge. Informed by the findings of his first empirical analysis, he tests whether a sociological mechanism can account for the full outcome, finding that it can account for France's final decision to accept enlargement but not for its change of position. Thus, neither mechanism can fully explain the outcome (neither is sufficient alone, and they are not sufficient in combination with each other), finding them both "wanting in the 'pure' form" (2001: 76). He then uses the empirical results of the first two iterations to formulate an eclectic combination of the two mechanisms that attempts to "provide the missing link between egoistic preferences and a norm-conforming outcome" by developing the idea of rhetorical action (the strategic use of norm-based arguments) (76).

The eclectic conglomerate mechanism composed of the three individual mechanisms provides a sufficient explanation of the historical outcome. Sufficiency is confirmed when it can be substantiated that there are no important aspects of the outcome for which the explanation does not account. In all three iterations, Schimmelfennig is tracing causal mechanisms. However, taken individually, the rationalist, sociological, and rhetorical action mechanisms are more generally applicable, whereas the eclectic combination of all three is much more case-specific and therefore cannot be exported per se to other historical cases.

CHAPTER 5

Causal Inference and Process-Tracing Methods

Social scientists use theories in the same manner that we use maps—to simplify an immensely complex reality. Yet whereas cartographers engage in descriptive inference when they make maps, social scientists are also interested in going a step beyond describing what happens to study causal relationships, explaining how and why social phenomena occur. Theories of causal mechanisms are, for example, simplifications of reality that predict what causal forces are important in explaining the occurrence of a phenomenon. Yet social scientists are not interested in theories as purely hypothetical thought experiments. Theories need to be empirically validated to make sure that they accurately represent reality.

This chapter deals with the interrelationship between theory and empirical reality. After a theory is developed, we need to empirically validate its accuracy. We do so by testing whether empirical evidence strengthens or weakens our confidence in the validity of the theory as an explanation of a phenomenon.

Given the difficulty of measuring complex social phenomena such as democracy, we cannot fully measure what is happening in reality. Even with the best measuring instruments, we can gain only a selected sample of observations of a given phenomenon. Therefore, we are forced to infer from a small set of empirical observations that a theory was the cause of the phenomenon. In other words, we make an inferential leap from what we can observe empirically to conclude that an underlying causal explanation exists.

What enables us to jump from a set of empirical observations to infer whether a causal mechanism exists in a specific case in process-tracing research? Is the logic that enables inferences to be made the same in process-tracing as the frequentist logic of inference that underlies the methodological prescriptions for qualitative case study research as suggested by King, Keohane, and Verba (KKV)(1994)?

In process-tracing case studies, we attempt to analyze whether a theorized causal mechanism exists in an individual case. Therefore, we are interested in making what can be termed *within-case inferences,* meaning that we use empirical evidence collected from a particular case to infer that all of the parts of a hypothesized causal mechanism were actually present in that case. Process-tracing methods cannot be used to make cross-case inferences that involve concluding based on evidence drawn from a sample of comparable cases that a causal relationship exists across a population of a given theoretical phenomenon. Other forms of inferential tools, such as comparative methods, are necessary to make cross-case inferences.

In this chapter, we discuss why mainstream inferential tools used, for example, in classical statistical analysis and comparative cross-case methods cannot be used to make within-case inferences about causal mechanisms. Here, we continue the argument that our methodology must be brought in line with ontology (Hall 2003). In particular, we illustrate that given that the ontology of causality used in process-tracing differs from that of both classical statistical analysis and comparative methods, the inferential tools used in these methods do not apply in process-tracing. This discussion is followed by the presentation of the Bayesian logic of inference as a solution to the problem of making within-case inferences in process-tracing. The chapter concludes by discussing in more detail the types of inferences that can be made using process-tracing methods and, equally important, what types of inferences cannot be made.

5.1. The Type of Inferences Made in Process-Tracing

Process-tracing methods are used when we want to investigate whether causal mechanisms are present or absent in an in-depth case study (theory-testing), when we want to build a theorized causal mechanism based on an in-depth examination of the evidence in a single case (theory-building), or when we want to explain a particular outcome, such as why Nazi Germany was not effectively deterred from aggression against Poland by threats from France and the United Kingdom (explaining-outcome).

In all three variants of process-tracing, we are investigating a causal mechanism (or mechanisms) in what is effectively a single-case study. An important distinction across the variants is whether the ambition is to generalize beyond the single case (theory-centric) or is more focused on accounting for the outcome in the single case (case-centric). In a theory-centric single-case study, the researcher is interested in studying a delimited phenomenon such as the occurrence of war and making generalizations from the single case to the population level. The single case of war is treated as a selected example of the broader population of the phenomenon. Both theory-centric variants employ cases studies in this manner, although inferences within the single case about the presence/absence of a causal mechanism are made using process-tracing methods whereas inferences beyond the single case are not made using these methods. Instead, cross-case inferences are based on comparative methods or frequentist methods (see chapter 8). Cross-case inferences to a broader population are, for example, made possible using comparative cross-case methods such as fuzzy-set QCA that allow us to detect least-likely cases. Here, the logic would be that if evidence of a causal mechanism is found in a least-likely case, we can expect to find the mechanism elsewhere in the population.

Case-centric ambitions are prevalent in explaining-outcome process-tracing studies, where the scholar is interested in accounting for the key aspects of particularly important and puzzling outcomes, such as why the Soviet Union peacefully relinquished hegemonic control of Eastern Europe in 1989–90 or why EU governments decided to adopt the Euro in the Treaty of Maastricht. Indeed, many qualitative-oriented scholars contend that outcomes such as the end of Soviet domination of Eastern Europe have so many unique features that they are noncomparable with other cases of the broad phenomenon, such as the collapse of the Habsburg Empire in the aftermath of World War I (see also Collier and Mahoney 1996). Yet all three variants of process-tracing share the ambition of making within-case inferences.

Before we turn to the elaboration of why process-tracing methods build on a different inferential logic than other social science methods, it is instructive to develop an example of what a typical causal mechanism looks like—in particular, the types of evidence that must be gathered to enable an inference that all of the parts of a hypothesized causal mechanism are present in a particular case.

Owen (1994, 1997) has developed a five-part causal mechanism that explains how democracy produces peace.[1] Owen identifies the entities and activities that make up each part of the hypothesized causal mechanism that transmits causal forces from mutual democracy (X) to produce peace (outcome Y). Owen (1994) tests whether these phenomena are present in four case studies, but given that the evidence gathered in each case study is not comparable across the cases, these are in effect four parallel single-case process-tracing studies. Table 5.1 depicts the causal mechanism, with entities underlined and activities in italics.

Part 5 of his causal mechanism best illustrates the transmission of causal forces from X to Y that we want to study empirically in process-tracing analysis. Part 5 says that we should expect to see liberal elites agitate on behalf of their policies during war-threatening crises. The entities are liberal elites (n_5), and their activities ($\rightarrow$) that transmit causal forces are their agitation against war with other liberal democratic states.

In his case study of the Franco-American crisis of 1796–98, Owen investigates whether available evidence supports the idea that liberal elites were agitating, with the theory being operationalized in a case-specific manner that directs his attention toward the actions of liberal elites in the news media and other public forums. Observations include speeches by a key liberal actor (Republican vice president Thomas Jefferson) along with the views of prominent liberal newspapers (Owen 1997: 86–87). After these observations are assessed for their accuracy and interpreted in their context, Owen uses them as evidence to infer that the part of the causal mechanism was present in the case.

Two crucial differences between process-tracing case studies and other social science methods can be seen here. The first relates to the types of material being collected; the second is in the analytical aims of causal inference.

TABLE 5.1. The Five Parts of Owen's Causal Mechanism whereby Democracy Produces Peace

Part of the Mechanism	Conceptualization of Mechanism and Its Parts (entities and activities)
Context	Crisis between states that can result in war
Independent variable (X)	Pair of states where analyzed state is democratic and where opponent is either democratic (liberal) or autocratic (illiberal) state
Part 1 ($n_1 \rightarrow$)	Liberals will *trust* states they consider liberal and *mistrust* those they *consider* illiberal
Part 2 ($n_2 \rightarrow$)	When liberals *observe* a foreign state becoming liberal democratic by their own standards, they will *expect* pacific relations with it
Part 3 ($n_3 \rightarrow$)	Liberals will *claim* that fellow liberal democracies share their ends and that illiberal states do not
Part 4 ($n_4 \rightarrow$)	Liberals will *not change* their assessment of foreign states during crises unless those states change their institutions
Part 5 ($n_5 \rightarrow$)	Liberal elites will *agitate* for their policies during war-threatening crises
Outcome (Y)	During crises, statesmen will be constrained to follow liberal elites, thereby not going to war with other liberal states

Source: Owen 1994.

Quantitative statistical studies attempt to make inferences about the size of the causal effects that independent variables have on a dependent variable in the population of the phenomenon (cross-case inferences), whereas process-tracing research aims to make inferences about the presence/absence of hypothesized causal mechanisms in a single case (i.e., within-case inferences are being made).[2]

What Type of Empirical Material Is Used to Make Inferences?

First, the predicted evidence that has to be collected to test whether part 5 of the mechanism is present is very different from the types of evidence that are relevant to test the presence/absence of the other parts of the mechanism. For example, evidence that can test whether liberals trust other states that they consider liberal is very different from evidence for part 5. Put simply, evidence of part one is noncomparable with evidence of part 5 within the individual case. Evidence is also noncomparable across the four cases that Owen investigates. The evidence that Owen collects for other cases, such as Anglo-American relations from 1803 to 1812, differs greatly from that collected for the Franco-American crisis. Furthermore, pieces of evidence are attributed different inferential weight based on their case-specific probability (chapter 7), with the pronouncements of key liberal actor Jefferson seen as a particularly important bellwether for liberal elite agitation.[3]

Collier, Brady, and Seawright (2010b: 184–88) have introduced a useful distinction between the types of empirical material gathered in quantitative statistical analysis and qualitative case study research. In statistical analysis, the ambition is to gather what can be termed *data-set observations* (DSOs), defined as all of the scores in a row in a rectangular data set for a given case for both the dependent and all of the independent variables (see also Bennett 2006). If we transformed Owen's mechanism into a standard X/Y theory, the data-set observations of his study could be depicted as seen in table 5.2.

TABLE 5.2.   Data-set Observations of Owen's Liberal Democratic Peace Theory

Case	X = Perceptions of Opponent as Liberal Democracy?	Y = Armed Conflict?
F-US crisis (1796–98)	Yes	No
UK-US crisis (1803–12)	No	Yes
UK-US crisis (1861–63)	Yes	No
UK-US crisis (1895–96)	Yes	No

Source: Based on Owen 1994.

In the data set, we can see that there is a clear correlation between perceptions of an opponent as a liberal democracy (X) and a lack of armed conflict (Y). However, the mechanism whereby causal forces are transmitted from X to produce Y is black-boxed.

In contrast, in process-tracing, another type of empirical material is gathered. Collier, Brady, and Seawright suggest that this type of material be termed *causal process observations* (CPO), defined as "an insight or piece of data that provides information about the context or mechanism and contributes a different kind of leverage in causal inference. It does not necessarily do so as part of a larger, systematized array of observations" (2010b: 184).[4]

Unfortunately, the term *causal process observation* conflates observations with evidence. Observations are raw material data; they become evidence only after being assessed for accuracy and interpreted in context (chapter 7). This distinction is analogous to how the two terms are used in criminal proceedings, where observations by themselves have no evidentiary importance; empirical material must be assessed for accuracy and interpreted in its context to be admitted to court as evidence for/against a specific theory about why a crime occurred.

In process-tracing, this assessment is undertaken using case-specific contextual knowledge; therefore, we can depict the evaluation process symbolically as o + k → e, where o is an observation, k is case-specific knowledge, and e is the resulting evidence produced by the evaluation process. After evaluation, empirical material can be termed *evidence*, which can then be used to make inferences that update our confidence in the presence of a hypothesized causal mechanism (see chapter 7).

With regard to part 5 of Owen's hypothesized mechanism, evidence includes speeches by leading liberal elites (e.g., Jefferson) and editorials published in leading liberal newspapers. This evidence seeks to measure the activities (agitation) by the theorized entity (liberal elites) and thus can capture the transmission of causal forces from X to Y in ways that are impossible to measure using standard DSOs.

Even more important regarding the possibility of making cross-case inferences, evidence in the Franco-American crisis case is not comparable with evidence of the same part in the other three cases, making these in effect four parallel single-case studies. Mechanisms have different empirical manifestations in different cases. For example, in testing part 5 of the mechanism in the 1796–98 Franco-American crisis case, relevant evidence includes actions by Jefferson-led Republicans in Congress against a war declaration along with the finding that "the Republican press shrieked in protest" (Owen 1994: 107). In contrast, the evidence produced in the Anglo-American crisis during the Civil War includes the statement that "the [Emancipation] Proclamation energized evangelical Christian and other emancipation groups in Britain" and that mass rallies took place in Manchester at the end of 1862 and in London in the spring of 1863 against British recognition of the Confederacy (112). Given the very case-specific nature of the observable implications of the mechanism in the different cases, what counts as evidence in one case is not necessarily evidence in the other. What is improbable evidence in one case can be probable in another, also making observations noncomparable across cases (see chapter 7). Consequently, the cases cannot be compared directly, making within-case inferential tools necessary.

The Nature of Cross-Case versus Within-Case Inferences

Within qualitative methods, a distinction exists between quantitative-inspired researchers such as KKV, who argue for a "unified" logic that seeks to make inferences about the size of causal effects of independent variables on dependent variables in a population of a given phenomenon (King, Keohane, and Verba 1994; see also Gerring 2005), and qualitative scholars, who contend that in-depth case study methods such as process-tracing have a fundamentally different inferential ambition, which is to detect whether a hypothesized causal mechanism is present in individual cases (Bennett 2008b; Collier, Brady, and Seawright 2010a; Mahoney 2008; McKeown 2004; Munck 2004).

Arguments for making inferences about the size of mean causal effects in a population of a phenomenon build on the combination of the regularity and probabilistic understandings of causality. In KKV's understanding, causal effect is defined as "the difference between the systematic component of observations made when the explanatory variable takes one value and the systematic component of comparable observations when the explanatory variables takes on another value" (King, Keohane, and Verba 1994: 81–82). Here the aim is to make cross-case inferences about mean causal effects of systematic independent variables for the whole population of a given phenomenon based on a selected sample of cases (usually five to twenty), making an inferential leap from the magnitude of the mean causal effects of the independent variables in the sample to the entire population of a given phenomenon.

KKV argue strongly for the position that a single-case study is an invariant research design that prevents us from making causal inferences about causal effects: "Nothing whatsoever can be learned about the causes of the dependent variable without taking into account other instances when the dependent variable takes on other values" (King, Keohane, and Verba 1994: 129). To overcome this problem, they argue that scholars should disaggregate single cases by creating multiple DSOs of the independent and dependent variables. This can be achieved by, for example, disaggregating spatially by transforming a country-level study into its geographical subunits (states, counties, and so forth) or by disaggregating a case into a series of cases over time by testing variables at different points in time (t_0, t_1, t_2 ... t_n) (217–28). However, KKV view the disaggregation strategy as second-best as a consequence of the lack of independence between DSOs made in the disaggregated "cases." For example, values of variables in t_0 will be expected to affect values at t_1, thereby violating the conditional independence of observations rule that makes inferences possible across cases in the frequentist logic of inference (94–97).

Process-tracing research has a different inferential ambition. What we are doing in process-tracing is making inferences about whether causal mechanisms are present in a single case. We naturally want to know that the independent variable(s) and the ensuing causal mechanism have nontrivial causal effects on the outcome, but we are not interested in assessing the magnitude of the causal effects of the combination of an independent variable and the ensuing mechanism on a dependent variable. Instead, we are interested in how a causal mechanism contributed to producing Y or, in explaining-outcome process-tracing, in how a combination of mechanisms produced the particular outcome. We want to know whether evidence suggests that a causal mechanism is present in a particular case.

In contrast to what quantitative-inspired methodologists contend (King, Keohane, and Verba 1994), we contend that strong within-case inferences are possible based on a single in-depth case study using process-tracing methods. This involves adopting a different inferential logic than that suggested by KKV. The difference in the inferential logics in the two understandings of case study research can best be understood by analogy. The understanding of case study research espoused by KKV resembles a medical experiment that studies whether a treatment given to a group of patients has a substantial impact in comparison to a control group that receives placebo treatments. In contrast, inference in process-tracing is more analogous to a court trial, where the researcher assesses our degree of confidence in the existence of a causal mechanism linking X with Y based on many different forms of evidence collected to test the existence of each part of the hypothesized causal mechanism (McKeown 2004). Here, one piece of evidence can be enough to infer that a part of a causal mechanism exists based on the Bayesian logic of inference (Bennett 2008b).

5.2. What Type of Inferential Logic Can Be Used in Process-Tracing?

How can we make within-case causal inferences about whether the parts of a theorized causal mechanism are actually present? We investigate whether mainstream inferential logics such as the frequentist logic of inference espoused by King, Keohane, and Verba or the comparativist logic of elimination used in comparative methods can be used to make strong within-case inferences about the presence/absence of the parts of a causal mechanism. We argue that neither provides a basis for making within-case inferences about whether a causal mechanism is present. As a result, we need to adopt a different inferential logic to bring methodology in line with process-tracing's ontology of causality.

Table 5.3 illustrates the differences in the three types of inferential logics: the frequentist logic as it has been adapted by KKV to qualitative case study research, the comparativist logic of elimination, and Bayesian logic of subjective probability. Both the frequentist and the comparative method build on a regularity understanding of causality, although they diverge regarding whether we should adopt a deterministic or probabilistic understanding.[5] In contrast, process-tracing utilizes a mechanismic and deterministic understanding.

The types of evidence that form the basis for inferences are also different, with the frequentist logic drawing on homogenous DSOs, whereas process-tracing inferences are made using noncomparable process-tracing evidence. The comparative method utilizes a form of DSO, although they are typically a thicker and more in-depth controlled comparison of two or more cases than the type of observations advocated by KKV (see Mahoney and Rueschemeyer 2003).

The frequentist logic of inference assesses the magnitude of causal effects of X on Y, or the degree to which the presence of X raises the probability of Y in a population (Gerring 2005). In contrast, the comparative method aims at assessing necessary and/or sufficient conditions that produce Y (either in a population or a small number of cases) (Mahoney 2008), whereas process-tracing seeks to detect the transmission of causal forces through a causal mechanism to produce an outcome in a single case.

TABLE 5.3. Three Different Logics of Inference in Social Research

	Frequentist Logic in Qualitative Case Study Research (KKV)	Comparativist Logic of Elimination	Bayesian Logic of Subjective Probability (process-tracing)
Ontological understanding of causality	Regularity and probabilistic	Regularity and deterministic	Mechanismic and deterministic
Inferences made using:	Classic probability theory and predicted probability that a found association is random or systematic	Mill's methods of agreement and difference and variants of them	Bayes's theorem about the expected likelihood of finding specific evidence in light of prior knowledge
Types of causality assessed	Mean causal effect of X's upon Y	Necessary and/or sufficient conditions that result in Y	Presence/absence of causal mechanism (i.e., transmission of causal forces from X to produce Y)
Types of observations used to make inferences	Relatively large set of "thin" data-set observations (5–20 according to KKV)	Smaller set of "thicker" DSO's (typically 2–5 in-depth case studies)	Evidence ($o + k \rightarrow e$), where one piece of evidence can be enough to make an inference depending upon its probability
What counts as an observation?	Independent observations of X and Y across a comparable and relatively randomly selected set of cases	Individual cases of the phenomenon (e.g., Denmark and Sweden)	Observed evidence of whether we find the expected observable manifestations of each part of a causal mechanism
Analytical priority	Theory-centric focus, generalization from sample of observations to general population of phenomenon	Both theory- and case-centric focus	Both theory- and case-centric focus
Types of inferences made	Cross-case inferences (to population of phenomenon) or within-case inferences if congruence method used	Cross-case inferences (but smaller scope population) [contextualized])	Within-case inferences

The frequentist logic of inference can be used to make population-wide inferences about the mean causal effects of independent variables on a dependent variable, inferring from the sample of observations to the broader population of the phenomenon using the frequentist logic adapted from classic probability theory. Comparative methodology and process-tracing are typically more case-oriented in that thicker studies of each particular case are made. However, only process-tracing can in our view be used to make within-case inferences about causal mechanisms; comparative methods use the comparativist logic of elimination that by definition can only make cross-case inferences.

We now turn to a discussion of why the frequentist logic and the comparativist logic of elimination cannot be used in process-tracing research.

The Frequentist Logic of Inference in Qualitative Case Study Research

KKV contend that "the differences between the quantitative and qualitative traditions are only stylistic and are methodologically and substantively unimportant. All good research can be understood—indeed, is best understood—to derive from the same underlying logic of inference" (King, Keohane, and Verba 1994: 4). The inferential logic that KKV advocate is in essence the same frequentist logic that is used in classic statistical analysis.[6]

For frequentist-oriented scholars, the gold standard of scientific research is the experimental design. In a medical experiment, for example, researchers examine the size of the effects that a given treatment (X) has on a group of patients in comparison to a control group that receives placebo treatments (not X). The size of the causal effect of the treatment is then found by assessing the value of Y in the group where the treatment is administered in comparison to the value where it is not given (the control group). However, even in the best-designed experiment, we cannot measure the effect of treatment and nontreatment on the same patient at the same time. This is what Holland (1986) terms the fundamental problem of causal inference—it is impossible to observe the effect of X and not X on the same unit of Y.

Building on classic probability theory, Holland offers what can be termed a frequentist logic of inference as a second-best solution to the fundamental problem of causal inference. The gist of the logic is that when certain assumptions hold, we can proceed as if we were able to measure both treatment and nontreatment on the same unit, using classic probability theory to assess whether any found associations between X and Y are the product of chance or are the result of a systematic correlation that can be interpreted as a causal effect of X on Y. Four main assumptions need to be fulfilled when using the frequentist logic of inference to make casual inferences (Holland 1986). First, the units of a sample must be homogenous, enabling comparisons that approximate a treated group/control comparison of the same unit. Second, X must temporally occur prior to Y. Third, the DSOs of each unit must be independent of each other, usually the result of random selection of the sample. Finally, we must be able to assume that the size of the average causal effect of X is constant on every unit in the population.

In the frequentist logic of inference in quantitative social research, a large number of DSOs are analyzed using statistical models such as linear or logistic regression to test whether there are any systematic correlations in the empirical patterns of association between X and Y. In terms of classic probability theory, the association is tested to see whether it is the product of nonsystematic (i.e., random) or systematic variation. Social scientists can then base their inferences that a causal relationship exists between X and Y on the classic statistical probability that the found correlation is not a product of chance (expressed in terms of statistical significance and p-levels). In the frequentist logic, the inferential heavy lifting is done by the laws of classic statistical probability theories about the distributions of populations, such as the central limit theorem.

For example, in a study in international relations of whether three liberal variables (democracy (X_1), economic interdependence (X_2), and membership in international institutions (X_3) resulted in more or less conflict between states (Y), Oneal, Russett, and Berbaum (2003) use a logistic regression model to analyze the association between the liberal independent variables and the dichotomous dependent variable (war/peace), controlled for a series of competing independent variables such as alliances. The size of the sample is 231,618 DSOs. They find a statistically significant relationship among all three Kantian Xs and the dependent variable. More important, they also estimate the marginal effects measured in terms of the predicted probabilities of war for each of the independent variables, finding a relatively large impact of democracy in comparison to the two other independent variables (table 2, p. 382). What enables Oneal, Russett, and Berbaum to make the inferential leap from their sample of observations to conclude that there is a substantively important causal relationship between democracy and peace more generally in the population are classical statistical laws of probability that assess the degree of probability that the association between X_1, X_2, and X_3 and Y estimated by the statistical model is one of chance.

KKV have adapted the frequentist logic of inference so that it can function as the foundation for methodological prescriptions for qualitative case study research (King, Keohane, and Verba 1994). KKV suggest that to make inferences about the mean causal effect of an X on Y, we should have between five and twenty independent observations of values of X and Y (DSOs). When the assumptions of unit homogeneity and what they term the conditional independence of observations hold,[7] KKV argue that inferences about the magnitude of causal effects can be made using case study methods.

Can this frequentist logic of inference be utilized in process-tracing studies? The short answer is no. As discussed earlier, KKV's frequentist logic of inference builds on logic similar to a medical trial, whereas process-tracing is more akin to a court trial.

In a typical process-tracing research design, the only assumption of Holland's that is usually fulfilled is the temporal one, where most tests of mechanisms involve also testing whether each part of the mechanism is temporally prior to the outcome. The assumption about unit homogeneity is not fulfilled in a process-tracing case study, as the manifestations of causal mechanisms differ both with regard to the individual parts of a mechanism and across cases. In addition, the inferential weight of individual pieces of evidence can also differ markedly.

For example, in Owen's (1994) study, the evidence collected for part 1 is not comparable with the evidence for parts 4 or 5. In contrast, using KKV's understanding, a case study would fulfill the assumption of unit homogeneity, given that by disaggregating over time we could observe the scores of X and Y at t_0, t_1, t_2, enabling them to be treated as comparable with each other. This is how congruence methods enable within-case inferences to be made.[8] Further, given the lack of comparability of evidence across the different parts of the mechanism, the assumption of independence loses its relevance when testing whether causal mechanisms are present. Basically, it matters little whether evidence of parts 1–5 are independent if we cannot compare them.

One could argue that the tests of whether each of the parts of a mechanism is present can be thought of as individual case studies that should be further disaggregated to create a sufficient number of comparable observations to enable the employment of the frequentist logic of inference. However, this approach would conflict with the nature of evidence that is collected in process-tracing research. While we do have multiple pieces of evidence of each part of the causal mechanism, they are noncomparable with each other. The difference between DSOs and evidence results from the different purpose that evidence serves in process-tracing research. In terms of the Owen example, we cannot just disaggregate the examination of part 5 of the mechanism ("liberal elites agitate") to multiple observations of whether or not elites agitate. Indeed, a single piece of highly improbable evidence, if found, can be enough to substantiate that the part of the mechanism was present (Bennett 2008b).

In process-tracing case studies, pieces of evidence should not be thought of in terms analogous to individual patients in a medical trial; instead, they can be seen as resembling evidence at a court trial. For example, in a trial dealing with a robbery, a part of the theory of the crime would be the suspect's motive. If it is theorized that the suspect committed the robbery to fund a drug habit, we would predict that we would find different types of evidence of the habit, such as witnesses who testify to having seen the suspect using drugs and physical evidence such as traces of drugs or drug paraphernalia found at the suspect's residence. Not all of these pieces of evidence would need to be found; indeed, our confidence in the validity of the part of the theory would be substantially increased if even one piece of highly incriminating evidence was found (e.g., a syringe used to shoot heroin with only the suspect's fingerprints on it).

In process-tracing, we never possess a sample of observations that enable us to use the frequentist logic of inference to make causal inferences. However, the nonapplicability of the frequentist logic does not result from a lack of stringent research design, as KKV would argue. Instead, it is an explicit choice. While it limits our ability to make cross-case causal inferences to a population of a phenomenon, process-tracing enables us to make stronger within-case inferences than would be possible using the frequentist logic.

The Comparative Method's Logic of Elimination

Comparative methods deal primarily with finding and/or eliminating necessary and/or sufficient conditions that produce a given outcome. For example, using comparative methods, Skocpol (1979) found that a combination of state breakdown and peasant revolt were sufficient conditions for producing social revolution in agrarian-bureaucratic states. Necessary conditions are defined as causes that must always precede Y for Y to occur; Y will not occur if X is absent. Sufficient conditions are causes that, if present, always produce Y, but Y is not always preceded by X.

While it uses the same regularity understanding of causality as the frequentist logic, comparative methodology utilizes another logic to make causal inferences that can be termed the comparativist logic of elimination. The basic idea of the logic of elimination in comparative methodology is based on John Stuart Mill's methods of agreement and difference. Mill's method of agreement is used to eliminate potential necessary causes. Here, all of the instances of Y (e.g., social revolutions) are examined,[9] and all potential conditions that are not present in all of the cases are eliminated as necessary conditions. While being able to make strong negative inferences (elimination), the method enables only very weak positive inferences. Mill suggested that conditions that survived the test were only possibly associated with the outcome, as it could not be ruled out that future cases would be discovered where the outcome occurred but the posited necessary condition was not present (George and Bennett 2005: 155–56). The method of difference is used to test for sufficient causation, where two or more cases that have different outcomes are compared. Conditions that are present in both types of outcomes are then eliminated as potential sufficient conditions. Mill's methods have been further developed to account for multiple causal paths to the same outcome, using more complex set-theoretical logic that draws on the same notion of a logic of elimination (Ragin 1988, 2000, 2008; Rihoux 2006).

The logic of elimination used in comparative methodology cannot form the basis for causal inferences in process-tracing research for two reasons. First, comparative case studies by definition deal with cross-case inferences based on a controlled comparison of cases, whereas process-tracing studies aim at within-case inferences about whether a causal mechanism is present in a particular case. The comparativist logic of elimination does not give us any inferential leverage to determine whether a part of a mechanism is present in a particular case study, as the comparative method's use of the regularity understanding results in the actual mechanism being black-boxed; instead, patterns of correlations are assessed using the logic of elimination.[10]

Further, even if we could find two fully comparable cases, when we delve into testing whether the theorized parts of a mechanism are present in both, the types of evidence that would be utilized for each part are noncomparable. What counts as strong evidence in one case might differ substantially from another case. Comparative methods offer us no tools for assessing the inferential weight of different process-tracing evidence in particular cases. For example, in Owen's study, to what extent does the observation of the key liberal actor, Jefferson, making statements supporting liberal France in the Franco-American crisis increase our confidence in the presence or absence of part 5 of the causal mechanism? Here, process-tracing—in particular, the Bayesian logic of subjective probability—gives us a set of inferential tools that enable us to evaluate in a transparent manner the inferential weight of different pieces of evidence.

5.3. The Bayesian Logic of Inference and Process-Tracing

Bayesian logic provides us with a set of logical tools for evaluating whether finding specific evidence confirms/disconfirms a hypothesis that a part of a causal mechanism exists relative to the prior expected probability of finding this evidence. Drawing on arguments developed by Bennett (2006, 2008b), along with Collier, Brady, and Seawright (2010b), we argue that Bayesian logic should be utilized as the inferential underpinning of process-tracing methods, enabling us to evaluate transparently and systematically the confidence that we can place in evidence confirming/disconfirming hypothesized causal mechanisms.

In Bayesian logic, the analyst gives greater weight to evidence that is expected a priori to be less probable based on previous knowledge of the phenomenon. "What is important is not the number of pieces of evidence within a case that fit one explanation or another, but the likelihood of finding certain evidence if a theory is true versus the likelihood of finding this evidence if the alternative explanation is true" (Bennett 2006: 341).

This reasoning is based on Bayes's theorem, which is a simple and uncontroversial logical formula for estimating the probability that a theory is supported by evidence based on the researcher's degree of belief about the probability of the theory and probability of finding given evidence if the theory is valid before gathering the data (Buckley 2004; Howson and Urbach 2006; Jackman 2004; Lynch 2005; Western and Jackman 1994).

The simplest version of Bayes's theorem is **posterior ∝ likelihood × prior.** This theorem states that our belief in the validity of a hypothesis is, after collecting evidence (posterior), equal to the probability of the evidence conditional on the hypothesis being true relative to other alternative hypotheses (likelihood), times the probability that a theory is true based on our prior knowledge. Here, we use the term *hypothesis* to refer to hypotheses about the existence of each part of a theorized causal mechanism.

Before we go further into a discussion of the different parts of Bayes's theorem, the idea that a theory, here understood as the existence of the parts of a causal mechanism, can be confirmed contradicts the Popperian falsification ideal of science that still forms the basis of many methodological textbooks in the social sciences. KKV approvingly quote Popper's categorical statement that "theories are not verifiable" (King, Keohane, and Verba 1994: 100). In contrast, Bayesian logic posits that we can both confirm and disconfirm our confidence in the validity of a theory—although given the uncertain nature of empirical observation, we can never be 100 percent confident about either confirmation or disconfirmation. Bayesian logic is closer to the actual practice of science, where we tend to have stronger confidence in the validity of theories that have withstood numerous independent empirical tests (Howson and Urbach 2006: 4). Bayes's theorem also predicts that a theory test that merely repeats existing scholarship with the same data will do little to update our confidence in the validity of the theory. This is due to the Bayesian principle of "updating," where the findings of a previous study form the prior for the next study; given that the data has been assessed in previous studies, finding the data is not surprising (high likelihood), and therefore little or no updating of the posterior takes place (Howson and Urbach 2006). In contrast, our belief in the validity of a theory is most strongly confirmed when we engage in new scholarship and find evidence whose presence is highly unlikely unless the hypothesized theory actually exists. For example, within international relations, confidence in the validity of democratic peace theory increased significantly in the 1990s as new scholarship tested the theory in different ways and with different forms of evidence. However, after initial tests, repeated tests of the thesis using the same data and methods do little to further update our confidence in the validity of the theory.

Confirmation—or, more accurately, an increase in our confidence about the validity of a theory—is achieved when the posterior probability of a theory exceeds the prior probability before evidence was collected. If there is a high prior probability (i.e., existing scholarship suggests that we should be relatively confident about the validity of a theory) and the evidence collected is the same as used in previous studies, additional tests do little to update our confidence in the theory.

The three elements of Bayes's theorem are posterior probability, likelihood, and the prior. The full theorem can be expressed as follows (Howson and Urbach 2006: 21):

$$p(h|e) = \frac{p(h)}{p(h) + \dfrac{p(e|\sim h)p(\sim h)}{p(e|h)}}$$

The term $p(h|e)$ is the posterior probability, or the degree of confidence we have in the validity of a hypothesis (h) about the existence of a part of a causal mechanism after collecting evidence (e). The term $p(h)$ is the prior, which is the researcher's degree of confidence in the validity of a hypothesis prior to gathering evidence, based on existing theorization, empirical studies, and other forms of expert knowledge. The likelihood ratio is the expected probability of finding evidence supporting a hypothesis based on the researcher's interpretation of the probability of finding it in relation to the hypothesis and background knowledge informed by previous studies, compared with the expected probability of finding the evidence if the hypothesis is not true (p(e|~h). This is expressed in the formula as p(e|~h)/p(e|h). A prediction by a soothsayer that you will meet a tall dark stranger is highly probable to occur, meaning that observing it does little to update our confidence in the hypothesis that the soothsayer can predict the future. However, if the soothsayer correctly predicted the number of hairs on the stranger's head, this evidence would seriously increase our confidence in the validity of the hypothesis (Howson and Urbach 2006: 97).

It must be noted that no evidence confirms or disconfirms a theory with 100 percent certitude: Confirmation is a matter of degree. When we develop strong tests for the presence/absence of the parts of a hypothesized causal mechanism that can discriminate between predictions of evidence that confirm h and the alternative hypothesis, and when the observations collected are quite accurate, we can use Bayesian logic to update our degree of confidence in whether a causal mechanism existed.

This formula introduces a degree of subjective choice by the researcher in terms of expectations of the probability of the likelihood of finding certain evidence and the interpretation of our confidence in a theory based on existing theorization (the prior). This has been the subject of extensive critique by non-Bayesian scholars, who contend that it introduces an unacceptable degree of subjectivity into the scientific process. Bayesian scholars contend that these expected probabilities are not purely subjective but are based on the existing body of prior research (Chalmers 1999; Howson and Urbach 2006). In addition, even if priors are somewhat subjective, after a series of empirical tests that increase confidence in the validity of a theory, the final posterior probability would converge on the same figure irrespective of whether two different values of the prior were taken initially (Howson and Urbach 2006: 298).

Further, Bayesians counter that many subjective decisions are also made when using the frequentist logic of inference, such as significance levels, the choice of null hypothesis, and the statistical estimation method. These choices are usually not very transparent and are often quite arbitrary (Howson and Urbach 2006; Lynch 2005: 137; Western 1999: 11). In the Bayesian logic of inference, "subjective" choices are made explicitly and transparently, and they are less subjective than they would appear since they are informed by existing scientific knowledge, documented for example in the form "Based on sources X, Y and Z, we have a relatively high level of prior confidence in theory A."

Given the resemblance of process-tracing to detective work, we illustrate the relevance of Bayesian logic for causal inference in process-tracing using an example drawn from a classic Sherlock Holmes story, *Silver Blaze* (A. C. Doyle 1975). The crime in the story is the mysterious abduction of a racehorse, Silver Blaze. After Holmes develops a theory of a mechanism that hypothetically can explain the crime based on his prior experience, he travels to the scene of the crime to investigate whether evidence supports the existence of each part of his hypothesized mechanism. One of the parts of this theorized mechanism deals with whether the perpetrator is a stranger or an insider. Holmes utilizes the observation that a particularly obnoxious stable dog did not bark on the night of the crime to evaluate the validity of this specific part of the mechanism.

> "You consider that to be important?" he asked.
> "Exceedingly so."
> "Is there any other point to which you would wish to draw my attention?"
> "To the curious incident of the dog in the night-time."
> "The dog did nothing in the night-time."
> "That was the curious incident," remarked Sherlock Holmes.
> (A. C. Doyle 1975: 24)

Expressed mathematically, let us say for illustrative purposes that Holmes's degree of confidence in hypothesis h (the hypothesis on the part of the mechanism that an insider was the culprit) is quite low (e.g., 20 percent), meaning that the prior (p (h)) is 20 percent and the more probable alternative hypothesis (~h) is 80 percent probable. The low value for the prior reflects the relative improbability of the part of the mechanism that hypothesizes that an insider abducted his own horse in comparison to more probable alternative explanations such as theft by a stranger of such a valuable asset.

After multiple visits to the stable, Holmes and Watson both experienced firsthand and heard testimony from observers that the stable dog always barked when strangers are near. Therefore, based on these observations and the improbability of alternative explanations of "no bark,"[11] we would expect that it is highly likely that the evidence of the dog that did not bark (e), if found, would support h (p (e|h) = 90%; p (e|~h) = 10%). Note that the inferential weight of evidence is evaluated in relation to case-specific knowledge.

Inserting the prior and the likelihood function into Bayes's theorem, we get the following posterior probability that expresses our degree of confidence in the hypothesis after collecting and evaluating the evidence:

$$69.2\% = \frac{0.2}{0.2 + (0.1/0.9) \times 0.8}$$

This example shows how the Bayesian theorem provides us with an inferential tool that allows us to update the degree of confidence we have in a hypothesis after evaluating the inferential weight of collected evidence. In the Holmes example, after finding the evidence of the dog not barking, based on the probabilities we attached in the preceding, we find that Holmes was justified in holding a much higher degree of confidence in the validity of the hypothesis after evidence was gathered (from 20 percent to 69.2 percent).

The key point here is that one piece of evidence significantly increased our confidence in the validity of the hypothesis—something that never would be the case when using the frequentist logic of inference. In other words, pieces of evidence do not necessarily have the same inferential weight in process-tracing (Bennett 2008b). Inferential weight is instead a function of the expected probability of a piece of evidence given the hypothesis in relation to the expected probability of finding the evidence given the alternative hypothesis.

When we are using the Bayesian logic of inference in process-tracing, we usually do not express priors and likelihood functions in mathematical terms (although there is no logical reason why this cannot be done), but the Bayesian logic plays the same essential role in evaluating causal inferences that frequentist logic plays in quantitative large-*n* research.

We find it unfortunate that many qualitative scholars using process-tracing do not make their priors and likelihood ratios explicit in their analysis. The result is that their work all too easily falls prey to the criticism that their inferential reasoning is soft. In our view, priors and likelihood ratios should be made as explicit as possible in one's analysis. They should be explicitly described in terms of what we believe to be probable based on the existing theoretical debate and empirical studies using the terminology prior probability and the likelihood ratio of finding evidence.

For example, if we are studying the disintegration of the Soviet empire in the late 1980s/early 1990s, based on what we already know from realist theories of declining powers and historical studies (e.g., Gilpin 1981; Kennedy 1988), we would expect that Soviet decision makers would contemplate a last throw of the dice by engaging in foreign military adventures during the power transition. This prior probability would inform our inferences when studying the disintegration of the Soviet empire. Therefore, if we are testing sociological hypotheses about the development of norms of cooperation and we find evidence that matches the predicted evidence that would support the sociological hypothesis (which would predict that Soviet decision makers never even contemplated violence), this found evidence, given that it is not likely unless the sociological thesis is true, would greatly increase the degree of confidence we have in the validity of the sociological hypotheses in comparison to our existing knowledge of past power transitions.

Bayesian logic is what enables process-tracing scholars to make within-case causal inferences in the same manner that frequentist logic and the logic of elimination enables cross-case causal inferences to be made in quantitative and comparative social research.

In the next section, we discuss what type of valid inferences can be made when we are using process-tracing methods. Finally, we discuss in more detail the limits to the types of inferences that can be made using process-tracing methods.

5.4. Making Causal Inferences in Process-Tracing Methods— Uses and Limits

While process-tracing enables strong causal inference to be made with regard to the presence of causal mechanisms in single cases (within-case) and in particular whether the individual parts of a whole mechanism are indeed present in the particular case, it is not compatible with generalizations beyond the individual case (cross-case inferences). When we attempt to generalize beyond the single case, we can no longer rely on process-tracing methods and the underlying Bayesian logic of subjective probabilities but instead need to adopt cross-case comparative methods that are built on either the frequentist logic or the comparativist logic of elimination (see chapter 8).

The types of causal inferences being made in process-tracing depend on which variant of process-tracing is used. As introduced in chapter 2, theory-centric variants of process-tracing (building/testing) have the inferential ambition to detect whether there is evidence suggesting that a causal mechanism was present in a case. Here inferences are first made about whether each part of the mechanism is present. Given that each part is theorized as being individually necessary, if there is evidence that significantly increases our confidence in the presence of each part, we can infer that the whole mechanism is present. Theory-centric process-tracing cannot make inferences about the necessity or sufficiency of the mechanism in relation to the population of the phenomenon. In contrast, explaining-outcome process-tracing seeks to produce a sufficient explanation of a particular outcome, made possible by the adoption of pragmatic methodological ideas (see chapter 2).

Inferences in Theory-Centric Process-Tracing

The scope of inferences that can be made using theory-centric variants of process-tracing is restricted to whether or not a mechanism is present in a case. Neither inferences about necessity nor sufficiency of a mechanism in relation to the population of a phenomenon can be made. To prove necessity or sufficiency of conditions in relation to a population requires cross-case comparative methods, such as investigating all cases where Y is present to see whether the mechanism is also always present when Y occurs (see Braumoeller and Goetz 2000; Seawright 2002).

However, when we engage in theory-building or testing process-tracing research, the necessity and/or sufficiency of the theorized cause (X) has usually already been tested using more appropriate cross-case methods. In the case of democratic peace theory, many large-n cross-case studies have suggested that mutual democracy (X) is a sufficient explanation for peace between two states (Y) (e.g., Russett and Oneal 2001). Confirming the existence of a causal mechanism in a particular case (especially a "least-likely" case) substantiates a robust correlation between an explanatory variable (X) and an outcome that has been found using cross-case comparative or statistical methods, we can infer based on the process-tracing study that the correlation is actually a causal relationship where an X is linked with an outcome through a causal mechanism.

The belief that theory-centric process-tracing can be used to test two competing theories against each other is widespread but erroneous in most situations. In the complex social world, most outcomes are the product of multiple mechanisms acting at the same time. The inferences that can be made with theory-centric process-tracing are therefore restricted to claiming that a mechanism was present in the case and that it functioned as expected. No claims can be made about whether the mechanism was the only factor that resulted in outcome Y occurring—in other words, we cannot claim sufficiency based on a single theory test.

When engaging in theory testing, alternative theoretical explanations of the predicted evidence for a part of the causal mechanism form the ~h element of the likelihood ratio. However, in most situations, alternative theoretical mechanisms will not be able to form ~h for each part of a mechanism.

For example, if we are testing a rational decision-making mechanism, part 1 of our mechanism is that decision makers gather all relevant information. Testing this mechanism might involve a likelihood ratio where h is the part of the rational mechanism, while the most relevant alternative explanation (~h) for the predicted evidence could be a normative explanation. But for part 2, defined as identifying all the possible courses of action, the most plausible alternative explanation (~h) for the predicted evidence might be a bureaucratic politics explanation. In other words, a single competing mechanism will usually not provide the most plausible alternative explanation of evidence for each part of the causal mechanism.

The only exception is when it is possible to conceptualize and operationalize two competing mechanisms in a manner where they are composed of the same number of parts, each of them the polar opposite of the other and mutually exclusive. For example, Moravcsik's (1999) research design (see chapter 4) put forward a supranational entrepreneur mechanism formulated in a manner that was the diametrical opposite of an intergovernmental bargaining mechanism. If the analysis found that one existed, then the other logically could not exist. Each of the parts was operationalized in a manner where the competing theory logically formed ~h, enabling a competing theory test to be performed. Yet this is a rare situation in social research; more common is the situation where theories are acting at the same time. Therefore, we can only infer that a mechanism was present, cognizant that other mechanisms can also contribute to producing Y.

A more viable alternative for testing competing theories is to engage in a two-step research design, where competing theories are evaluated using the congruence method either before or after a process-tracing theory test. If congruence is used first, the competing theory (theory X_2) is conceptualized and tested as a causal theory ($X_2 \rightarrow Y$) instead of being transformed into a mechanism, as in process-tracing. Based on the value of the independent variable in the case (X_2), the congruence method involves testing whether the prediction about the outcome that should follow from the theory is congruent with what is found in the case (Blatter and Blume 2008; George and Bennett 2005: 181–204). If the predicted observable implications of the competing alternative are not found when examining the outcome of the case, then the analyst can proceed with the second step, using process-tracing to test whether a theorized mechanism (X_1 and a mechanism) existed and functioned as expected. If the mechanism is found, the conclusion can be drawn that X_2 was unable to account for the outcome of the case, whereas X_1 was causally related to the outcome through a found mechanism.

Using congruence after a process-tracing theory test is a way to check that the findings are not excessively biased toward what Khong terms "overly subjective interpretations of the raw data" (1992: 66). Here, alternative explanations of the outcome are tested using the congruence method, assessing whether they have greater congruence or consistency with the outcome than theory X_1 and a mechanism. Khong used this type of two-step analysis to bolster his inferences in a theory test about the role that an ideational mechanism (historical analogies) played in the case of U.S. decision making in the Vietnam War. After finding that the predicted outcomes of alternative theories did not match those of the case, he can make a stronger inference that the ideational mechanism was causally related to the decisions taken.

Inferences in theory testing are made for each part of a causal mechanism based on the Bayesian logic of inference, where each part of the mechanism is tested to see whether we can update our confidence in its presence or absence. Each part is theorized as being individually necessary. Therefore, if our confidence in the presence of one part is significantly decreased, we can infer that the mechanism as a whole was not present in the manner in which it was theorized. Our inferences about the presence of the whole mechanism are therefore only as strong as the weakest link in our empirical tests (see chapter 6). If we are unable to infer that the mechanism was present, the result is either the conclusion that the mechanism was not present or a round of theory building should be done to develop a more accurate causal mechanism.

Inferences in Case-Centric Process-Tracing

When the aim of a process-tracing study is to explain a particular outcome, the study is in effect attempting to confirm the sufficiency of an explanation. More precisely, we should seek to provide a "minimally sufficient" explanation with no redundant parts (Mackie 1965). An everyday example of sufficiency is that if the requisite background factors are present (power is available and the circuit and lightbulb are unbroken), when I turn on a switch, the light will always turn on when the mechanism linking the power source and the lightbulb becomes activated. In the same fashion, advocates of democratic peace theory postulate that having two democratic countries is sufficient to produce peace even in situations where the countries otherwise have such strong conflicts of interests that there is a significant risk of war.

Explaining-outcome process-tracing studies can start deductively or inductively (see chapter 2). For example, when we are attempting to explain a given instance of an otherwise well-studied phenomenon, analysts can proceed in a deductive manner, testing existing theories in a comparative theory test to see what aspects of the specific outcome they can explain. When we are studying a little-studied phenomenon, the analyst can proceed in a manner more analogous with forensic science (as popularized by the TV show *CSI*). Here, the investigator starts with a corpse (the particular outcome) and then works backward to build a plausible theory based on the available evidence gathered from a multitude of different sources. The forensic evidence takes the form of physical evidence, such as hair samples, but the investigator also relies on other forms of evidence, such as the testimony of witnesses. This form of inductive study may appear to start from scratch, but in all but the most extreme instances, the investigator will draw inspiration from past experiences and existing theories.

In most circumstances, a single theorized causal mechanism is not sufficient to explain the outcome and therefore must be supplemented with new parts from other compatible theories or new theories to achieve minimal sufficiency. However, all the parts of this more complex mechanism must be individually necessary for the mechanism, and the overall mechanism need only achieve minimal sufficiency. These requirements focus our analytical attention on achieving as parsimonious an explanation as possible.

How do we know a minimally sufficient explanation when we see it? A good example can be seen in Schimmelfennig (2001). Here he takes as his point of departure two competing theorized causal mechanisms from rationalist and sociological theories of international cooperation to explain the existing EU member states' positions toward eastern enlargement. Not surprisingly, Schimmelfennig finds that neither can fully explain the outcome (neither is sufficient), and he therefore engages in theoretical synthesis, working backward from the outcome to fashion a more complex theoretical mechanism that is logically coherent, involving "rhetorical action." He provides strong evidence that the more complex mechanism is present in the case and that it is sufficient to account for the outcome. Sufficiency is confirmed when it can be substantiated that there are no important aspects of the outcome for which the explanation does not account (Day and Kincaid 1994).

We cannot, however, use process-tracing methods to determine how frequently a given mechanism is sufficient in relation to a broader population of relevant cases as a consequence of the inclusion of nonsystematic parts and case-specific conglomerate mechanisms, and because the outcome is unique (it is not a case of something). Basically, explanations are case-specific here (Humphreys 2010: 269–70). Therefore cross-case comparative designs are more appropriate if we want to study sufficiency across a population (such as a positive on cause design) (see Dion 1998).

Sufficiency naturally does not mean that mechanism X is the only true path to Y but merely that if mechanism X occurs, it is sufficient to produce Y. A classic example used by Mackie (1965) is how we can explain what caused a fire in a house (Y = house fire). In a specific case, a short-circuit, the absence of a suitably placed sprinkler, and the presence of flammable materials were sufficient to produce the fire. However, alternative paths to a house fire are possible, including a gas explosion or lightning coupled with the lack of sprinklers and the presence of flammable materials.

Conclusions

Table 5.4 illustrates what forms of inferences can and cannot be made using process-tracing methods. Process-tracing methods can be used to confirm/ disconfirm the necessity of the individual parts of a causal mechanism. While cross-case comparisons could be utilized if we conceptualized a mechanism as a set of intervening variables that can be compared across cases, we would then lose sight of the causal forces that hypothetically cause the mechanism to produce an outcome.

We have argued that explaining-outcome process-tracing can confirm/ disconfirm the minimal sufficiency of a mechanism in a single-case study but not for a broader population. Process-tracing methods cannot test for the necessity of a mechanism, and we therefore need to rely on other, cross-case comparative methods to test for overall necessity of a mechanism as a cause of a phenomenon.

In practice, most existing applications of process-tracing methods are

TABLE 5.4.   Research Situations where Process-Tracing Methods Can Be Used to Make Causal Inferences

Testing for the Necessity of the *Parts* of a Causal Mechanism in Single Case	Testing for the Necessity of a Mechanism as a *Whole* at the Population Level	Testing for the Sufficiency of a Mechanism in Single Case	Testing for the Sufficiency of a Condition at the Population Level
Process-tracing (all variants)	Not process-tracing. Use instead comparative cross-case designs (e.g., positive on outcome design— all Y's).	Explaining-outcome process-tracing	Not process-tracing. Use instead comparative cross-case designs (e.g., positive on cause design, all X's).

hybrid studies. Process-tracing studies often are comprised of a set of two to five individual process-tracing case studies. Internally, each process-tracing study utilizes a mechanismic understanding of causality to engage in causal inferences about whether the individual parts of the mechanism are present and whether the mechanism as such is sufficient either to produce a specific outcome or to test whether the causal mechanism is present in the given case (thereby demonstrating a causal relationship between X and Y instead of a mere correlation). Here, within-case inferences are made using process-tracing. However, cross-case inferences are made using comparative designs, selecting for example a least-likely case or set of cases (see chapter 8).

CHAPTER 6

Developing Empirical Tests of Causal Mechanisms

Chapter 4 dealt with how we should develop theories, where a causal theory $(X \rightarrow Y)$ should be reconceptualized into a theorized causal mechanism composed of a set of parts, each of which can be thought of as a hypothesis (h) about which we have expectations of the prior probability of its existence (p(h)). In the Bayesian inferential logic described in chapter 5, the purpose of empirical tests is to update our degree of confidence in a hypothesis in light of the empirical evidence that has been found. Our ability to update the posterior probability of a hypothesis is contingent on the probability of evidence and the ability of our empirical tests to discriminate between evidence that supports h and alternative hypotheses (~h). This chapter discusses how empirical tests of hypothesized mechanisms are developed in process-tracing research.

Testing theorized causal mechanisms involves formulating case-specific predictions about the expected observable manifestations of each part of a causal mechanism that we should see if it is present. We define these observable manifestations as evidence that we should expect to find in the case if each part of a causal mechanism is present. In developing these case-specific predictions, we deploy our contextual knowledge of individual cases. Predicted evidence is analogous to what Adcock and Collier (2001) term *empirical indicators* for theoretical concepts, although we use the term to refer to the predicted evidence for each part of a mechanism instead of just X and Y.

We begin this chapter by further developing the Bayesian foundations for empirical tests of theorized causal mechanisms in process-tracing, illustrating how our ability to update our confidence in the presence of a causal mechanism and all of the parts depends on (1) the probability of the evidence (p(e)), (2) the likelihood ratio (p(e|~h)/p(e|h)), and (3) the theoretical prior. The second section discusses the different types of evidence utilized in process-tracing analysis, distinguishing among pattern, sequence, trace, and account evidence. The third section develops four test types for developing predictions for what evidence we should expect to find if h is valid, arguing that we should attempt to maximize both the certainty and uniqueness of our predictions to maximize our ability to update our confidence in the hypotheses in light of empirical evidence (van Evera 1997). We provide practical suggestions for maximizing both the certainty and the uniqueness of our predictions. Finally, we illustrate the challenges relating to developing empirical tests using a bureaucratic politics mechanism as an example.

6.1. Bayesian Updating

The key to testing theories in process-tracing analysis is to maximize the inferential power of our empirical tests for whether the parts of a hypothesized causal mechanism exist. The stronger the test, the more we can update our degree of confidence in the presence/absence of the parts of the hypothesized mechanism. To understand test strength and in particular the power of evidence to update our confidence, we need to look more closely at three terms in Bayesian theory: the probability of evidence, the likelihood ratio relating hypotheses to evidence, and theoretical priors.

The importance of the probability of evidence (p(e)) is most clearly seen in Bayes's original theorem, or what has been termed the first form of the Bayesian theorem (Howson and Urbach 2006: 20–21). This is a simpler version of the theorem than the one presented in chapter 5.

$$p(h|e) = \frac{p(e|h)\, p(h)}{p(e)}$$

Here the posterior (p(h|e)) is equal to the probability of the evidence conditional on the hypothesis being valid multiplied by the probability of the hypothesis, divided by the probability of the evidence taken by itself. Because p(e) is in the denominator, as the probability of the evidence decreases, the ability of evidence to update the posterior increases, other things equal. More surprising evidence (low p(e)), if found, results in larger increases in our confidence in a hypothesis than less surprising evidence. Given its unlikelihood, a man-bites-dog story, if found, has a stronger inferential weight than a more typical dog-bites-man story. We return to the question of the probability of evidence p(e) in our discussion of evaluating evidence in chapter 7. The second term of interest in Bayesian updating is the likelihood ratio, the effect of which is most clearly seen in the third form of Bayes's theorem from chapter 5. The likelihood ratio is p(e|~h)/p(e|h). The likelihood ratio should be read as the probability of finding the predicted evidence (e) if the alternative hypothesis (~h) is true in comparison to the probability of finding the evidence if the hypothesis is true. The ratio captures an empirical test's ability to discriminate between predicted evidence that supports h and ~h. If h predicts e, the occurrence of e will raise our confidence in the validity of h, depending on the size of likelihood ratio. When p(e|h) is high and p(e|~h) is low, finding e results in a large increase in confidence. While the ratio depicts ~h as a single alternative, it can also be defined as any plausible alternative to h.

$$p(h|e) = \frac{p(h)}{p(h) + \frac{\underline{p(e|\underline{\sim}h)}p(\sim h)}{p(e|h)}}$$

In practical research situations, we often lack a clearly demarked alternative hypothesized explanation of a part of a causal mechanism, and even if we have a relatively clear alternative, it is often difficult to design tests that do not privilege h over ~h, or vice versa. For example, in testing ideational versus material interest mechanisms as explanations for the lack of force used by the Soviets in 1989 to stop the revolutions in the Warsaw Pact countries, Tannenwald suggests that tests of mechanisms that take material factors as their starting point privilege materialist explanations, and vice versa (2005: 22–23). She states that "the larger issue of whether one starts with ideas or material factors in assessing the role of ideas is ultimately impossible to resolve and will remain a fundamental point of disagreement among scholars." However, she pragmatically attempts nonetheless to develop balanced tests of h and ~h—for example, by looking at the range of options considered by actors to see whether certain options were considered unthinkable (role of ideas) or whether all plausible options were considered (material interests) (23, 24).

Even if there is a well-developed alternative, the testing of two contending hypotheses for a part of a mechanism (h and ~h) against each other can degenerate into the sort of gladiatorial contest seen in the movie *Mad Max beyond Thunderdome*, where two men enter, one man leaves. In these gladiator-like contests, ~h is often depicted in such a highly simplified form that its fate is sealed even before the analysis starts (Checkel 2012).

Therefore, we agree with Bennett's suggestion that we should cast our net widely for alternative plausible explanations of predicted evidence of a particular part of a mechanism, attempting to avoid crude either/or analyses (2008a: 707). The questions that we can ask when testing each part of a mechanism include, Can plausible alternative mechanisms be formulated? Are there any other plausible explanations for the predicted evidence?

The final step is to define theoretical priors, understood as the expected probability that a given hypothesized mechanism (and its parts) is valid (p(h)). When we are engaging in causal inferences in the empirical analysis, the process of updating our level of confidence in the validity of the parts of a mechanism is informed by our prior beliefs about our confidence in the presence of a mechanism as a whole.[1]

If we are testing whether a democratic peace mechanism exists, our prior would be our confidence, based on what we know, in the existence of a mechanism. But answers to the question of the level of prior expectations vary across different research traditions in political science. Regarding democratic peace, skeptics from the realist tradition of international relations contend that the thesis has a very low prior probability of being true (low p(h)) despite the large number of quantitative and qualitative studies that have been undertaken. For example, realists have contended that the found correlation between democracy (X) and peace (Y) is the product of confounding variables such as the distribution of democracies on one side of the divide during the Cold War (Farber and Gowa 1997; see also Layne 1994; Rosato 2003). A realist would therefore start a process-tracing analysis with a low prior as a starting point in a particular case.

As discussed briefly in chapter 5, the use of priors introduces a degree of unavoidable subjectivity into the analysis. In Bayesian statistical analysis, the standard procedure is to test posteriors' sensitivity on prior estimates by simulating how the posterior changes depending on different priors (Jackman 2004). We cannot do this in qualitative research; therefore, when the literature exhibits significant disagreement about a prior, the best bet is to use conservative estimates of p(h) relative to p(~h). In other words, we prejudice our analysis away from h and toward alternative theories (Lynch 2005).

Further, priors inform all scientific research, and by explicitly stating them, we make their incorporation transparent (Chalmers 1999; Howson and Urbach 2006). For example, in process-tracing analysis, we should state that "based upon prior research, we are a priori relatively confident that theoretical proposition X is valid." This prior then informs the subsequent evaluation of the degree of updating of our confidence in the theory after it has been empirically tested in our case study.

Most important, priors tend to wash out after repeated meetings with empirical evidence (Howson and Urbach 2006: 298). A realist and liberal scholar who engaged in research on the democratic peace mechanism would start with different priors but after repeated empirical studies would converge on the same posterior, assuming that strong empirical tests were developed that did not privilege one of the theorized mechanisms and that the empirical evidence was accurate.

6.2. Types of Evidence in Process-Tracing

Testing whether causal mechanisms are present in process-tracing analysis involves investigating whether our theory-based predictions for what we should see in the empirical record are matched in reality. Do we find the predicted evidence of the parts of the mechanism? Here, the term *relevant evidence* used in evidence law is appropriate. U.S. Federal Rule of Evidence 401 defines *relevant evidence* as "any evidence having any tendency to make the existence of any fact that is of consequence to the determination of the action more probable or less probable than it would be without evidence."

In comparison to data-set observations, predicted evidence in process-tracing is more analogous to what Collier, Brady, and Seawright (2010b: 184–88) term "causal-process observations" or what Bennett refers to as process-tracing observations (2006: 341). Pieces of evidence in process-tracing are noncomparable, as they take many different forms depending on what type of evidence is best suited to testing a particular hypothesized part of a causal mechanism. As discussed earlier, observations only become evidence after they have been evaluated using our contextual knowledge of the specific case ($o + k \rightarrow e$).

Four distinguishable types of evidence are relevant in process-tracing analysis: pattern, sequence, trace, and account. Pattern evidence relates to predictions of statistical patterns in the evidence—for example, in testing a mechanism of racial discrimination in a case dealing with employment, statistical patterns of employment would be relevant for testing parts of the mechanism. Sequence evidence deals with the temporal and spatial chronology of events predicted by a hypothesized causal mechanism. For example, a test of a hypothesis could involve expectations of the timing of events where we might predict that if h is valid, we should see that that event b took place after event a. However, if we then found that event b took place before event a, the test would suggest that our confidence in the validity of this part of the mechanism should be reduced (disconfirmation).

Trace evidence is evidence whose mere existence provides proof that a part of a hypothesized mechanism exists. For example, the existence of the official minutes of a meeting, if authentic, provides strong proof that a meeting took place. Finally, account evidence deals with the content of empirical material, such as meeting minutes that detail what was discussed or an oral account of what took place in a meeting. Khong (1992) uses this type of evidence when he illustrates the range of policy options considered by U.S. decision makers in the escalation of the Vietnam War.

In designing empirical tests, we need to state clearly what types of evidence we should expect to see if a hypothesized part of a mechanism exists. In the Moravcsik example (see chapter 4), a test of the hypothesis regarding the Commission possessing privileged information can be operationalized as "We should expect to see that the Commission in the most sensitive areas of negotiations was much better informed about the content and state of play of the negotiations than governments, possessing more detailed issue briefs and more accurate and updated information on the state of play of the negotiations." In a case testing this hypothesis, we should expect to see pattern evidence in the form of a greater number of internal study papers and papers documenting the state of play in the Commission archives than in national governmental archives. Here, the quantity of observations forms the evidence, with contextual knowledge playing only a lesser role in evaluating that each document was a study paper or a description of the state of play (what different actors wanted at specific points in the negotiations). Second, another type of relevant evidence would be account evidence, where we should expect that participants in the negotiations would verify in interviews that the Commission was better informed both about the content of issues and the state of play of the negotiations. Contextual knowledge would, for example, be used to evaluate each interview to detect potential sources of bias.

6.3. Test Strength

The logic of empirical testing in process-tracing is that if we expected X to cause Y, each part of the mechanism between X and Y should leave the predicted empirical manifestations that can be observed in the empirical material. Detecting these manifestations, or fingerprints, requires the development of carefully formulated case-specific predictions of what evidence we should expect to see if the hypothesized part of the mechanism exists. The key difference between predicted evidence as used in process-tracing and other in-depth case study methods such as the congruence method is that in process-tracing, predictions should be formulated in a manner that captures both the entity and the activity involved in each part of a causal mechanism, whereas congruence tests typically test the same prediction for X and Y by themselves at different times during an empirical process (t_0, t_1, . . . t_n).

In other words, empirical tests in process-tracing should be designed in a manner that captures traces of the transmission of causal forces through the theorized causal mechanism. Bayesian logic suggests that when we design empirical tests, we need to maximize the inferential power of evidence to update our confidence in the validity of a hypothesis (Good 1991). This involves making strong predictions about (1) what evidence we should expect to see if a part of a causal mechanism exists and (2) what counts as evidence for alternative hypotheses, while taking into consideration (3) what we can conclude when the predicted evidence is not found—that is, what counts as negative evidence (~e). In operationalizing the parts of a causal mechanism into a series of tests, we need to think about our ability to use the empirical tests to update our confidence in the validity of h when we find e and when e is not found (~e).

Van Evera has introduced a helpful terminology for evaluating test strength that can be adapted for use in process-tracing testing and is compatible with the underlying logic of Bayesian updating (1997: 31–34).

First, what types of inferences can be made when we find the predicted evidence? Does finding e increase our confidence in the existence of the part of the mechanism in relation to plausible alternatives? Van Evera uses the term *unique predictions* to refer to the formulation of empirical predictions that do not overlap with those of other theories. Uniqueness corresponds to the likelihood ratio, where predictions are developed that maximize the value of $p(e|h)$ in relation to $p(e|\sim h)$. Therefore, if we have a hypothesis formulated in a manner that is highly unique and if we find the predicted evidence, our confidence increases in the presence of the part of the mechanism. In the Sherlock Holmes example from chapter 5, the prediction of finding that the dog that did not bark was highly unusual, with other explanations for the lack of bark quite implausible ($p(e|h)$ was high relative to $p(e|\sim h)$).

The second dimension relates to what types of inferences we can make when we do not find the predicted evidence. If we find ~e, can we update our confidence that the part of the mechanism does not exist? What empirical evidence do we have to see for h to be valid? Van Evera (1997) terms this a *certain prediction,* meaning that the prediction is unequivocal and the prediction (e) must be observed or the theory fails the empirical test. Logically, when $p(e|h) = 1$, then $p(h|\sim e) =$ zero, given that $p(h) > 0$ (Howson and Urbach 2006: 93). This means that if our prediction is maximally certain and we find $\sim e$, our posterior confidence in h is 0, meaning that we have maximally disconfirmed the existence of h. Popper was so fascinated by this logic that he used it as the basis for his falsification principle. However, falsification is a misguided strategy, given that we never can be 100 percent sure that the evidence collected was accurate or that the test was 100 percent certain (93). Disconfirmation should therefore be understood as a matter of degree. If we find $\sim e$, we downgrade our confidence in the existence of the theorized part of the mechanism in relation to the degree of certainty of the empirical prediction. Yet given the ambiguity of social science data, we can never falsify a theory.

Van Evera classifies different types of tests of predictions along these two dimensions, resulting in four ideal-typical types of tests: straw-in-the-wind, hoop, smoking gun, and doubly decisive (1997: 31–34). These dimensions should actually be understood as continuums, based on the idea that through diligent refining of our predictions, we can push test strength further in the direction of more certain and more unique tests (see figure 6.1). At the same time, 100 percent certain or unique tests are a will-o'-the-wisp, impossible to attain as a result of the impossibility of perfect measurement of social phenomena. Therefore, test strength is a matter of degree and is best represented as a continuum.

The weakest type of test is a straw-in-the-wind test. These are empirical predictions that have a low level of uniqueness and a low level of certainty. These tests do little to update our confidence in a hypothesis irrespective of whether we find e or $\sim e$, as both passed and failed tests are of little if any inferential relevance. Bennett (2008a) suggests an example of a straw-in-the-wind test for whether ideas or material interests mattered for the Soviet nonuse of force in 1989. Looking exclusively at the views of Soviet premier Gorbachev and testing predictions from both hypotheses is inconclusive since "the policy views of any one individual, even an individual as historically important as Gorbachev, cannot definitively show that material incentives rather than ideas were more important in driving and shaping changes in Soviet policies" (716).

Hoop tests involve predictions that are certain but not unique; the failure of such a test (finding $\sim e$) reduces our confidence in the hypothesis, but finding e does not enable inferences to be made (Bennett 2006; Van Evera 1997). For example, in criminal trials, questions such as, "Was the accused in the town on the day of the murder?" and "Was the suspect too big to squeeze through the window through which the murderer entered the house?" are

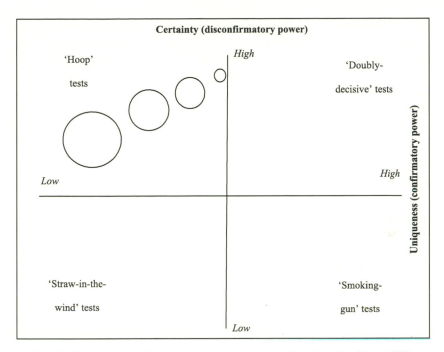

Fig. 6.1. Types of tests of parts of a causal mechanism. (Based on Van Evera 1997: 31–34.)

hoop tests through which a hypothesis would need to pass. However, finding that the suspect was in the town does not confirm the suspect's guilt, whereas finding that the suspect was out of the state would suggest innocence, contingent on the accuracy of the evidence supporting the suspect's alibi. In practice, hoop tests are often used to exclude alternative hypotheses.

Figure 6.1 depicts hoop tests as having different diameters, illustrating that as we strengthen the uniqueness and certainty of our hoop tests, we increase test strength. As the hoop through which the hypothesis must jump becomes progressively smaller, our ability to update our degree of confidence in the validity of the hypothesis is updated when we find either e or ~e. A prediction that a suspect is in the state at the time of a crime is a large hoop, whereas a much tighter hoop would be whether the suspect was in the neighborhood at the time a crime was committed. As the later test is much harder for a hypothesis to jump through, the inferential value of the test is greater.

Smoking gun tests are highly unique but have low or no certainty in their predictions. Here, passage strongly confirms a hypothesis, but failure does not strongly undermine it. A smoking gun in the suspect's hands right after a murder strongly implicates the suspect, but if we do not find the gun, the suspect is not exonerated. In Bayesian terms, the likelihood ratio is small, with finding e given h highly probable, whereas ~h is highly improbable, thereby greatly increasing our confidence in the validity of h if we find e. However, employing this type of test is a high-risk strategy given that a small likelihood ratio usually implies relatively improbable evidence (p(e) low), which by its nature makes e very difficult to find. Yet if we do not find e, we are unable to update our confidence in the validity of h. In other words, the dilemma is that unless we find e, a smoking gun test is pointless (no updating possible), but if we design a weaker test that increases the probability that we will find e (i.e., p(e) higher), our ability to update the posterior if we find e is reduced considerably.

Finally, doubly decisive tests combine both certainty and uniqueness. If the evidence is not found, our confidence in the validity of the hypothesis is reduced; at the same time, the test discriminates strongly between evidence that supports the hypothesis and alternatives (small likelihood ratio). In a criminal trial, a doubly decisive test could be the tape of a high-resolution surveillance camera from the scene of the crime. The prediction that the suspect should be identifiable in the tape is relatively certain, for if the expected evidence (suspect captured on the tape) is not found (and the tape has not been tampered with), we can with reasonable confidence conclude that the suspect is innocent. Further, if the tape shows the suspect committing the crime, this test confirms guilt unless there is evidence suggesting that the suspect was acting under duress (high uniqueness).

Doubly decisive tests are therefore ideal. However, in real-world social science research, it is also almost impossible to formulate predictions in such a manner given the difficulty of finding and gaining access to the type of empirical evidence that would enable doubly decisive tests. Furthermore, inverse relationships often exist between the uniqueness and certainty of tests in that the more unique the empirical predictions, the less likely we are to find the evidence, and vice versa.

We advocate seeking to maximize the levels of both certainty and uniqueness. However, when push comes to shove and we are forced to choose between certainty and uniqueness, we suggest prioritizing certainty over uniqueness in process-tracing test designs based on Bayesian logic. As we argue in chapter 3, each part of a causal mechanism should be seen as individually necessary. While passing a form of smoking gun test would substantially increase our confidence in the presence of a given part of a causal mechanism, the failure to find a smoking gun tells us nothing. Because we are operating with what are in effect single-case studies for each part of a mechanism, we need to design tests that have a relatively high degree of certainty (hoop tests), since the absence of the evidence (~e) of a certain prediction allows us to infer with a reasonable degree of certainty that the part of the mechanism was not present.

In addition, hoop tests can be employed in clusters in process-tracing research, where multiple independent hoop tests of what we must find in the evidence (certainty) are formulated for each part of a mechanism. When hoop tests are combined to test h, the result is an additive effect that increases our ability to update our confidence in the validity of h given that the probability of a nonvalid hypothesis surviving multiple independent hoop tests falls after each successive hoop. The greater the variety of independent evidence collected, the stronger the support for the hypothesis, other things equal (Howson and Urbach 2006: 125–26).

An Example—Improving Test Strength

We seek to maximize the strength of our tests of each part of a causal mechanism. In chapter 5, we discussed Moravcsik's (1998, 1999) theorization on the influence of supranational actors in EU negotiations. Moravcsik (1999) tests whether a causal mechanism exists that posits that supranational actors such as the Commission gain influence in EU negotiations because of their relative informational advantages. One part of the causal mechanism is conceptualized as "The Commission has privileged access to information."

A hypothetical example of a straw-in-the-wind test that puts forward uncertain and nonunique predictions to test the hypothesized part could be that we should "expect to see that the Commission has many civil servants." However, this is a weak test on both of van Evera's dimensions. First, the test has a low level of certainty, since the information we need is not the number of civil servants per se but whether these officials have relative informational advantages vis-à-vis national civil servants. Second, the uniqueness of the test is low, as finding many civil servants can also be explained by competing theories such as intergovernmentalist theory. Intergovernmentalism would argue that most of the civil servants are translators and therefore do not contribute to granting the Commission privileged access to information.

The test could be improved on both dimensions so that it approaches a doubly decisive test. This test could be formulated as we should "expect to see that the Commission in the most sensitive areas of negotiations was much better informed about the content and state of play of the negotiations than governments, possessing more detailed issue briefs and more accurate and updated information on the state of play." This test has a higher degree of certainty, as finding this evidence is vital in making the argument that the Commission possesses privileged information. Further, the predictions are quite unique in that this phenomenon is something we would not expect to see if competing alternative theories such as intergovernmentalism were correct. In Bayesian terms, formulating the hypothesis in this way help us to increase the likelihood ratio and thereby increase our confidence in the theory if we find evidence that supports our theory; at the same time, the level of certainty allows us to update our confidence in the nonexistence of the part of the mechanism if we do not find e but find ~e.

Conclusions

In operationalizing empirical tests of causal mechanisms, we develop predictions about what we should expect to see in the empirical record if a hypothesized part of a causal mechanism is present (predicted evidence), formulated in a manner that maximizes the level of certainty and uniqueness. When developing predictions of what type (or types) of evidence we should see for each part of the mechanism, it is useful to think in terms analogous to playing both sides (prosecutor and defense) in a criminal trial. What evidence must appear in the empirical record if the hypothesized part of the mechanism is present (certainty)? If found, can we explain the evidence using alternative hypotheses (~h) (uniqueness)?

The testing process takes place for each part of a causal mechanism. As mentioned in chapter 5, the strength of our inferences about the presence of a causal mechanism depend on the ability of the test of each part of a mechanism to update significantly our confidence (up or down) in its presence. Therefore, our inferences about the presence of a causal mechanism are only as strong as the weakest test, making it vital that we strive to maximize test strength for each part. In practice, we often find that testing the parts in between is much more difficult than testing the start and the outcome of a causal mechanism. When faced with this challenge, we suggest suitable caution regarding inferences about the presence and workings of the mechanism. The analysis must clearly flag the weakest link(s)—for example, by stating that part 3 can only be tested using a straw-in-the-wind test that does little to update our confidence in the presence/absence of the part. At the same time, we must be realistic, and if we can provide strong tests (ideally doubly decisive) of many of the parts of a mechanism and the predicted evidence is found, we can cautiously conclude that we have updated our confidence in the presence of the mechanism as a whole.

Testing in explaining-outcome process-tracing is often a much messier task given that we usually do not possess a simple mechanism; instead, we want to test the presence of multiple overlapping mechanisms with different parts, including nonsystematic mechanisms. However, in line with the ontological and epistemological position of pragmatism taken by scholars engaging in explaining-outcome process-tracing (see chapter 2), we also need to acknowledge that empirical tests here are usually much more instrumental. Theorized mechanisms are seen as heuristic tools that guide our inquiry toward a persuasive explanation (Humphreys 2010: 268). Empirical analysis is closer to what can be thought of as calibrating a case-specific explanation in an iterative research design to account for discrepancies between the theorized mechanisms and the data (Jackson 2011: 146–47) (see chapter 2). However, Bayesian logic and the strength of tests still provide the foundations for the causal inferences that are made, but they are used in a looser and more pragmatic fashion than in theory-centric variants of process-tracing, where the aim is the more instrumental one of assessing the similarity between the predicted evidence, what is found, and the ability of a given theorized mechanism to account for those results in terms of the likelihood ratio.

In the rest of the chapter, we present an extended example of how we should conceptualize and operationalize causal mechanisms in theory-testing process-tracing, illustrating the many challenges we face in practical research situations.

6.4. An Extended Example of Conceptualization and Operationalization of Causal Mechanisms: Studying Bureaucratic Politics

In this example, we attempt to build a design that can test the presence/absence of a hypothesized causal mechanism for bureaucratic politics in a single-case process-tracing study. The example illustrates some of the challenges in utilizing process-tracing methods and designing tests that can measure and evaluate the existence of the different parts of a hypothetical causal mechanism. The specific case involves the interministerial coordination of national positions on the issue of the transfer of sovereignty to the EU within EU constitutional negotiations. The basic question is whether politicians are in control of the formulation of national positions or whether bureaucratic self-interest plays a role in the translation of societal preferences into negotiable national positions.

Conceptualizing a Bureaucratic Politics Mechanism

There is a wealth of literature within public administration research and foreign policy analysis (FPA) that suggests that how the state is organized matters in domestic and foreign policy, with the manner of organization viewed as a crucial intervening variable between inputs (societal preferences) and outcomes (national positions). In the theory of bureaucratic politics, ministries attempt to pursue their parochial institutional interests in a bargaining game of pulling and hauling (Allison and Zelikow 1999; Bendor and Hammond 1992: 317–18; Caldwell 1977: 95; Hermann et al. 2001; Jones 2008; Michaud 2002; Peters 1995; Preston and 't Hart 1999; Rosati 1981). Policy outcomes are not merely the result of a rational matching of national interests and solutions but are better seen as the product of internal conflict, compromise, and negotiation among competing ministries. This definition differs from the revised model developed by Allison and Zelikow (1999) that they term governmental politics, which became more focused on the high-level political battles between different senior political figures (cabinet officials) and the president rather than with the lower-level interministerial battles among bureaucrats within a government. Here we are interested in explaining how interministerial battles (bureaucratic politics) produce outcomes that more reflect the bureaucratic self-interest of ministries than the "national interest" (i.e., the interests of domestic economic groups and other societal actors).

We know from principal-agent theorization that political officials (ministers) as principals are in a "Yes, Minister" relationship with their civil servants in ministries (agents) (e.g., Bendor, Glazer, and Hammond 2001; Epstein and O'Halloran 1994; Strøm 2000). The executive depends on bureaucrats to translate the basic positions that they lay out into detailed and negotiable national positions, granting bureaucrats extensive opportunities to skew outcomes toward their own preferences (Peters 1995). Conversely, ministers can use centralized coordination mechanisms to control what the bureaucracy is doing (Peters 1998).

While bureaucratic politics has been the focus of much theorization, most formulations of the model are not theories per se but are instead descriptive models of decision-making processes (Bendor and Hammond 1992: 317–18; Caldwell 1977: 95; Jones 2008). Therefore, our first step is to reformulate the model of bureaucratic politics into a causal theory. The independent

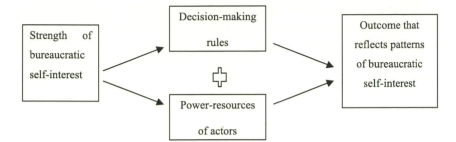

Fig. 6.2. A causal theory of bureaucratic politics

variable is the strength of the self-interest of bureaucratic actors, the intervening variables are the decision-making rules and the power resources of the actors, and the outcome should therefore be the impact of bureaucratic self-interests as mediated by the action channel used to make the decision. This is illustrated in figure 6.2.

The causal theory leads us to the following predictions that could be tested using congruence methods in a case study (Blatter and Blume 2008; George and Bennett 2005: chapter 9). First, we should expect that the strength of the dynamic of bureaucratic politics is a function of how strongly bureaucratic actors are interested in an issue. When bureaucratic actors have few self-interests in an issue (it has no real impact on the institutional power/prestige of their ministry), outcomes should reflect the national interest, and vice versa. Second, decision-making rules matter in that they determine whether the game involves coalition building around majority positions or is dominated by ensuring that the least interested actor is on board when decisions are made by unanimity (Hermann et al. 2001). Third, bureaucratic actors with procedural or hierarchical powers will be able to skew outcomes closer to their own preferred outcome. Therefore, we should expect that outcomes reflect the bureaucratic self-interest of actors as mediated by the decision-making rules and power resources of the participating actors.

For process-tracing, this causal theory then needs to be reconceptualized as a causal mechanism. However, before we do so, we briefly discuss the theoretical prior that would inform the tests of the empirical indicators in the specific case.

The Theoretical Priors

Given that the question of the importance of bureaucratic politics in the national preference formation process in EU constitutional negotiations has not been investigated empirically by other scholars, we could utilize Moravcsik's well-established findings as the prior for the whole mechanism. Moravcsik's liberal intergovernmentalist theory suggests that the state is a relatively neutral transmission belt between the preferences of domestic economic groups and national positions: "Groups articulate preferences, governments aggregate them" (Moravcsik 1993: 483). In his major study of EU constitutional bargains, Moravcsik finds some evidence suggesting that in situations where "producer groups were balanced by strong national macroeconomic ideas and institutions," the views of governments and central banks did matter (1998: 477). However, the overall conclusion is that the form of state organization does not matter, and we can therefore treat the state as more or less a black box.

Therefore, in Bayesian terms, based on our prior knowledge, we are relatively confident that the bureaucratic politics mechanism (and its parts) are not present in this case. Updating our confidence in the presence of bureaucratic politics requires finding strong evidence that is highly unlikely to be found unless bureaucratic politics are present.

Conceptualizing and Operationalizing a Bureaucratic Politics Causal Mechanism

To develop a causal mechanism, we need to reconceptualize the causal theory into a mechanism composed of a set of parts (entities engaging in activities) to study the dynamic transmission of causal forces through the mechanism to produce the outcome (policies that more closely reflect bureaucratic self-interest than we otherwise would expect). Here, we reconceptualize the theory as a mechanism with five distinct parts: (1) preferences (bureaucratic self-interest), (2) the battle over the choice of action channel, (3) debates within group determined by the decision-making rule, (4) actors exploiting their powers (procedural or hierarchical), and (5) outcomes that reflect patterns of bureaucratic self-interest. The full mechanism is illustrated in figure 6.3. and table 6.1.

The following discussion also illustrates how the mechanism could be operationalized into a set of case-specific predictions about what evidence we should expect to find if h is valid. Here, we need to ensure that the tests for each part of the mechanism are formulated in a manner that maximizes the certainty and uniqueness of the predicted observable implications, at the same time making sure that the test is realistically feasible (i.e., data can be collected that can actually measure what we intend to measure, and so forth).

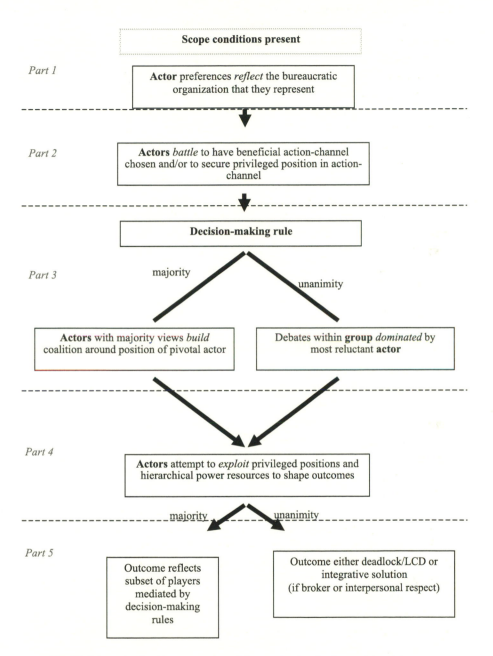

Part 1

Scope conditions present

Actor preferences *reflect* the bureaucratic organization that they represent

Part 2

Actors *battle* to have beneficial action-channel chosen and/or to secure privileged position in action-channel

Decision-making rule

Part 3

majority

unanimity

Actors with majority views *build* coalition around position of pivotal actor

Debates within **group** *dominated* by most reluctant **actor**

Part 4

Actors attempt to *exploit* privileged positions and hierarchical power resources to shape outcomes

majority

unanimity

Part 5

Outcome reflects subset of players mediated by decision-making rules

Outcome either deadlock/LCD or integrative solution (if broker or interpersonal respect)

Fig. 6.3. A hypothesized bureaucratic politics mechanism for interministerial bargaining

TABLE 6.1. A Conceptualization and Operationalization of a Bureaucratic Political Causal Mechanism

Conceptualization of Each Part	Predicted Evidence	Type of Evidence Used to Measure Prediction
1 **Actor** preferences *reflect* the bureaucratic self-interests of the ministry that they represent (competence maximizing and minimizing the disruptive effects of expected EU policy streams) (a) line ministries will attempt to *minimize* the level of disruption of EU rules upon domestic issues administered by them by minimizing or even opposing integration in their areas of competence (b) foreign ministries have interests in maintaining their coordinator position in EU affairs and therefore promote positions that reflect governmental preferences	Expect to see evidence of "bureaucratic politics talk" in the preferences of bureaucratic actors	Measured using account evidence from interviews with participants and/or internal documents produced by the ministries
2 **Actors** *battle* to have beneficial action-channel chosen and/or to secure positions with strong procedural powers in a given action-channel	Expect to see significant jockeying among actors for chairmanship of interministerial committees, etc.	Measured using sequence evidence (timing of events) and account evidence (participant accounts from interviews)
3 Debates within **group** *dominated* by either (a) (majority): Actors with majority views building coalition around position of pivotal actor (b) (unanimity): Most reluctant actor	Expect to see either (a) Minority views marginalized; coalition-building around majority view (b) Majority attempting to influence most reluctant actor to move away from SQ	Measured using account evidence from interviews with participants and/or meeting minutes
4 **Actors** attempt to *exploit* power resources (hierarchical positions or procedural powers) to shape outcomes	Expect to see actors with strong hierarchical positions and/or privileged positions in negotiation more dominant in debates and more successful in influencing outcome	Measured using account evidence from interviews with participants and/or meeting minutes

5	Outcome reflects either	Expect to see that outcome	Measured using pattern evi-
	(a) Subset of actors deter-mined by DM rule and privileged positions	reflects either (a) Subset of actors deter-mined by DM rule and privileged position	dence (level of congruence between outcomes and positions of ministries),
	(b) Deadlock/LCD	(b) Deadlock/LCD	account evidence from
	(c) Integrative solution if broker and/or interper-sonal trust present in group	(c) Integrative solution if broker and/or interper-sonal trust present in group	interviews with partici-pants, and final positions produced

Part 1: Actor Preferences

The key to any theory of bureaucratic politics is the behavioral assumptions that are supposed to drive civil servants. Scholars generally believe that bu-reaucrats have institutional interests based on where they sit. One widely utilized behavioral assumption is that bureaucratic actors will attempt to maximize their competencies—for example, by protecting their existing turf (Dunleavy 1991; Peters 1998; Pollack 2003: 35–36). With regard to the ques-tion of the transfer of national sovereignty within EU constitutional politics, competency-maximizing national ministries can be expected to have certain interests. First, we can expect that line ministries will attempt to minimize the level of disruption of "Europe" has for domestic issues administered by those ministries by minimizing or even opposing integration in their areas of competency—in effect, protecting their turf. In some instances, however, line ministries will support more integration—primarily where further de-velopments in the policy area are expected to result in the significant expan-sion of the ministry's competencies (e.g., in competition policy) or where it can be expected to result in a significant increase in the ministry's autonomy within the domestic system (Dunleavy 1991; Peters 1995). Second, we should expect that foreign ministries have interests in maintaining their coordina-tor position in EU affairs and therefore will promote positions that closely reflect governmental preferences to maintain governmental trust.

How, then, do we know bureaucratic politics talk when we see it in a spe-cific case study? In other words, how can we determine whether statements from line ministries and departments are expressing parochial institutional interests rather than faithfully translating governmental preferences into positions on the concrete issues? The baseline that can be utilized is that a faithful translation of government preferences into positions should follow the overall direction of what the government has previously stated—for example, in papers sent to Parliament prior to the start of a given set of constitutional negotiations. While most of this paper is drafted by civil servants from the foreign ministry, the key point is that it is written before the interministerial coordination process, that is, before bureaucratic politics potentially kick in. For instance, if the government stated that it is interested in transferring competencies to the EU on a specific issue but the line ministry that is responsible for the issue area opposes this transfer in study papers produced prior to a negotiation, this evidence would be an empirical indicator of bureaucratic politics talk. This could be measured using account evidence from interviews with participants both within the given ministry and in other ministries and/or internal documents produced by the ministries.

This evidence is relatively easy to gather and can provide strong evidence suggesting that the part is present/absent. This test is relatively certain in that it is necessary to observe that actors are taking positions that reflect bureaucratic self-interest so that we can be confident that the part of the bureaucratic politics mechanism exists. It is also relatively unique, as it would be difficult to otherwise explain why the line ministries most affected by EU regulation in a given issue area would also be the ones most opposed to the transfer of sovereignty on that issue.

Part 2: The Choice of Action Channel

Allison and Zelikow introduce a helpful term, *action channels,* defined as a "regularized means of taking governmental action on a specific kind of issue. . . . Action-channels structure the game by preselecting the major players, determining their usual points of entrance into the game, and distributing particular advantages and disadvantages for each game" (1999: 300–301). In this part of the mechanism, we theorize that self-interested bureaucrats will fight for the selection of an action channel that maximizes their relative powers and/or that they will attempt to secure a privileged position within a given action channel.

A test for the presence/absence of part 2 is more difficult to operationalize in a manner that permits the close observation of causal forces. We should first expect to see that actors will jockey for positions within interministerial coordination committees and that they will lobby for the selection of action channels that privilege them, other things equal. The predicted evidence of this jockeying, while difficult to gather, would, if found, update our confidence that the part of the mechanism is present. This hypothesized part could be measured using sequence evidence (timing of events) and account evidence (participant accounts from interviews).

However, the test is not particularly certain, as there can be many reasons that evidence for this jockeying is not present. For example, there can be standing precedents for which ministry serves as chair for a specific inter-ministerial group that are sufficiently strong to overpower any bureaucratic jockeying. This suggests that this part of the mechanism is perhaps not 100 percent necessary for the mechanism to operate and implies that a recon-ceptualization could be considered to take account of the novelty or level of precedence for the choice of specific coordinating procedures. Further, observing jockeying does not necessarily mean that bureaucratic politics is taking place (low uniqueness); instead, it could reflect that a given ministry simply believes it is the most competent to chair a given committee based on policy expertise in the area, a phenomenon that is not evidence of bu-reaucratic politics. This test is therefore a smoking gun test, where finding e significantly updates our confidence in h being valid (if we can ascertain that jockeying was based on self-interest) but finding ~e does little to update our confidence in either direction.

Part 3: Debates within the Action Channel

To determine which bureaucratic actor wins the internal power struggle, Allison and Zelikow suggest that we focus on how the rules of the game structure the action channels through which bureaucratic organizations act (1999: 300–302). Unfortunately, they develop no theory for how the rules of the game determine who wins or loses. Therefore, we supplement their ideas with Hermann et al.'s theorization on the impact of decision-making rules in foreign policymaking within groups—in particular, how majority versus unanimity impacts who wins and loses (2001: 143–45).

We should expect that when majority voting is used, minority views will be marginalized unless the majority respects a minority that has an intense view, with debates focusing on a subset of options that reflect the majority (Hermann et al. 2001). If the group's members have a high degree of inter-personal trust and respect, they will attempt to bring the minority on board through integrative measures such as the use of compromises, trade-offs, and innovative solutions. Conversely, if unanimity is required, we should expect either deadlock/lowest-common-denominator solutions, as debates revolve around getting the most reluctant actor on board, or a more integrative solu-tion in circumstances where a broker and/or interpersonal trust is present.

Operationalizing this part and the next part of the hypothesized mechanism is troublesome. The basic problem is that problems of access mean that it is usually very difficult to observe internal negotiating dynamics—it is difficult to formulate strong predictions for what evidence we should find if the parts of the mechanism exist. Instead, we are forced to rely on indirect and/or incomplete measurements. For example, while we may possess the minutes of interministerial meetings (in a best-case scenario), it is also possible that the formal institutional structures did not reflect the real workings of a negotiation. For example, it is possible that a smaller ad hoc group of influential actors met behind the scenes, fleshing out a deal in a manner that does not reflect the formal deliberations that took place in the committee and that we can observe with our data (meeting minutes). Furthermore, we risk conflating the actions undertaken by actors with influence, and we risk mistaking an actor who speaks loudly with an actor who is influential.

This said, we can operationalize part 3 by stating that we should expect that when majority decision making is used, minority views will be marginalized (except when the intense views of a minority are respected) and that we will see coalition-building dynamics taking place around a position held by a majority. Alternatively, when unanimity is used, we should expect to see discussions that are dominated by efforts to ensure that the most reluctant actor is on board. The tests formulated in this manner would be relatively unique in that these types of dynamics would be hard to explain if, for example, we theorize that foreign policy decision making is a rational and neutral process of determining the optimal solution to a given problem. However, the tests are not very certain as a consequence of the substantial empirical challenges in studying interministerial decision making; therefore, these tests are close to smoking gun tests.

It can be expected that there will be a divergence between the meetings portrayed by official minutes (which will probably not display the expected dynamics) and deliberations in the corridors between key actors (which probably will display the expected dynamics). As it is easier to collect information about what happened in official meetings than informal meetings, it can be very difficult to formulate this test with any degree of certainty unless evidence of sufficient quality is available to allow us to measure the following predictions: "We expect to see majority dynamics within the key decision-making forum (regardless of whether it is the official meetings or informal corridor deliberation)." Here we would need extensive account evidence, both from internal meeting minutes and from in-depth interviews with participants. This part could be measured using account evidence from interviews with participants and/or meeting minutes.

Part 4: Actors Attempt to Exploit Their Positions
(Procedural or Hierarchical)

The impact of hierarchical and procedural positions is undertheorized in the bureaucratic politics literature (Jones 2008). Here, we tentatively theorize that hierarchy in government also determines who wins and loses, in that, for example, a minister should be able to trump the views of an undersecretary of another ministry, other things equal. Second, drawing on rational institutionalist theories, we should expect procedural powers such as chairing an interministerial committee would grant the holder certain power resources that can be exploited (Peters 1995; Tallberg 2006). For example, a coordinating ministry has responsibility for writing the final recommendation for a position, a role that can be subtly (or not so subtly) exploited to push the ministry's own interests.

Regarding part 4, we should expect to see that actors with strong hierarchical positions and/or privileged positions in negotiation more dominant in debates and more successful in influencing outcome. This part could be measured using account evidence from interviews with participants and/or meeting minutes.

However, we cannot automatically conclude that if we do not find evidence of actors attempting to exploit their power resources that they did not attempt to do so behind closed doors. In other words, any realistic operationalization for part 4 has a relatively low degree of certainty, as it is very difficult to observe this informal, behind-the-scenes use of power resources. We often must infer the process from the outcome—for example, arguing that because actor X had a disproportional impact, he/she must have successfully exploited the chair position. Here, there is the significant risk of both false negatives (actions that were not observed being mistaken for nonpresent actions) and false positives (actions being conflated with influence).

Part 5: Outcomes Reflect Bureaucratic Self-Interests of Actors

Finally, we should expect that the outcome reflects the preferences of (1) a subset of bureaucratic actors as mediated by the relative procedural and hierarchical power resources of actors, (2) deadlock/LCD under unanimity, or (3) an integrative solution if a broker and/or interpersonal trust and respect were present in the interministerial group.

Comparing the outcome with what we would expect based on the institutional self-interest of bureaucratic actors as mediated by the decision-making rule and actor power and initial governmental positions should give us a final indication of whether bureaucratic politics was actually taking place. This test has both a high degree of certainty (in that it must be present for us to conclude that bureaucratic politics took place in the given case) and a high degree of uniqueness (as it is difficult to find any other explanation for an outcome that reflects bureaucratic self-interests of individual ministries as mediated by the action channel). The predicted evidence could be pattern evidence, such as the level of congruence between outcomes and positions of ministries, and account evidence from interviews with participants along with the final positions.

The Challenge of Conceptualizing and Operationalizing Causal Mechanisms

The basic question explored here was whether we can conceptualize and operationalize a bureaucratic politics mechanism that enables us to undertake a strong theory test in the case of national position development in EU constitutional negotiations. The tentative answer is that while we can formulate relatively strong (close to doubly decisive) tests for parts 1 and 5, we cannot formulate very strong tests for the parts in between. Instead, these are mostly smoking gun tests that attempt to assess predictions that are very difficult to measure in practice.

We conclude that we would have substantial difficulties in testing the mechanism unless we have access to both extensive primary documentation and a series of participant interviews collected either during or immediately after the negotiations (Caldwell 1977; Clifford 1990). We are therefore forced to infer that bureaucratic politics took place from evidence of parts 1 and 5 and circumstantial evidence of parts 2, 3, and 4.

In contrast, when an issue is highly salient (especially a crisis such as the Cuban Missile Crisis), extensive secondary and primary documentation is often available, and participants can recall events even many years after they took place, enabling us to access evidence that allows the analyst to observe a causal mechanism more directly. But these are not cases of bureaucratic politics but instead are governmental politics, where battles involve high-level officials (president and ministers). Here, preferences are not based on the idea that where you stand is where you sit, and negotiations have different dynamics.

The broader lesson of this example is that in many practical research situations, it is difficult to live up to this book's ideal-typical prescriptions regarding the conceptualization and operationalization of causal mechanisms. Most research situations are not like the one faced by Owen when studying the democratic peace, where already extensive theoretical work had already been undertaken on which he could base his conceptualization and where an encompassing empirical record was available. As the example in this chapter shows, conceptualization is challenging when theories are less well developed, and empirical testing (operationalization) can be nearly impossible when we lack full access to the empirical record. Our inferences about mechanisms are only as strong as the weakest test of a part of a mechanism.

This does not mean we should give up the endeavor when we face difficulties, merely that we should be realistic and accept that when we are using process-tracing methods, our conceptualizations and operationalized empirical tests will be less than perfect. But we should continue to strive to push our tests in the direction of the ideal.

CHAPTER 7

Turning Observations into Evidence

"There is nothing more deceptive than an obvious fact."
—A. C. Doyle 1892: 101

Empirical material needs to be evaluated before it can be admitted as evidence on which to base causal inferences. But how can we know that what we have observed is the evidence that our theory tests had predicted? How can we assess the inferential value of individual pieces of evidence? This chapter deals with the evaluation process, where raw empirical observations are assessed for their content, accuracy and probability, enabling us to use them as evidence to update our degree of confidence in the presence of the hypothesized causal mechanism. This process needs to be both transparent and open to scrutiny to ensure that it is as objective as possible.

We use the term *observation* in this book to refer to raw data prior to the evaluation of its content and accuracy (i.e., degree of measurement error). After it has been assessed for its content and potential measurement error, we use the term *evidence,* indicating that it contains a certain level of inferential value.[1]

While numerous methodological texts discuss challenges relating to the collection and analysis of data, this chapter goes a step further by making these prescriptions compatible with the Bayesian logic of inference used in process-tracing, giving us a set of evaluative tools that can be used to assess our degree of confidence in the accuracy and content of the evidence collected in process-tracing research. The prescriptions are most applicable for theory-testing and explaining-outcome variants of process-tracing as a consequence of the development of predictions about what evidence we should find in the case, capturing the need to match predicted evidence with found evidence.

The overall process of evaluating evidence is in many respects analogous to how evidence is admitted and evaluated within the U.S. legal system.[2] In a court of law, prosecutors and defenders produce different observations that can be used to make inferences about what happened. These observations include witness accounts, technical examinations, DNA tests, and so on. In a given court case, not all of the collected observations are accepted as evidence, since they can be inaccurate and/or the evidence can be so likely that it provides little inferential leverage in making an argument plausible (V. Walker 2007).

Before observations can be used in a court case, their accuracy and the probability of evidence must be evaluated. If we are dealing with a fingerprint match, we would treat a smeared print left on a surface at the scene of the crime, such as a train station, as potentially much less accurate than a print where clear ridges could be detected that would better enable comparison with a "rolled" print taken from the suspect. Regarding the probability of the evidence, a strong match between a DNA sample found on the victim and the DNA of the suspect is highly unlikely unless the two samples are the DNA of the same suspect. Combined, an accurate measure that is highly unlikely ($p(e)$ is low) would have strong inferential weight in a court case, enabling the judge to infer with a reasonable degree of confidence that the suspect most likely was the culprit.

Taken as a whole, the judge's role is evidence evaluation—deciding which evidence is relevant and evaluating the accuracy and the probability of the evidence (V. Walker 2007: 1696). This means that a prosecutor cannot just show up in court with a gun and postulate the suspect used it to perpetrate a murder. To be admitted by the judge as evidence of a theory that a given suspect committed the crime, forensic material and/or testimony must either establish beyond a reasonable doubt or makes it highly plausible that (1) the victim was killed by a gun, (2) the gun was actually in the possession of the suspect at the time of the crime, and (3) the gun was the weapon used in the murder. In this evaluation process, the defense questions whether sources of measurement error raise doubt about the accuracy of the evidence. For example, if the testimony linking the weapon and the suspect comes from the suspect's estranged wife, should we even admit the observation as evidence when she has a revenge motive that raises serious doubts about the veracity of her testimony? Further, what is the probability of the found evidence? For example, what is the range of error of the ballistics tests used to link the weapon with the crime? Could the matching results of the ballistics tests be the product of random chance?

Similarly, in a process-tracing case study, we need to assess the content and accuracy of our empirical observations before they can be admitted as evidence with which to update our confidence in the presence or absence of causal mechanisms; we then need to assess the probability of the evidence. The analyst needs to act as judge, prosecutor, and defense, providing arguments for why we can be confident about the content and accuracy of our observations while critically assessing our level of confidence.

Evaluating evidence involves four distinct steps that should be transparently described in one's research. Based on the predictions for what type of evidence we should expect to see if the hypothesized causal mechanism is present, we collect empirical data. Here, we need to evaluate whether we have enough data. More is not necessarily better. Instead, we need to collect strategically observations that allow us to assess our empirical tests. Further, we need to be realistic and be aware of resource limitations.

Second, we assess the content of our collected observations, using our contextual knowledge to determine what our observations tell us in relation to what evidence was predicted to occur.

Third, can we trust that the observations we have collected are in fact evidence of what we intended to measure? That is, are they accurate? Is the observation what it purports to be? What are the potential sources of error, and can we correct for them so that we can use the observation as evidence in a theory test to update the posterior probability of the hypothesized causal mechanism? This involves evaluating our confidence in the accuracy of our measure in terms of the estimated probability that the measure is accurate, depicted in Bayesian logic as $p(a)$. We discuss the risks that nonsystematic and systematic measurement error in our collected evidence pose for our ability to update the posterior probability of a hypothesized causal mechanism.

Finally, when using the Bayesian logic of inference, we can make stronger inferences when the evidence is highly unlikely. We therefore have to evaluate the probability of the evidence by itself. This process was illustrated in chapter 6, where we saw that the more improbable the evidence ($p(e)$ low), the stronger our ability to update our confidence in the posterior probability of the validity of a theorized mechanism when we find e. The probability of specific pieces of evidence ($p(e)$) therefore needs to be assessed using our knowledge of the context of the particular case.

This chapter proceeds as follows. The first section discusses some of the common challenges that all sources of empirical material share, focusing on the four stages of evaluation (collection, content evaluation, assessment of accuracy, and probability of evidence). We focus in particular on the assessment of accuracy and probability of evidence. This is followed by a presentation of the most common forms of empirical sources used in process-tracing case studies, ranging from participant interviews and archives to newspaper accounts. For each of these types of sources, we present the most common forms of measurement error and offer practical suggestions that can reduce these risks, thereby also increasing our confidence that our observations are measuring evidence that enables us to update the posterior probability in one direction or another. Different types of evidence (pattern, sequence, trace, account) can come from different types of sources. For example, account evidence can be gathered from both secondary sources (newspapers) and primary sources (participant interviews).

7.1. How Observations Are Turned into Evidence

"The facts . . . are like fish swimming about in a vast and sometimes inaccessible ocean. . . . What the historian catches will depend partly on chance, but mainly on what part of the ocean he chooses to fish in and what tackle he chooses to use."

—Carr 1961: 26

The Collection of Observations

The collection of empirical observations is not a random, ad hoc process but should instead be steered by theory, focusing on testing whether the predicted evidence for a hypothesized part of a mechanism is present in the empirical record. In process-tracing, we deliberately search for observations that allow us to infer whether the hypothesized part of a causal mechanism was present.

For example, if we are testing a hypothesized mechanism dealing with supranational entrepreneurship by the EU Commission, an empirical test of one part of the mechanism could be that we expected to find trace evidence that the Commission tabled many proposals relative to governments during a given negotiation. Relevant observations would be all of the Commission and governmental proposals during the negotiations.

It is vital to understand that we are not merely cherry-picking observations that fit a favored hypothesis when we do research. We are attempting to test whether the predicted evidence is present, meaning that we do not just go out and try to find supporting evidence; instead, we strategically seek to collect empirical material that would enable us to determine whether the predicted e or ~e is present. We therefore collect observations that enable us to put our hypothesized causal mechanism to a critical test (usually in the form of hoop tests, but in certain circumstances double-decisive tests). The researcher has to evaluate, at each stage of the process, whether the data collected is enough, whether the residual uncertainty is acceptable, and whether additional data should be collected to find sufficient evidence for the existence of e or ~e.

The collection of observations (either primary or secondary) always incurs the potential risk of bias as a consequence of the nonrandom selection strategy used. This might result in skewed inferences that are based on a sample that is not representative of the population of potential evidence (Collier 1995: 462). According to Collier and Mahoney, selection bias occurs when "some sort of selection process in either the design of the study or the real-world phenomena under investigation result in inferences that suffer from systematic error" (1996: 58–59).

This danger is particularly acute in process-tracing research. Sources often select the researcher—for example, where availability concerns determine which sources we use (Thies 2002: 356). There can be reasons why a particular record has survived through time, whereas others might have been deliberately destroyed. Further, our access to relevant sources might be restricted, limiting our ability to get the material we need to collect to test our hypotheses in an unbiased fashion.

Selection bias might also occur even when secondary rather than primary sources are used. Lustick (1996) has suggested that a researcher's choice of a particular historical monograph can be seen as holding the potential for selection bias. A historian may misinterpret the evidence, drawing incorrect inferences about past events, or may leave out important facts about the event, making the account unfair or unbalanced. Another concern is the selection effects of the social scientist when she chooses to focus on a particular historian's work and consciously—or unconsciously—excludes the work of others (Larson 2001; Lebow 2001). In the worst-case scenario, the two problems are combined, and the social scientist with a particular theoretical and conceptual predisposition purposefully selects certain historians who share this bias and whose work is already tainted, producing faulty confirmation of the social scientist's theory (Lustick 1996: 606). In most cases, we should not rely on a single historical work but rather should try to incorporate different historians who belong to different historiographic schools in our analysis (Lustick 1996).

Testing whether a causal mechanism is present involves assessing whether our theory-based predictions of what evidence we should see in the empirical record are matched in reality. The predicted evidence can take the form of pattern, sequence, trace, or account evidence. Relevant evidence depends on what empirical manifestations were predicted by the tests. Collecting different types of evidence raises different types of challenges. Pattern evidence in the form of a number of proposals in a negotiation can be time-consuming to collect, and important holes can exist when documents are unavailable for one reason or another. Conversely, collecting accurate elite interviews that provide account evidence about what happened in a given negotiation raises numerous challenges regarding access to high-level decision makers and regarding the independence of their accounts. In collecting data for process-tracing, the most appropriate analogy is that of a detective, with the collection of relevant evidence involving the expenditure of much shoe leather (Freedman 1991).

Finally, the collection of empirical material should be seen as a cumulative process. Even with the most strenuous efforts, the evidence we gather can always be improved in subsequent studies. Drawing on an analogy with astronomy, until recently, the theory that other solar systems had earth-like planets was merely a hypothetical conjecture. Recent advances in telescope technology have enabled the collection of evidence showing the existence of earth-like exoplanets. Future technological developments will allow for more accurate measurements to be taken that will increase our confidence in the theory. Similarly, in process-tracing research, evidence gathered will always have a preliminary form, and the results of our research (the posterior probability) can always be updated by new evidence. Important archival evidence can be declassified, memoirs are published, and scholars who critically analyze existing evidence can develop more accurate interpretations of e that either increase or decrease our confidence in the presence of hypothesized causal mechanisms. Therefore, scholars using process-tracing methods need to be as aware as historians that any result can be updated when new sources are found that better measure e. In the words of Elman and Elman, "Historians know that there are likely to be other documents, indeed whole collections of papers that they have not seen. Accordingly they are inclined to view their results as the uncertain product of an incomplete evidentiary record" (2001: 29).

Assessing the Content of Observations

Once we have collected observations, we need to evaluate critically what those observations tell us in light of our background knowledge about the context. This is the first phase of evaluating whether our observations are evidence (o + k → e). The next phase involves assessing accuracy.

What does the observation tell us? What is the source of the observation and the context in which it was produced? Answering these questions requires considerable background knowledge. For example, how does the given political system work? Is there anything amiss in the events that have been uncovered? What is normally included in the type of source (e.g., minutes of a cabinet meeting)? It is important to interpret documents within their historic, situational, and communication contexts. We need to understand the purpose of the document and the events leading up to it to interpret its meaning correctly (Larson 2001: 343). According to George and Bennett, the analyst should always consider who is speaking to whom, for what purpose, and under what circumstances (2005: 99–100). The inferential weight of what is contained in a document often cannot be reliably determined without addressing these questions. Similarly, when conducting elite interviews, it is vital to consider whom is being interviewed and his or her motivations for doing so.

This means that each observation should be evaluated relative to what is known about the actors, their intentions, their interactions, and the situation in which they found themselves (Thies 2002: 357). When analyzing documents, one must ask what purpose the document was intended to serve and what agenda the author might have. How did the document fit into the political system, and what is the relation to the stream of other communications and activities within the policymaking process? It is also important to note the circumstances surrounding the document—why has it been declassified or released and for what purpose—and what has not been released?

Evidence might also be what is not mentioned in the text or in an archive. This type of evidence can be called *e silentio* evidence—based on silence or the absence of an expected statement or message in a text or in an archive. If we expect an author to have a strong interest in presenting an event in a certain light or we would expect the author to take credit for a given decision, and such is not the case, this omission might have inferential weight in our analysis. When a certain event is not mentioned in the text, one possible explanation might be that the event did not take place. Conversely, if we are very confident based on other sources that an event took place, its omission in a source could be a highly improbable piece of evidence with strong inferential weight. As the "dog that did not bark" example showed us, silence or the absence of something can in certain circumstances be the strongest evidence.

Evaluating the Accuracy of Observations

The next stage of the evaluation process is to assess its accuracy. In the measurement of social phenomena, we can never aspire to 100 percent accurate measurements, but through a critical evaluation of the size of measurement error, we can increase our degree of confidence that our collected observations are what we think they are.

Is the observation what it purports to be? Are we measuring what we intended to measure? Inaccurate measures can be the product of either non-systematic or systematic errors in the measuring instrument we use to collect observations. Nonsystematic (or random) error is commonly termed *reliability*, whereas systematic error is defined here as the *bias* in our measuring instrument. For example, a telescope that has random imperfections in its mirrors will produce a blurrier image. The result would be haphazard pictures that prevent us from making accurate observations regarding the exact location of stellar objects. However, the error is random. In contrast, bias is the product of a measuring instrument that produces systematic errors. If there is an error in a mirror that results in the image being skewed systematically two millimeters to the left, this is a much more serious form of error, as it distorts the picture in a systematic pattern, resulting in invalid inferences.

These two forms of measurement error and the risks that they pose for causal inferences can be expressed in Bayesian terms. Unreliable measurements decrease our confidence that we have actually measured e, which then reduces the ability of our empirical tests to update our confidence in the presence/absence of a part of a mechanism (the posterior probability). Accuracy can be expressed in terms of probability $(p(a))$, where an unreliable measure has a low probability of being accurate, and vice versa. Entered into Bayes's theorem, an unreliable measure reduces the ability of evidence to update our confidence in whether or not a hypothesis is true.

Howson and Urbach provide a Bayesian reasoning for this statement (2006: 111). The probability of accuracy $(p(a))$ enters the calculation of the posterior probability of a hypothesis through the likelihood function. The nominator of the likelihood ratio is $p(e|{\sim}h)$, which logically equals $p(e|{\sim}h \,\&\, a)p(a) + p(e|{\sim}h \,\&\, {\sim}a)p({\sim}a)$. The latter means that the probability of e being found if the hypothesis is not true when the measure is accurate is multiplied by the probability of the accuracy of the instrument. This sum is then added to the product of the probability of e being found if h is not true and the instrument is not accurate multiplied by the probability that the instrument is not accurate. In the denominator, $p(e|h) = p(e|h \,\&\, {\sim}a) \times p({\sim}a)$ means that the probability of e being found if the hypothesis is true equals the probability of e being found if h is true when the measure is inaccurate times the probability of the measure being inaccurate. Taken together, these calculations show that a very unreliable measure increases the size of the denominator and decreases the nominator in the likelihood ratio. If we find e but $p(a)$ is low, finding e does little to update our confidence in the veracity of the hypothesis, meaning that the posterior probability is not updated substantially.

The best solution to the problem of unreliable measures is to collect multiple independent observations. This approach is commonly referred to as *triangulation* and can refer to collecting observations either from different sources of the same type (e.g., interviewing different participants) or collecting observations across different types of sources (e.g., archives and interviews) or different types of evidence, if available (i.e., pattern, sequence, account, trace). However, triangulation does not help unless we can substantiate that the sources are independent of each other. Doing three interviews and postulating that sources have been triangulated is not enough—the researcher needs to substantiate the fact that the interviews are independent of each other.

The importance of the independence of sources can be understood using Bayesian logic. If pieces of evidence are truly independent, it is highly unlikely that the measures will result in the same evidence (e) unless e is actually a true measure (Howson and Urbach 2006: 125). If we are conducting interviews to measure what happened in a political negotiation and three participants in the negotiations offer similar accounts, and if we can verify that the accounts are independent of each other, we would increase our confidence in the accuracy of the evidence of the account of the negotiations. It would be highly unlikely to find similar accounts unless the observed e is a true measure. However, finding similar accounts could also mean that the participants met afterward to agree on a common account of the events. If they had met, finding that the accounts were similar would do little to update our confidence in the accuracy of the evidence. And finding that the accounts are too similar should actually decrease our assessment of the accuracy of the measure quite dramatically, as it is highly unlikely that we would find 100 percent correspondence unless the measure is not accurate.

Biased observations mean that the error has a systematic pattern. The risk of this problem is particularly acute in process-tracing research, where the observations we collect are not a random sample. We need to be particularly concerned with systematic error when the bias is systematically related to the patterns predicted by (e|h) or (e|~h). This worst-case scenario can occur either inadvertently (when the measuring instrument produces evidence that systematically confirms or disconfirms h) or when a researcher deliberately chooses observations that either confirm or disconfirm the pattern expected by (e|h) or (e|~h). In this scenario, the evidence collected is either too good or too bad to be true (Howson and Urbach 2006: 116–18). If the found e fits the hypothesis perfectly, we should be very suspicious, as this result is improbable in the real world. Howson and Urbach use Bayes's theorem to show why collected evidence that perfectly fits with either (e|h) or (e|~h) does not result in the updating of the posterior probability. Rigging the results would mean that we would expect to find e regardless of whether or not h was true, meaning that the probability of finding the evidence when using a highly inaccurate measure (~a) would be high regardless of whether the hypothesis was true or not (p(e|h & ~a) = p(e|~h & ~a)). When this is the case, it can be shown that the posterior probability (p(h|e)) equals the prior (p(h)), meaning that when e is rigged, no updating of the posterior takes place.[3]

In contrast to the problem of reliability, there are no quick fixes to correct for systematic bias in our measurements. Therefore, being suspicious is a rule of thumb in evaluating observations. Observations that appear to be too good to be true are probably false. Second, corrections can be made by critically evaluating the size and direction of bias. This can be accomplished by a critical assessment of the source of each observation and by comparing the observation with other independent observations in a triangulation process to assess the size and direction of bias. We should focus in particular on assessing the degree of systematic error that either favors or disfavors the hypothesis.

Evaluating the Inferential Weight of Evidence: How Probable Is the Evidence?

Finally, once we are reasonably confident that the evidence we collected is accurate, we need to evaluate the probability that particular pieces of evidence exist, tying our evaluation into the Bayesian theorems presented in chapters 5 and 6. The term p(e) in the first form of Bayes's theorem states that the inferential weight of evidence is contingent on its probability in the context of the specific case. This refers to evidence independent of its relation to a hypothesis, whereas when the relationship between theory and evidence is considered in the likelihood ratio, this relates to considerations of test strength that were discussed in chapter 6.

We evaluate p(e) based on our contextual knowledge of particular cases. The contextual sensitivity of evidence is one of the strongest comparative advantages of in-depth, qualitative case study methods, where expert substantive knowledge of individual cases is used to evaluate what constitutes evidence and whether it is highly improbable or probable to find specific pieces of evidence in a particular case.

The probability of evidence relates directly to the question of how many pieces of evidence are necessary to update our confidence in the validity of a hypothesis. If p(e) is very low, even one piece of evidence can be enough to update significantly our confidence in the validity of a hypothesis. For example, using an example from the *Silver Blaze* story, another part of the hypothesized mechanism explaining the crime was that Straker planned to injure the prize racehorse by cutting its tendon so that it could not run in the race. This part of the mechanism relates to how the crime was planned.

Holmes tests this part by developing a prediction that Straker would have had to practice the delicate tendon-nicking technique before he attempted it on the racehorse. The evidence that Holmes collects to test this prediction is that three of the "few sheep in the paddock" had recently gone lame. To evaluate the inferential weight of this evidence in relation to updating his confidence in the part of the mechanism, Holmes assesses the probability that three out of a handful of otherwise healthy sheep went lame in a short period of time. He concludes that the probability of finding this evidence was highly unlikely, enabling him to use the found evidence to make a strong inference about the part of the mechanism. In contrast, if sheep were known to commonly have hip problems like those that plague certain large dogs, the probability of finding the evidence (lame sheep) would have been quite high, meaning that little updating would have been possible based on the found evidence.

The key point here is one single piece of evidence, if sufficiently improbable, can significantly increase our confidence in the validity of the hypothesis. Schultz explicitly uses this type of reasoning when he presents evidence in a case study of the 1898 Fashoda crisis between France and the United Kingdom.

> As predicted . . . signals from the government were sent in a way that entailed high and visible audience costs. They were made publicly, in full view of the British electorate, and they were designed to arouse public opinion so that it would be difficult for the government to later back down. The most prominent example of such signaling came on October 10, when Salisbury took the *unusual step* of publishing a blue book on the crisis, a collection of key dispatches between the two countries. Until this point, the negotiations had taken place in private. With the publication of the blue book, the positions taken and arguments made by both sides were out in the open. The British public could see for its own eyes the uncompromising position of the government, as well as the audacity of French claims. Salisbury's action was *not only unusual but a breach of prevailing diplomatic norms:*

"as a matter of courtesy, records of diplomatic negotiations are not generally given to the public until the negotiations with which they are concerned are ended." . . . At the same time, the move had tremendous signaling value. By publicizing Britain's stance in such an *unusual manner,* Salisbury effectively painted himself into a corner: retreat from this position would entail substantial political costs." (2001: 186–87; emphasis added)

The word *unusual* appears numerous times to hammer home the point that one piece of improbable evidence (here, making public the blue book) is enough to substantiate the claim that the U.K. government was creating high and visible audience costs for itself. Evaluation of p(e) is case-specific. What is unusual in one case might be common evidence in another. Schultz substantiates the unusual nature of publicly airing the blue book by mentioning that publishing key dispatches is something that not only deviates from normal U.K. government behavior at the time but also is a "breach of prevailing diplomatic norms." By itself, the observation is just an observation; combined with contextual knowledge, it is evidence that is highly improbable and therefore has a stronger inferential weight than more probable pieces of evidence.

All evidence is not created equal. The Bayesian logic of inference and the role that the probability of evidence plays in it implies that we should attempt to design bold predictions for finding relatively improbable evidence. However, this raises two dilemmas. First, our empirical tests must be practical. Surprising or improbable evidence is difficult to access, and if we have access, very difficult to find. Second, we need to ensure that our selected evidence is representative of general trends in the evidence. A single piece of evidence like the blue book could be an anomalous observation. Therefore, when using highly improbable evidence, it is important to establish that the single piece of evidence reflects broader trends.

Consequently, in most empirical tests, we make predictions that rely on multiple pieces and sources of evidence. However, it can be argued that utilizing multiple different pieces and sources of evidence that are independent of each other actually decreases p(e): How probable is it that we find the same confirming evidence when we utilize different sources of evidence? In a study of the Cuban Missile Crisis, finding the same evidence in U.S. and Soviet archives would be highly improbable unless our observations are measuring e, whereas finding that U.S. participant accounts in memoirs and interviews matches U.S. archival records is much more probable.

Depending on the type of evidence, very different forms of evaluating its probability can be appropriate. If we are assessing pattern evidence, classic statistical probabilities can be relevant to assess the probability of finding e given what we know about the normal distribution of populations and the like. However, even here, we are using reasoning that is more analogous to detective work. Freedman offers a good example of the evaluation of the probability of pattern evidence based on Snow's work on the causes of cholera: Snow "made a more complete tally of cholera deaths in the area. His 'spot map' displays the location of cholera fatalities during the epidemic, and the clustering is apparent from the map" (2011: 226–27). Crucial here is the evaluation of the probability of the pattern (p(e))—for example, by using statistical tests to determine the expected probability of a correspondence between distance to infested water supplies and the incidence of cholera. Conversely, if we are evaluating sequence evidence, how unusual would a given pattern of meetings be given what we know about the context?

7.2. Sources of Evidence in Process-Tracing

The selection of sources in process-tracing research is not driven by random sampling; instead, we select sources based on the type of evidence that is best suited to enable us to engage in a critical theory test. In other words, source selection is theory-driven.

Different sources of evidence are commonly used in process-tracing analysis, and each has its own benefits and pitfalls. We first introduce one way in which primary and secondary sources can be delineated, using the widely accepted Anglo-Saxon terminology (e.g., Trachtenberg 2006). We then discuss the shortcomings associated with particular sources and tools that can be used to improve the accuracy of measurements based on these sources.

The Distinction between Primary and Secondary Sources

We define primary sources as eyewitness accounts of a given process—for example, documents produced by participants at the time an event occurred. Secondary sources, in contrast, are produced based on primary sources. Thus, the work of a historian studying primary sources (e.g., the documentary record of a negotiation) is a secondary source.

It can often be difficult to determine whether a source is primary or sec-

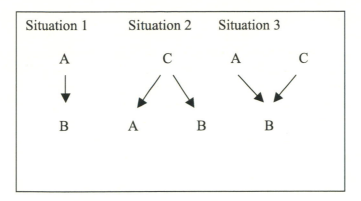

Fig. 7.1. Dependence between sources. (Based on Erslev 1963.)

ondary. An interviewee can be a primary source; however, if the respondent did not actually participate but has the information from other participants, the interview would be a secondary source.

We can use tools such as the dating of documents and text analysis to determine which sources are primary and secondary (Milligan 1979). For example, if source A has the same linguistic phrasing as source B and we can show that the production of source A preceded source B, this suggests that source B should be treated as secondary material that builds on source A, as it is highly unlikely that they would have used the same phrasing unless source B draws on source A.

Logically, there are three ways that a source A can be related to source B (figure 7.1.). First, source B has the information from source A. Here, source A is primary and B is secondary. We should therefore, other things equal, attribute higher inferential weight to A rather than B. Second, if sources A and B are reports drawn from a common source C and C is unknown for us, then A and B are both primary to us. However, they are not independent of each other given the common source. Therefore, when we possess A, adding B would not provide any new additional evidence. If C is known, then A and B should be considered secondary and C primary. We should therefore use C instead of A and B. Third, if parts of B draw on A, but B also reports something from C and C is unknown for us, then A is primary, the parts of B that draw on A are secondary, while those parts that rely on the unknown C are primary to us. However, if both C and A are known, then they are primary sources, while B is secondary (Erslev 1963: 44–45).[4]

Interviews

One of the most commonly used sources of evidence in process-tracing research is interviews, be they elite interviews, where the respondents provide information about events or their motivations therein, or interviews with persons who are treated as representatives of a particular worldview. This discussion focuses on elite interviewing, since the goal of many process-tracing studies is to gain information about political events by interviewing the key actors in the process (Tansey 2007). Interview observations are primarily used to supply account evidence, where we are interested in participants' recollections of different aspects of a process, and sequence evidence, where we want to gather information about the sequence of events that took place in a process.

Before the content of individual interviews is assessed, one needs to consider whether the selection of sources is biased in one direction. If we are analyzing a political negotiation, have we spoken to both the winners and losers? To quote a proverb, "Success has many fathers; failure is an orphan."

The account provided by an interview must be assessed. What does the respondent say? That is, what is the observation? One of the advantages of elite interviews is that they provide the opportunity to interview the persons who actually participated in the case under investigation. Participant accounts potentially offer a more direct measure of a causal mechanism, depending on how the theoretical test has been operationalized. Further, interviewing allows the researcher to move beyond the written accounts and gather information about the underlying context of events.

Once we have determined the content of the observation, we need to assess the degree of accuracy of evidence in terms of reliability and bias. The first question to ask is, What was the interviewee's role in the process? Should the observation be treated as primary or secondary material? A primary source was directly involved in an event, while the secondary source was not present but instead draws on information from other sources (e.g., other participants or the minutes of meetings).

Normally, we should expect that the accuracy of a primary source is higher than that of a secondary source, but this might not always be the case. A participant who was either unable to comprehend what was happening or who perceived events incorrectly is less accurate than a secondary account by an expert observer who had full access to the documentary record and many different participant accounts. However, if the observer is biased toward a particular theory about why events happened, the secondary account would also contain significant measurement errors that would decrease the accuracy of the observations.

A particular challenge is raised by the fact that respondents sometimes overstate their centrality in a political process. Could the respondent have known what took place behind closed doors? Kramer gives the example of former Soviet ambassador to the United States Anatoly Dobrynin, whom some historians have used as an inside source for observations about the Soviet decision-making process leading to the Cuban Missile Crisis. However, despite Dobrynin's claims, Kramer argues that Dobrynin was not privy to the highest-level deliberations (1990: 215). Most damningly, Dobrynin was not informed about the deployment of missiles until after the United States had discovered them (215). Therefore, we would assess his account of the high-level deliberations as being less accurate, other things equal.

When we are dealing with secondary sources, the observations might be unreliable if the interviewee has relied on hearsay. In this type of interview, the researcher needs to ask the respondent about the sources for his/her claims about what happened in a political process. Does the respondent build his/her claims on the minutes of the meetings or from detailed discussions with participants immediately after the negotiations took place?

Another pitfall is the length of time between an event and when the interview is conducted. Participants interviewed immediately after a negotiation can be expected to have a reasonable recollection of the details about what took place, but lapses of memory over time will result in observations that are less reliable. More insidious is the risk that participants will, by reading other accounts and talking with other participants, change their interpretation of what happened to match other accounts, resulting in potential bias in our observations if we interview these participants long after the fact.

To assess potential bias in the observations, one needs to ask whether the respondent has a potential motive for presenting a skewed account of events? Indeed, one needs to ponder why the respondent has chosen to be interviewed. If one is interviewing only the winners in a political negotiation, this should raise warning flags about the potential bias of the material provided.

As a consequence of the imperfections of human memory, interviews will never be a perfectly reliable measuring instrument. Reliability can, however, be improved through the careful use of triangulation both across different persons and between different kinds of sources (interviews, archival observations, and so forth).

However, for triangulation to work, we need to establish that the sources are independent of each other. If we are triangulating across interviews, we need to make sure that we have conducted interviews with participants from different sides to establish the independence of sources. If we are investigating a case involving a negotiation of a bill in the U.S. Congress, we would say that triangulation across independent sources has occurred if we interviewed members of both parties in the House and Senate, along with their aides and lobbyists who were involved, together with White House representatives who took part in the negotiations. If we find the same account evidence in multiple independent sources, it would be highly unlikely to find this unless e is an accurate measure of e.

Triangulation across different kinds of sources can also be used to check the accuracy of interview observations (Tansey 2007), again contingent on the independence of the different sources. If we interview a person who took part in a meeting and then find the same observations in the minutes of the meeting, this could increase our confidence in the accuracy of the observations. However, if the person we interviewed also wrote the meeting minutes, finding the same observation in two different kinds of sources would do nothing to increase our confidence in the accuracy of our observations.

Archival Material

Process-tracing scholars often aspire to produce case studies that build on what social scientists have often termed "hard" primary evidence—for example, official internal documents produced by public authorities that describe what took place behind closed doors (e.g., Moravcsik 1998: 80–85). While even internal documents can include measurement error, when they are generated as a nonpublic record of what took place, we can be reasonably confident that they are accurate: As Trachtenberg notes, "What would be the point of keeping records if those records were not even meant to be accurate?" (2006: 147). Archival material can provide all four types of evidence. Pattern evidence could, for example, entail counting the number and length of documents. Sequence evidence could be in the form of documents, describing what meetings took place over a period of time (e.g., agendas for meetings). Trace evidence could take the form of meeting minutes as proof that a meeting actually took place (a trace). Finally, meeting minutes could also be used as account evidence for what took place there.

The first step in evaluating the accuracy of archival material is to examine the authenticity of a document. If something seems amiss in the authorship, time period, style, genre, or origin of a document, we have to uncover its past to evaluate whether the source can tell us anything. Relevant questions are: (1) Has the document been produced at the time and place when an event occurred, or has it been produced later and/or away from where the events took place? (2) Is the document what it claims to be? (3) Where and under what circumstances was it produced? (4) Why was the document created? and (5) What would a document like this be expected to tell us? Naturally, if the document is not authentic, it has no inferential value for us.

The rest of this section deals primarily with challenges related to dealing with official archives, such as foreign ministerial archives. However, for many of the research questions in which social scientists are interested, this type of archive can be either uninformative or irrelevant. The personal archives of participants can also be relevant, but daunting challenges of access can arise. For many research questions, there are no relevant archives, meaning that the historical record must be traced using other types of sources.

The historical record is usually quite ambiguous (Wohlforth 1997), and we do not suggest that ambitious scholars enter the archives before they have operationalized strong tests of the presence/absence of each part of the hypothesized causal mechanism. Finding answers in archival records is often akin to finding a needle in a haystack. Without a clear set of theory tests to guide one's search in the archives, it is more akin to finding some small object in the haystack without knowing what that object is. The utility of using a theory-driven search for data is illustrated by an exchange from the Sherlock Holmes story *Silver Blaze*:

> Holmes took the bag, and descending into the hollow he pushed the matting into a more central position. Then stretching himself upon his face and leaning his chin upon his hands he made a careful study of the trampled mud in front of him.
>
> "Halloa!" said he, suddenly, "what's this?"
>
> It was a wax vesta, half burned, which was so coated with mud that it looked at first like a little chip of wood.
>
> "I cannot think how I came to overlook it," said the Inspector with an expression of annoyance.
>
> "It was invisible, buried in the mud. I only saw it because I was looking for it." (A. C. Doyle 1975: 17)

Before we can admit observations gathered in archival material, we need to assess what the observation is in light of our background knowledge (e.g., the context in which it was produced) and the potential sources of measurement error that can exist in the document.

Basic questions include the document's source. Can we assume it is authentic? Why was the document created, and what were the circumstances and motives surrounding its creation (Thies 2002: 357, 359)? Trachtenberg (2006: 141) gives examples of questions one could ask to put documents in context in a particular international conflict: What did each country want? What policies were they pursuing? In what kind of thinking was the policy rooted? What did each side actually do? How does the document fit into this story? Here, we need to assess the purpose of the document and the empirical process leading to its creation to enable an accurate interpretation of what evidence the observation provides (Larson 2001: 343). That is, we need to evaluate $o + k \rightarrow e$.

What does the source tell us? Can it inform us about the part of the causal mechanism we are examining? Is the evidence a trace of a hypothesized part of a causal mechanism, where the mere existence of given piece of evidence substantiates that a hypothesized part of the mechanism existed? For example, the existence of an internal study paper could substantiate the claim that the government put at least some effort into a negotiation. Or is the source an account of events that allegedly took place, like the minutes of a meeting? In addition, was the source produced when the event took place or much later? Did the author personally take part in the event, or was the document produced based on the accounts of others? For example, diplomatic cables often report secondary accounts of meetings or contain a leader's interpretation of a situation as recounted by one of his aides.

In assessing archival sources, it is useful to consider what this kind of document usually contains. This can be termed the genre of a document. What is usually included in the minutes of a National Security Council meeting or a CIA study paper?

After we have assessed the observations in light of what we otherwise know about the genre of document and the context in which it was produced ($o + k$), we need to evaluate whether the observation has any plausible measurement error. Does the source give a reliable account of what it alleges to measure (Trachtenberg 2006: 146)? If the source alleges that it records what took place in a meeting, does other evidence also show that the meeting was held (146)? If the meeting was between governments, do we find accounts in the archives of the other governments (146)? If the document was produced much later than the meeting, we should, other things equal, expect it to be less reliable.

Do the observations contain any form of systematic error? We know that high-level actors attempt to skew the historical record to favor their own accounts (Wohlforth 1997). One way in which this can occur is that documents are selectively declassified, with the sources available all slanted toward the account of events favored by authorities. We therefore have to ask ourselves why this particular document has been declassified while others have not. Does this selective declassification have potential bias?

Further, what is the likelihood that the observations themselves have been manipulated? In other words, do the minutes of meetings reflect what took place or the account favored by a decision maker? The risk of this form of bias is particularly problematic in centralized dictatorial systems such as the Soviet Union, where official records only reflect what leaders want them to say (English 1997). In the Soviet archives, there are strong indications that the documentary record reflects the views of leaders, especially during the Stalin years.

But the problem also exists in democratic systems. The BBC TV series *Yes, Prime Minister* illustrates the problem in a (hopefully!) exaggerated example of a fictional exchange between two civil servants, Bernard (B) and Sir Humphrey (SH), regarding the production of minutes of cabinet meetings:

SH: What I remember is irrelevant. If the minutes don't say that he [the Prime Minister (PM)] did, then he didn't.

B: So you want me to falsify the minutes?

SH: I want nothing of the sort! . . .

B: So what do you suggest, Sir Humphrey?

SH: The minutes do not record everything that was said at a meeting, do they?

B: Well, no of course not.

SH: And people change their minds during a meeting, don't they?

B: Yes . . .

SH: So the actual meeting is actually a mass of ingredients from which to choose from. . . . You choose from a jumble of ill-digested ideas a version which represents the PM's views as he would, on reflection, have liked them to emerge.

B: But if it's not a true record . . .

SH: The purpose of minutes is not to record events, it is to protect people. You do not take notes if the PM says something he did not mean to say, particularly if it contradicts something he has said publicly. You try to improve on what has been said, put it in a better order. You are tactful.

B: But how do I justify that?

SH: You are his servant.

(BBC 1987)

Another challenge with archival documents relates to intelligence esti-mates and reports from embassies. Here, we need to think of the relationship between the producer of the document and the consumer. A classic example occurred in the early 1960s during the Vietnam War, where assessments of the situation produced by junior CIA officials in the field were consistently very pessimistic (Ford 1998). However, more senior CIA officials were cog-nizant of what the consumers of intelligence in Washington, D.C., wanted to hear. Therefore, they pressured junior officials to "get with the team" and edit documents in a more optimistic direction. If we are testing a part of a causal mechanism dealing with whether high-level decision makers knew the real situation on the ground in Vietnam, our results would be very dif-ferent depending on whether we gain access to the first, unedited pessimistic version or the redacted final optimistic version sent to Washington, D.C.

As with interviews, triangulation can be used to assess and potentially to correct for measurement error, contingent on the different sources being independent of each other. If we find the same account of an event in the ar-chives of two different governments, it is highly unlikely that we would find these two observations unless they actually are measuring what took place.

Memoirs, Public Speeches, and Other Forms of Primary Sources

We now turn to a variety of primary sources that are generally treated as "soft" primary sources—the memoirs and diaries of participants, private let-ters, and public statements and speeches. Common to these primary sources is that they are usually intended to be made public. Only the most naive per-son would expect that private letters that detail important events will remain private after one's death. Therefore, even private letters can be expected to be written with the understanding that they might be made public at some point. We can, however, use these sources to provide account evidence—taken with more than a few grains of salt. In contrast, we can usually trust these softer sources for sequence evidence, although in particularly sensitive negotiations, there also can be strong motives for participants to distort even the timetable of events.

Memoirs are intended to be made public, and therefore are only an ac-curate picture of what an actor wants others to believe happened. Private diaries and letters of participants in historically important events can also be expected to be biased as a consequence of the high probability that they will someday be made public. Like memoirs, they therefore are an accurate measure only of the participant's take on events for public consumption.

When assessing these sources of observations, we need to ask the same questions that we ask of interview observations: How close was the person to the events? Did the person participate, or is the information from hearsay? Does the source have a motive to present an accurate account of the events? For example, politicians might have a tendency to overstate their importance in a series of events, whereas civil servants often downplay their roles to maintain the appearance of neutrality.

We should be particularly cautious in claiming that an observation is accurate when the information contained in it aligns with the interests/motivations of the source. Conversely, if the author gives an account that is against his or her interests, we are not likely to find this observation unless it is accurate, meaning that we can attach more confidence to its accuracy.

Public statements and speeches can be used as evidence in specific circumstances. Speeches often are used to justify policy choices and therefore cannot be used to measure the real motivations behind a decision. For example, public justifications for war in Iraq included speeches by Bush about weapons of mass destruction that were not necessarily the real motivation behind the invasion. However, if we find the same justifications in private settings where policymakers can speak more freely, it is unlikely that we would find the same statements in both the public and private record unless they accurately reflect policymakers' motivations (Khong 1992: 60).

Historical Scholarship

When we are doing process-tracing research, we are usually very dependent on secondary historical scholarship. In the words of Skocpol, "Redoing primary research for every investigation would be disastrous; it would rule out most comparative-historical research. If a topic is too big for purely primary research *and* if excellent studies by specialists are already available in some profusion—secondary sources are appropriate as the basic source of evidence for a given study" (quoted in Lustick 1996: 606). Historical work can be used as sequence and account evidence.

When utilizing historical reports, we must first remember that historical work is not "the facts." We need to assess carefully the reliability and potential bias of each observation that we use from historical scholarship.

Historians are people, too, meaning that they can make mistakes. Historians may misinterpret primary sources, resulting in incorrect descriptive inferences about what happened. This does not mean that we cannot use historical accounts but merely that we must be aware of the fact that any given work is potentially unreliable. To reduce this risk, we should triangulate observations from multiple historical sources to ensure that we reduce the risk of random measurement error.

More problematic is the fact that the work of historians reflects their implicit (or sometimes explicit) theories. The "historical record," therefore, is not a neutral source of information but instead reflects these theories (Lustick 1996). There is a substantial risk of bias when a social scientist with a particular theoretical and conceptual predisposition purposefully selects work produced by historians who share this bias, resulting in the mistaken confirmation of the social scientist's preferred theory (606).

For example, in scholarship on the start of the Cold War, the first generation of work in the 1950s tended to favor the theory where the Soviet Union and either the innate expansionistic tendencies inherent in communist doctrine (the "neurotic bear") or Soviet behavior as a traditional great power were the cause of the Cold War (e.g., White 2000). This school was followed by the revisionist accounts in the 1960s that pinned blame on the United States, contending that U.S. expansion as a consequence of capitalist economic interests triggered the Cold War (e.g., Williams 1962). A third theory was put forward in the 1970s by the postrevisionist school, which saw the Cold War as primarily the product of misunderstandings that could have been avoided at least to some degree (e.g., Gaddis 1972). If we are interested in testing a liberal theory dealing with the impact of perceptions and misperceptions, we would find supporting evidence for the theory in the postrevisionist school and disconfirming evidence in the previous two schools. In Bayesian terms, this form of bias implies a form of rigging of test results that undermines our ability to update our confidence in the accuracy of hypothesis.

Lustick's solution to this bias problem is first to know the historiographic schools and then to triangulate across them. The researcher should select the historical work that is best suited to provide a critical test. If one is choosing to test an ideational mechanism dealing with actor perceptions, one should not choose work from the postrevisionist school as a source of evidence.

Newspaper Sources

Finally, newspaper and other journalistic sources can, in certain circumstances, provide accurate observations of what we intend to measure. In the case of Owen's tests of part 5 of his hypothesized democratic peace mechanism (see chapter 5), editorials in the liberal press about views toward France were a form of primary evidence of "liberal elites agitating." Newspapers can provide pattern evidence (e.g., number of articles dealing with a subject), sequence evidence (timetable of events), and different forms of account evidence.

However, the accuracy of newspaper sources often can be difficult to assess. In the words of Moravcsik, "Journalists generally repeat the justifications of governments or the conventional wisdom of the moment without providing much with which to judge the nature or reliability of the source. Second and more important, even . . . if reliable, their sheer number and diversity means that the ability of an analyst to present such evidence tells us little or nothing" (1998: 81). Here we agree with Larson, who suggests that these forms of secondary sources can provide important background material about the context in which decisions were made and what events took place they cannot be used as evidence in process-tracing research unless the observations are triangulated with other types of sources. In other words, newspaper sources are often better at supplying k than they are at supplying o in the formula o + k → e.

CHAPTER 8

Case Selection and Nesting Process-Tracing Studies in Mixed-Method Designs

Explaining-outcome process-tracing studies are almost by definition stand-alone single-case studies. In contrast, single-case studies using either theory-building or theory-testing variants are not intended to stand alone; instead, they seek to contribute with their specific comparative advantages to what we know about a broader social phenomenon. A case study of two democracies that did not go to war despite severe conflicts of interest updates our degree of confidence in the existence of a more general causal relationship between mutual democracy and peace, at the same time shedding light on the mechanisms that explain how mutual democracy produces peace.

Yet how can single-case studies contribute to our broader knowledge of causal relationships? This chapter illustrates how the theory-building and -testing variants of process-tracing can be nested into a broader research program, something that is possible given that they share the theory-centric ambition of studying systematic elements of causal relationships with other social science research methods. But nesting is possible only through case selection techniques building on cross-case inferences made using other methods. Furthermore, explaining-outcome process-tracing studies cannot be embedded in a nested analysis because of the inclusion of nonsystematic, case-specific mechanisms in explanations.

As introduced in chapter 2, choosing which variant of process-tracing to employ depends on the purposes of the study. First, is the purpose of the study to explain a particularly interesting outcome, or does the study have theory-centric ambitions? If the former is the answer, then the explaining-outcome design is chosen, with the focus of crafting a minimally sufficient explanation of the particular outcome. In contrast, ambitions to understand causal relationships across a population of cases lead to the choice of either theory-building or theory-testing designs.

Second, when choosing between theory-building and -testing variants, are there well-developed theoretical conjectures for empirical correlations between known independent and dependent variables or conditions, or are we in a situation where there is either no well-developed theory explaining a phenomenon or where existing theories have been disconfirmed in prior empirical analysis? In the first situation, we choose theory-testing designs, whereas theory-building designs are chosen when we lack plausible theoretical mechanisms to account for outcomes.

Case selection strategies in process-tracing differ for each of the three variants of process-tracing, a fact that the existing methodological literature on case selection in process-tracing has overlooked by treating process-tracing as a single method. We discuss why existing methodological prescriptions for selection strategies are not always applicable for the different variants of process-tracing (e.g., Gerring 2007a; King, Keohane, and Verba 1994; Lieberman 2005). Prescriptions are developed for case choice in the theory-building and -testing variants of process-tracing, in particular focusing on how these prescriptions differ from existing guidelines. In contrast, cases are chosen in explaining-outcome designs not on the basis of research design strategies but instead because the cases are substantively important (e.g., the French Revolution), although explaining-outcome studies also have the potential to contribute insights to ongoing theoretical debates in the field.

Common to all three variants, however, is the need for the analyst to be explicit about the case selection strategy, detailing the reasoning behind the selection of specific cases. Given that the perfect case for a particular research purpose usually does not exist, arguments need to be put forward that substantiate why the case can fulfill the research's goals.

After discussing case selection strategies and how they enable nesting of only theory-centric process-tracing studies into broader mixed-method designs, we discuss the challenges in making the results of process-tracing research communicate with those from other research methods. Whereas methods such as frequentist, large-n statistical methods or small-n comparative methods analyze patterns of regularity between X and Y, process-tracing methods look at both X and the mechanism linking it with Y. Therefore, there is the risk that the two talk past each other, with analyses of the causal effects of X on Y potentially incompatible with analyses of the causal relationship of X and a mechanism with Y. We now turn to a discussion of case selection strategies in the three process-tracing variants.

8.1. Theory-Testing Process-Tracing

Case Selection Strategies

Theory-testing process-tracing has at its core the ambition to go beyond correlations that have been found using large-n methods, attempting to test whether hypothesized causal mechanisms are to be found between X and Y. According to Lieberman, "Given the potential for problems of endogeneity and poor data in statistical analyses carried out at the country level of analysis, statistical results alone rarely provide sufficient evidence of the robustness of a theoretical model. Almost inevitably, strong questions arise about causal order, heterogeneity of cases, and the quality of measurement. SNA [small-n designs such as process-tracing] provides an important opportunity to counter such charges" (2005: 442).

Theory-testing process-tracing strategies are used in two situations. First, theory-testing is used when there are well-developed theoretical conjectures but we are unsure whether they have empirical support. In Moravcsik's (1999) test of a supranational entrepreneur mechanism (see chapter 4), there was a well-developed theory that could be tested but there was uncertainty regarding whether there was an actual empirical correlation between X and Y.

Second, and more common, is when theory tests are performed after a regular association between X and Y has been found with other methods (often large-n studies). Here, the analytical ambition is to test whether there is evidence that a causal mechanism links X and Y. In this situation, typical cases are chosen to test whether a hypothesized causal mechanism is present, with a typical case selected on the basis of the previous large-n analysis (Gerring 2007a: 89; Lieberman 2005: 444–45). A typical case is "representative of a population of cases (as defined by the primary inference)" (Gerring 2007a: 96).

How do we identify a typical case that is appropriate for theory-testing process-tracing? The answer to this question depends on whether the preceding large-n analysis was undertaken using frequentist methods or using comparative, set theoretic methods such as fuzzy-set QCA.

Looking first at case selection after frequentist analysis, existing methodological prescriptions suggest that after we have performed a regression analysis, a typical case is the case with the smallest residuals (Gerring 2007a; Lieberman 2005). According to Lieberman, when we are using small-n methods to test a theory, our case selection strategy should be informed by the best fitting statistical model that has been found using regression analysis (2005: 444–45). Cases that are on or close to a regression line that plots the actual dependent variable scores against regression-predicted scores are identified as possible candidates for in-depth analysis as a consequence of their low residuals.

In this case selection strategy, a case on the regression line (on-lier) enables the analyst to check for spurious correlation and can help to fine-tune the theoretical argument by elaborating the causal mechanisms linking X and Y (Lieberman 2005). The logic behind the selection strategy is presented in figure 8.1, which illustrates how we could depict the empirical results of large-*n* statistical analyses of the economic development thesis using interval-scale variables for levels of economic development and democracy. Increasing values of economic development are expected to result in an increase in the level of democracy in a country (e.g., Burkhart and Lewis-Beck 1994). Candidates for typical cases would be cases 1, 2, 3, and 5, since they are on-line cases with small or zero residuals. We would not consider cases 7 and 8 as candidates because of their larger residual values in relation to the regression line, whereas cases 4 and 6 would be less attractive than 1, 2, 3, and 5.

According to Lieberman, our confidence would be updated even more if we select two or more on-liers that have a wide range of observed scores on the outcome (2005: 444). In figure 8.1, this would involve selecting cases 1 and 5 for two parallel theory tests.

Yet these existing recommendations for case selection strategy ignore the purpose of theory-testing process-tracing: to investigate whether the hypothesized causal mechanism was present in a case. Both X and Y need to be present in the chosen case for the hypothesized causal mechanism to be present, even in theory. It therefore makes no sense to test whether a hypothesized causal mechanism was present in a case when we know a priori that it could not be present, given that either X or Y was not present. Further, the scope conditions that enable the mechanism to function also have to be present.

Cases with low values of X and/or Y are in practice cases where X and/or Y are not present. In figure 8.1, if we are interested in testing whether there is a hypothesized economic development causal mechanism that can be found using in-depth process-tracing methods, choosing case 1 (an economically backward, autocratic country) would do nothing to update our confidence in whether an economic development mechanism exists, nor would it shed light on how it functioned.

In theory-testing process-tracing, cases should be chosen where X and Y are present, along with the relevant scope conditions. Yet frequentist methods offer us few tools for determining whether these conditions are present

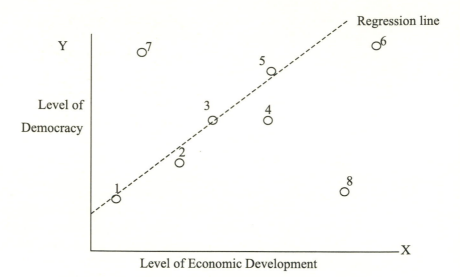

Fig. 8.1. The conventional wisdom for case selection in theory-testing process-tracing after a frequentist analysis illustrated using hypothetical data for the economic development thesis.

except when X and Y are conceptualized as dichotomous variables. If we are operating with an interval-scale variable, at which value can we say that X is actually present?

Comparative methods using set theoretic logic give us more useful tools for selecting a typical case for theory-testing process-tracing. As we argued in chapter 4, X and Y should be conceptualized in terms of set-theoretical terms instead of as variables when we are engaging in process-tracing. Whereas variables describe the full variation of a concept, including both poles, a set-theoretical conceptualization of X and Y understands them in terms of presence or absence.

This can take two forms. In crisp-set logic, concepts take either two values: fully in or fully out of the set. In terms of figure 8.2, cases to the right of the qualitative threshold line are scored as members of the set democracy and vice versa. More realistically, fuzzy-set logic describes concepts as either being a member of a set or not (differences in kind) but opens up the possibility that cases can either be more in than out, or vice versa (differences in degree) (Ragin 2008). The key difference between fuzzy sets and variables is that there is a qualitative threshold that marks membership of cases in the set, demarcating them from cases that are outside of the set. Understood in fuzzy-set terms, the threshold lines in figure 8.2 would mark the qualitative

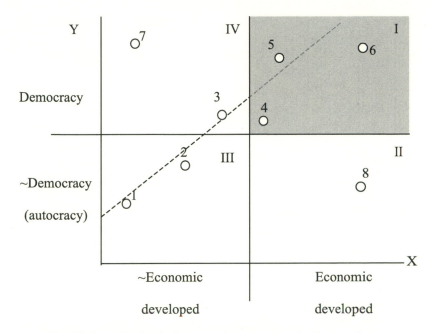

Fig. 8.2. Case selection in theory-testing process-tracing illustrated using hypothetical data for the economic development thesis.

thresholds that determine membership within the set, whereas the placement within the quadrants is based on the degree of membership in the set (more in than out, fully in, and so forth). Using real data, the placement of cases within quadrants would usually be different in fuzzy sets than using normal interval-scale scores, depending on how fuzzy sets are calibrated (see Ragin 2008, chap. 4). For heuristic reasons we keep the same placement in all of the figures.

The importance of conceptualizing in set-theoretical terms and how it impacts case selection is illustrated in figure 8.2. Instead of an interval variable, we have substituted hypothetical fuzzy-set scores for the cases. (The basic prescriptions for case selection are the same regardless of whether crisp- or fuzzy-set scores are used.) Fuzzy-set scores of 1 equal full membership in the set, a value of 0.5 is the qualitative threshold between being in or out, and a value of 0 is fully out of the set.

The critical distinction between figures 8.1 and 8.2 is that the inclusion of a qualitative threshold line for membership in the sets of democracy and economic development enables us to detect which typical cases are relevant for testing whether there is a causal mechanism linking X and Y. Cases that can be chosen are those that are members of the set of democracy and economically developed countries, depicted in the shaded quadrant I (cases 4, 5, 6).

Whereas cases 1, 2, and 3 were appropriate based on Lieberman's suggested strategy, choosing them would do little to update our confidence in the existence of a hypothesized economic development causal mechanism. Cases 1 and 2 are cases of nondeveloped and autocratic countries, whereas case 3 would be a deviant case where we should expect that mechanisms other than economic development are contributing to produce democracy. Cases 4 and 6 become more relevant for theory-testing process-tracing, as despite having relatively large residuals in relation to the regression line found using interval-scale variables (reproduced solely for heuristic purposes in figure 8.2), both cases fulfill the most important criteria for selection—both X and Y are members of the set of X and Y. If we are using fuzzy-set scores, the best typical case would be the one that was in the middle of a distribution of cases in quadrant I. Beyond X and Y, the scope conditions for the operation of the mechanism also need to be present.

In summary, typical cases that can be selected for theory-testing process-tracing are those where both X and Y are present (at least hypothetically), along with the scope conditions that allow the theorized mechanism to operate.

There are, however, differences of degree between typical cases when concepts are formulated in fuzzy-set terms, ranging from most-likely to least-likely cases depending on how conducive the context is to the operation of the mechanism and the degree of membership that X and Y have in the set (Eckstein 1975: 118–20; Gerring 2007a: 116–21). These differences of degree are also captured to some extent when X and Y are formulated as interval-scale variables, although using traditional interval-scale variables, we lack information regarding the cutoff marking whether X and Y are present. Therefore, we suggest that fuzzy-set QCA scores provide more relevant information for selecting most- and least-likely cases in theory-testing process-tracing because they capture both the distinction between differences in kind (present or not) and differences in degree (most versus least likely). Cases that are within the zones of most likely (case 6) and least likely (case 4) are depicted in figure 8.3, whereas case 5 remains merely a typical case.

Most-likely typical cases are cases where we would most expect that a hypothesized causal mechanism was present given that X and Y have high fuzzy-set scores and the scope conditions that enable the mechanism to function are highly favorable. Using fuzzy-set scores, both X and Y would have

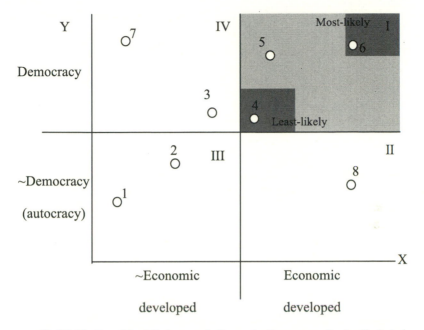

Fig. 8.3. Most- and least-likely cases in theory-testing process-tracing illustrated using hypothetical data for the economic development thesis. (The zone of most-likely cases is depicted as the box in the upper right corner of quadrant I. The zone of least-likely cases is depicted as the box in the lower left corner of quadrant I.)

high membership scores (case 6 in figure 8.3). In contrast, least-likely typical cases are cases where we should least expect that a hypothesized causal mechanism would be present; X and Y are present (but to a lower degree when fuzzy-set scores used, depicted as case 4 in figure 8.3), and the scope conditions lead us to predict that the mechanism is less probable to be present. Regarding the scope conditions, an analogy would be to testing a fire causal mechanism. A most-likely case context would be one where the scope conditions were strongly conducive (plenty of oxygen, massive amounts of dry fuel, etc., and so forth), whereas a least-likely case context could be one where the facilitating scope conditions were not plentiful (e.g., there was little oxygen, the fuel was relatively damp, and so on) but where fire was at least still theoretically possible.

Most-likely single cases serve two functions. First, most-likely cases can be used when we are unsure about whether a hypothesized causal mechanism exists at all. Here, our prior about the presence of the mechanism in a population of cases (p(h)) would be very low. A single theory test that found the mechanism was present would increase our initially very low confidence in the existence of the mechanism by raising the posterior ($p(h_p|e)\uparrow$), enabling us to infer with greater confidence that the mechanism exists. However, based on the single most-likely case, we are unable to make any inferences about the range of its existence in a broader population of cases. Further, additional most-likely case studies that found the mechanism to be present would do little to update our confidence once the prior has been updated above a very low level.

Second, most-likely studies enable cross-case inferences to be made in the direction of decreasing our confidence in the existence of a causal mechanism, or what Eckstein terms "invalidation," when the causal mechanism and/or Y are not found (Eckstein 1975: 119). When Moravcsik found that supranational actors did not have influence and that the causal mechanism that was hypothesized to link X and Y was not present in a most-likely case, this enabled a cross-case inference to be made that updated the confidence in the supranational entrepreneur mechanism in a downward direction in the whole population of comparable cases (Moravcsik 1999).

Least-likely cases enable cross-case inferences to be made when a causal mechanism is found in a single case, based on what Levy refers to as a "Sinatra inference"—"if I can make it there, I'll make it anywhere" (2002: 144). Testing a theory using a least-likely case can be considered as a high-risk strategy, since the potential for failure is relatively high. Failure is understood as a research outcome that enables no updating to take place. If the mechanism is not found in a least-likely case, we cannot update our confidence in its presence in the broader population given that we initially had little hope of finding it present. Conversely, this might also be considered a potentially high-benefit strategy since if we are able to find the mechanism in a non-favorable setting, this significantly increases our confidence in the existence of the casual mechanism in a wider population of cases.

In both instances, what enables cross-case inferences to be made is classification of a case as most/least likely based on a larger-n comparative analysis using a fuzzy-set theoretical definition of concepts. In other words, cross-case inferences are not made based on the findings of the single process-tracing study but instead are only enabled by nesting the single case into the broader research program by using comparative fuzzy-set methods. On its own merits, a single process-tracing theory test is unable to produce any cross-case inferences but can only update our confidence in the presence/absence of a causal mechanism in a particular case, enabling strong within-case inferences to be made but not cross-case inferences.

Cross-case inferences are stronger when we engage in multiple parallel theory tests of typical cases. It is important, though, to first underline that if we take seriously the mechanismic understanding of causality, the results of two or more theory tests of typical cases cannot be strictly compared against each other as causal mechanisms have case-specific manifestations. If we are studying a mechanism dealing with parliamentary dynamics, while the mechanism would be conceptualized as composed of comparable parts, the actual empirical manifestations in cases would be very different across cases and therefore would in principle be noncomparable. For example, a part of a mechanism could deal with interparty dynamics, which would look very different depending on whether we were studying the Dutch, French, or Spanish parliaments.

The number of typical cases necessary to enable us to infer with a reasonable degree of confidence that the mechanism exists in a population of cases depends on (1) the ability of the case to update our confidence in the presence/absence of a mechanism and (2) our assumptions regarding causal complexity and contextual specificity of mechanisms.

First, building on the Bayesian logic of inference and in particular on the idea of research as updating of confidence in the validity of theories, least-likely cases can often stand alone if a mechanism is found, although if it is not found, they do little to update our confidence. A least-likely case therefore has strong confirmatory power but little disconfirmatory power. Therefore, an iterative research strategy of a most-likely followed by a least-likely case study can often be a more productive line of attack, especially when we initially are not very confident in the validity of a theory. If the mechanism is found to be present in the most-likely, the least-likely can be used to establish the bounds of its operation.

However, our ability to assess the contextual specificity of a mechanism is contingent on our assumptions about causal complexity. Simplifying slightly, for causal inferences to be made using frequentist methods, assumptions about causal homogeneity are made that imply that there are not multiple different causal mechanisms that could link any given X to Y. That is, equifinality is assumed away. If we assume causal homogeneity, one typical case would strongly increase our confidence in the presence/absence of a mechanism across a population of cases. In contrast, in both small-n comparative and process-tracing methods, it is assumed that causal relationships are much more complicated, with multiple paths to the same outcome (equifinality is ever-present). This, then, severely limits our ability to make cross-case inferences based on a single typical case, as we cannot infer that if we found a causal mechanism between X and Y, the same mechanism operates in other comparable cases as there can be multiple mechanisms that contribute to producing the same outcome. In this situation, we would need to engage in multiple tests of typical cases before we could make cross-case inferences.

8.2. Theory-Building Process-Tracing

Theory-building process-tracing research aims to build theories of causal mechanisms that are applicable beyond a single case. Given the theory-centric ambition, only systematic parts that are theorized to have causal effects across the population of cases are included in the theorized mechanism.

Case selection strategies depend on whether the purpose is to (1) uncover a mechanism between X and Y or (2) whether we are attempting to build a theory when we know the outcome but are unsure about what mechanism(s) made it happen.

The first situation is when we know that a correlation exists between X and Y but we are in the dark regarding potential mechanisms linking the two. In this form of X-Y-centric theory-building, the analyst should choose to examine a typical case to identify a plausible causal mechanism that can be tested empirically in subsequent research (Gerring 2007a: 91–97). Here, a typical case is defined as one that is a member of the set of X and Y; moreover, the scope conditions required for it to operate are present. The candidate cases for theory-building under these circumstances are the same as the candidates for the theory-testing variant (cases 4, 5, and 6 in quadrant I in figure 8.4). Case 8 is a deviant case when studying how economic development contributes to producing democracy, which would be relevant to compare with typical cases to learn in what context the mechanism does not work.

An example of a typical case selection strategy for building a new theorized causal mechanism is Janis's (1983) investigation of groupthink. Knowing both the value of X (whether a decision was made in a small group) and Y (a poor decision-making process), Janis chose a typical (though quite puzzling) case on which to build his theory by studying the decision-making process in which a group of the "best and the brightest" officials in the Kennedy administration decided to support the Bay of Pigs invasion by exile Cubans, assisted by U.S. assets.

The second situation is where the outcome (Y) is known but we are unsure about what caused it to happen. A sufficient explanation is not being built; instead, a relatively parsimonious mechanism is uncovered that contributes to Y occurring but does not fully explain it.

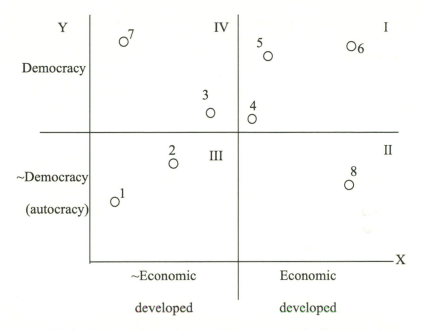

Fig. 8.4. Case selection in theory-building process-tracing illustrated using hypothetical data for an economic development causal mechanism.

Case selection in this second situation resembles a deviant case selection strategy. Gerring defines a deviant case as one "that, by reference to some general understanding of a topic (either a specific theory or common sense), demonstrates a surprising value [outcome]" (2007a: 105). A deviant case is therefore defined in relation to existing knowledge. The outcome of a deviant case may prove to have been caused by mechanisms that have been previously overlooked but whose effects are well known from other research (George and Bennett 2005: 111). The new theorized causal mechanism derived from studying the deviant case can then be tested either using large-*n* methods or a theory-testing process-tracing case study.

Candidates for case selection in the Y-centric variant of theory-building would be cases 3 or 7 in quadrant IV if we want to explain alternative mechanisms that can contribute to producing the outcome democracy in nondeveloped countries. The outcome democracy has to be present, but a deviant case implies that an existing X (economic development) cannot account for the outcome, meaning that cases in quadrant I are not deviant cases. In cases 3 and 7, an economic development mechanism cannot explain democracy as a consequence of the lack of economic development. Instead, case studies of 3 or 7 could be used to build a plausible alternative democratization causal mechanism in nondeveloped countries. Cases in quadrants II and III are not deviant cases, as the outcome democracy is not present.

Existing recommendations suggest that it is beneficial to compare typical and deviant cases to detect omitted variables (Gerring 2007a; Lieberman 2005). Yet as with existing suggestions for case selection in theory-testing process-tracing, this reflects a lack of taking causal mechanisms seriously. What analytical leverage can be gained by comparing a case investigating the economic development mechanism with a completely different mechanism? Traction in building and testing theories can be gained only by comparing mechanisms that contribute to producing the same outcome.

8.3. Explaining-Outcome Process-Tracing

"Not all cases are equal. Some have greater visibility and impact
because of their real-world or theoretical consequences. World War I
is nonpareil in both respects. Its origins and consequences are also
the basis for our major theories in domains as diverse as political
psychology, war and peace, democratization, and state structure."

—Lebow 2000–2001: 594

The purpose of explaining-outcome process-tracing differs from the two other variants. In explaining-outcome process-tracing, we try to establish a minimally sufficient explanation for why an outcome has been produced in a specific case. Explaining-outcome process-tracing includes both systematic parts and more case-specific (nonsystematic) parts. This type of process-tracing leans more heavily toward being a case-centric case study instead of a theory-centric ambition to generalize to a broader population. The distinction is fittingly described by Przeworski and Teune (1970) as the difference between cases described using proper nouns preceded by definite articles (case-centric cases like *the* French Revolution) and those described by common nouns coupled with indefinite articles (theory-centric—*a* revolution).

Case selection strategies in explaining-outcome process-tracing are driven by a strong interest in accounting for a particular outcome. However, this does not mean that there is no interest in accounting for outcomes across cases. For example, Jervis's (2010) analysis of intelligence failures by the U.S. national intelligence community attempts to build minimally sufficient explanations of failure in two cases: the failure to detect the coup against the Iranian shah in 1979 and the belief that weapons of mass destruction were present in Iraq in 2003. Yet the conclusions discuss the lessons that can apply to other comparable cases, lessons that can be understood as potentially systematic mechanisms that can be investigated in further research in other cases.

Therefore, we should not draw the line between explaining-outcome and theory-building process-tracing too sharply. The difference between them is more a matter of degree rather than a difference in kind, and explaining-outcome process-tracing case studies often point to specific systematic mechanisms that in principle can be tested in a wider population of cases or that can act as building blocks for future attempts to create generalizable causal mechanisms that can explain outcomes across the population of relevant cases.

The conclusion, however, is that the inclusion of nonsystematic mechanisms in explaining-outcome process-tracing studies makes it impossible to nest this type of process-tracing case study explicitly in a mixed-method research design (Rohlfing 2008: 1494–95).

8.4. Challenges of Nesting Theory-Centric Process-Tracing Studies in Mixed-Method Designs

Theory-testing studies are often explicitly nested in a broader mixed-method research program as case selection strategies based on the results of larger-n analyses. Two challenges must be tackled to nest a theory-testing process-tracing study into a mixed-method research design.

First, the type of theory being tested using process-tracing needs to be compatible with that tested in the large-n analysis. As discussed in chapter 2, testing a probabilistic theory in a single-case study basically makes no sense in that if we do not find the hypothesized mechanism, we do not know whether the theory is faulty or whether the particular case was an exception that proves the general rule. However, the requirement that theories be deterministic poses a daunting challenge when attempting to combine process-tracing theory-testing with frequentist large-n methods that understand theories in a probabilistic fashion. It is, however, theoretically possible to transform a probabilistic theory into a deterministic theory by reconceptualizing a theory formulated as "When X increases, we should expect that Y will tend to increase" into a theory such as "X is a necessary condition for Y" (for further discussion of this challenge, see Goertz and Starr 2003; Mahoney 2008).

Second, frequentist and comparative methods are basically studying different types of causal relationships than process-tracing (see chapter 2). The problem relates to what exactly we are inferring about. In frequentist, large-n, and comparative methods, inferences are made about patterns of regularity between X and Y, whereas in process-tracing, we are making inferences about the presence of a causal mechanism between X and Y. A typical frequentist analysis will investigate the causal effects of X on the incidence of Y, whereas a process-tracing study will investigate whether a mechanism was present in a case, investigating whether X $\rightarrow$ [($n_1 \rightarrow$) $\times$ ($n_2 \rightarrow$)] Y. Investigating mechanisms means that the focus is on what takes place between X and Y, whereas frequentist approaches focus on X and Y. In effect, we are studying two different things: causal effects versus causal mechanisms. Using an analogy to eating a pizza, in a frequentist analysis, we would only taste the crust on each side, whereas a process-tracing study involves eating both crusts and all of the stuff in between.

How can we ensure that what we are studying in the process-tracing case study can communicate with the inferences made using other research methods? One potential solution to this conundrum is to investigate ways that process-tracing results can be exported by reconceptualizing X and a mechanism as a causal configuration that is compatible with QCA (Ragin 2000). For example, Owen's democratic peace causal mechanism could be reconceptualized as a causal configuration composed of democracy & liberal groups & responsive government that could then be analyzed using other methods such as medium-n QCA. In many instances, QCA uses a deterministic understanding of causality, making it more easily compatible with process-tracing tests.

Another solution is to be pragmatic, explicitly flagging the problem in one's analysis, while ensuring that one utilizes conceptualizations of X that are comparable with each other across methods. If our process-tracing theory test utilizes a conceptualization of X that is comparable to the X used to study the phenomenon in other methods, we can make two inferences in a process-tracing theory test: (1) based on the found evidence, we can infer that X and the mechanism were present in case A, and (2) given that case A was a least-likely case, we can infer that X and the mechanism are also present in the rest of the relevant population of cases. The first within-case inference is made using process-tracing, whereas the subsequent cross-case inference draws on a comparative logic that divides the population into most- and least-likely cases. However, a single (or small handful) of process-tracing theory tests cannot by themselves make cross-case inferences about the presence of X and a mechanism in a population.

A theory-building process-tracing case study does not seek to make cross-case inferences per se but instead seeks solely to build a plausible hypothetical causal mechanism based on induction from the empirical evidence. However, theory-building process-tracing does not build a theory for theory's sake. Theory-building process-tracing is nested either implicitly or explicitly in a broader research design, where the newly built hypothetical mechanism can subsequently be tested using either theory-testing process-tracing or other methods to detect whether it is present in other cases. This means that we run into the same problems as in theory-testing both with regard to causal theories versus mechanisms and in the understanding of causality used in different theories. This means that there are clear limits to our ability to build theories about causal mechanisms using process-tracing that then can be tested using other research methods where theories are formulated in a probabilistic fashion in a mixed-method design.

Additional challenges include the risk that in building a theorized mechanism, we overlook an important systematic part of a mechanism or misclassify a nonsystematic part of a mechanism as systematic, or vice versa (Rohlfing 2008: 1509–10).

8.5. Conclusions

Table 8.1 summarizes the key differences across the three variants of process-tracing with regard to purpose and ambition, case selection strategies, and the type of causal mechanisms that are included (systematic or nonsystematic).

First, theory-testing and -building share theory-centric theoretical ambitions that aim at developing generalizations about causal relationships within a population of a given phenomenon, whereas, when push comes to shove, explaining-outcome studies prioritize the particular case over generalizability.

Second, case selection strategies vary, with cases in theory-testing merely chosen because both X and Y are present. When we attempt to nest a theory test in a broader mixed-method design, within the group of cases where X and Y are present we attempt to choose most-likely cases when we are unsure whether there is any empirical basis for a mechanism. In contrast, when assessing a thoroughly studied empirical correlation like the economic development thesis, we might choose a least-likely case to enable stronger cross-case inferences about the presence of the mechanism.

TABLE 8.1. Differences in Research Design in the Three Variants of Process-Tracing

	Theory-Testing	Theory-Building	Explaining-Outcome
Ambitions of study	Theory-centric	Theory-centric	Case-specific
Purpose of analysis	Test causal mechanism linking X:Y	(1) Identify potential causal mechanism linking X:Y in typical case, or (2) Formulate mechanism that produced Y in deviant case	Build minimally sufficient theoretical explanation of particular outcome
Case selection strategy	X, Y, and scope conditions present	X + mechanism and Y hypothetically present (typical), or Y present (deviant case)	Interesting outcomes, both substantively and theoretically important
Case chosen because ambition is to . . .	Test the necessity of the parts in the causal mechanism in empirical test	Theorize a plausible causal mechanism based upon the empirical evidence	Prove minimal sufficiency of causal mechanism (or set of mechanisms) in a single important case
Uses of variant of process-tracing in a broader mixed-method design	(1) An X:Y correlation has been found but we are unsure of causality (2) A well-developed theory exists but we are unsure whether there is empirical support	(1) An X:Y correlation has been found but we are unsure of the mechanism whereby X produces Y (2) We are unable to explain what caused Y with existing theories, resulting in the building of a new theorized mechanism that can account for the deviant case	Not possible due to the inclusion of nonsystematic parts, although limited lessons can be drawn about potential systematic parts that merit further research in other cases

In theory-building, we choose typical cases when we know X and Y but are unsure of the mechanism linking the two, whereas deviant cases are chosen when we know Y but not X. Explaining-outcome studies choose particularly interesting outcomes, both because of their substantive and theoretical importance (e.g., the end of the Cold War, the start of World War II) and because we are unable to account for the particular outcome with existing theories.

Theory-testing process-tracing assesses whether there is empirical evidence that updates our confidence in the presence/absence of the theorized causal mechanism in a single case, whereas theory-building uses empirical evidence as the starting point, using backward induction to build a plausible theoretical causal mechanism linking X and Y based on the empirical evidence. Explaining-outcome process-tracing studies involve a series of steps in which existing theorized mechanisms are tested for their explanatory power, followed by theoretical revisions based on the lessons of the first analytical cut, and so on until a minimally sufficient explanation of the outcome is crafted.

Finally, while both theory-building and -testing process-tracing can be nested into broader mixed-method research designs, explaining-outcome studies cannot be incorporated as a consequence of their inclusion of non-systematic parts in the analysis. However, for either theory-building or theory-testing to be utilized in a mixed-method design, theories need to be formulated in a deterministic manner, and when we export the findings of a process-tracing analysis to a regularity approach, we need to make sure we are studying roughly the same thing (either an X:Y regularity or X and a mechanism).

Appendix

A Checklist for Process-Tracing Analysis

This appendix presents a set of questions that can act as a checklist when using the three variants of process-tracing based on the arguments put forward in the book. We start by specifying the types of research situations that are relevant for using process-tracing and which variant can be applied in the specific circumstances. We then walk through the phases of the research process for each of the three variants, focusing on case selection, conceptualization, developing empirical tests, and the evaluation of evidence.

A.1. When Can Process-Tracing Be Used, and Which Variant Should We Choose?

Process-tracing is chosen when you want to study causal mechanisms using in-depth qualitative case studies. Are you more interested in making strong within-case inferences regarding the presence of mechanisms in a particular case, or do you want to make cross-case inferences that are applicable to the wider population of the phenomenon? If the former, use process-tracing methods; if the latter, use other methods such as fsQCA or combinations of process-tracing with comparative methods (see chapter 8).

The following questions should be asked:

- What type of causal inference do you intend to make?
- If testing for the necessity of the parts of the mechanism in a single case (i.e., was the mechanism present or absent?), use either theory-testing or explaining-outcome process-tracing.

- Do you have theory-centric or case-centric ambitions?
  - If you have the case-centric ambition of accounting for the outcome of a particular case, use explaining-outcome process-tracing.
  - If you have theory-centric ambitions, choose either theory-building or theory-testing process-tracing.

When choosing between the different variants of process-tracing:

- Choose theory-building when either (1) there is a well-established empirical correlation between X and Y but we are in the dark regarding a potential mechanism between the two; or (2) we know the outcome but are unsure of what mechanism contributed to causing it.
- Choose theory-testing when there is a well-developed theoretical conjecture on which a plausible mechanism can be deduced that can then be tested in a single-case study.
- Choose explaining-outcome when you have a particular interesting and puzzling outcome that needs to be explained.

A.2. Checklist for Theory-Testing Process-Tracing

Conceptualization of the Causal Mechanism(s)

Key theoretical concepts should be defined as systematized concepts, formulated in set-theoretical terms. Thereafter, a causal mechanism should be conceptualized, disaggregated into a series of parts composed of entities engaging in activities. Conceptualizing in these terms enables us to capture theoretically the actual process whereby causal forces are transmitted through a causal mechanism to produce an outcome. Causal mechanisms describe scope conditions, the initial condition of a causal mechanism (X) and the outcome (Y), and, equally important, the theoretical mechanism between X and Y that produces the outcome.

- Does your systematized conceptual definition of X and Y include the characteristics that are causally relevant for the mechanism?
- Are your concepts defined in a set-theoretical manner? (Is there a qualitative threshold?)
- Do formulated theoretical causal mechanisms already exist, or do you have to conceptualize one based on causal theories?

- Can the mechanism be disaggregated into a set of different parts $(n_1 \rightarrow) \ldots (n_n \rightarrow)$ in a plausible manner?
- Are the parts included in the theorized mechanism systematic or nonsystematic?
  - If nonsystematic, exclude them from your causal mechanism.
- Have you conceptualized the parts in your mechanism in a way that they contain entities and activities, formulated as nouns and verbs?
- Is each part of the mechanism an individually insufficient but necessary part of the whole mechanism?
- What would be the appropriate level for conceptualization and testing the causal mechanism? At which level are the predicted empirical manifestations best studied?
  - Structural mechanism (macrolevel)
  - Situational mechanism (macro- to microlevel)
  - Action formation mechanisms (microlevel)
  - Transformational mechanism (micro- to macrolevel)
- What is the temporal dimension of the mechanism? Does it work in the short or long term, and what is the time horizon of the outcome becoming apparent?
- What type of theoretical explanation are you working with? Include the common building blocks of the appropriate type of theory (structural, institutional, ideational, or psychological).
- Have you explicitly formulated your theoretical prior for the whole mechanism, and if possible, for each of the parts?
- What is the theoretical proposition a case of? What is the relevant population of the proposition—that is, what is the scope of the theorized mechanism you are studying? What are the scope conditions in which it is expected to operate (context)?

Case Selection

In theory-testing process-tracing, the purpose is to investigate whether the hypothesized causal mechanism was present in a case. Both X and Y must be present in the chosen case for the hypothesized causal mechanism to be present in theory. It therefore makes little sense to test whether a hypothesized causal mechanism was present in a case when we know a priori that it could not be present, given that either X or Y were not present. Do not select cases based on a regression-line type of logic.

- Are X and Y and the relevant scope conditions present in the case?
- Choose a typical case, potentially a most- or least-likely case if the analysis is done using concepts formulated in fuzzy-set terms.
- Consider how your theoretical conclusions can be nested in a broader research design.

Operationalization of Empirical Tests

After conceptualization and case selection, empirical tests for the different parts of the mechanism should be operationalized. The logic of empirical testing in process-tracing is that if we expected X to cause Y, each part of the mechanism between X and Y should leave the predicted empirical manifestations that can be observed in the empirical material. Predictions about what evidence we should find translate the theoretical concepts of the causal mechanism into case-specific tests.

Tests that are as unique and certain as possible should be formulated based on our case-specific knowledge. The predicted evidence should not simply be a list of empirical events leading up to an outcome Y. Instead, they should be seen as empirical manifestations of the parts in the conceptualized theoretical causal mechanism, focused on measuring the activities of entities that transmit causal forces.

- Have the empirical predictions of evidence that should be found been formulated in a manner that enables us to capture traces of the transmission of causal forces through the theorized causal mechanism?
- When designing empirical tests, the Bayesian logic of inference suggests that we need to maximize the inferential power of evidence to update our confidence in the validity of a hypothesis. This involves making strong predictions about:
  - What evidence we should expect to see if a part of a causal mechanism exists?
  - What counts as evidence for alternative hypotheses?
  - What we can conclude when the predicted evidence is not found—that is, what counts as negative evidence ($\sim e$)?

There are two dimensions of test strength to consider:

(1) Do your tests attempt to maximize the level of uniqueness in a manner where predictions of empirical manifestations do not overlap with those of other theories (likelihood ratio)? (confirmatory power)

(2) Do your tests attempt to maximize the level of certainty of the prediction, meaning that the prediction is unequivocal and that the prediction (e) must be observed or the theory fails the empirical test? (disconfirmatory power)

Evaluating the Empirical Material

In a process-tracing case study, we need to assess the content and accuracy of our empirical observations before they can be admitted as evidence that can be used to update our confidence in the presence or absence of causal mechanisms. We then need to evaluate how probable the evidence was in the context of the particular case: More improbable evidence enables stronger causal inferences to be made, other things equal.

- Collect empirical data based on the empirical predictions for what type of predicted evidence we should expect to see if the hypothesized causal mechanism is present.
- Assess the content of our collected observations; determine using our contextual knowledge whether our observations are evidence.
- Can we trust the evidence that we have collected? What are the potential sources of error, and can we correct for them so that we can use the observation as evidence in a theory test to update the posterior probability of the hypothesized causal mechanism? (That is, assess $p(a)$).
- What is the probability of finding the predicted evidence in light of the context of the case? (evaluate $p(e)$).

A.3. Checklist for Theory-Building Process-Tracing

Conceptualization of Theoretical Concepts

- Do you know X and Y, or have you identified only Y?
- Are your concepts (X and/or Y) defined in a set-theoretical manner? (i.e., with qualitative thresholds)

Case Selection

Case selection strategies depend on the reasons why theory-building process-tracing was chosen. There are two different situations. The first situation is when we know that a correlation exists between X and Y but are in the dark regarding potential mechanisms linking the two. In this form of X-Y-centric theory-building, the analyst should chose to examine a typical case to identify a plausible causal mechanism that can be tested empirically in subsequent research. The second situation is where the outcome (Y) is known but we are unsure what caused it to happen. In this variant of theory-building, the purpose is to identify one or more Xs and to attempt to build a plausible mechanism for how X and Y are causally related. Case selection in this situation resembles a deviant case selection strategy. It is then hoped that the new theorized causal mechanism derived from studying the deviant case is applicable to other similar (deviant) cases.

- Choose deviant cases for theory-building when Y is known but we are unsure about what has contributed to causing X.
- Choose typical cases when X and Y are present but we do not know what the mechanism is.

Building Theoretical Mechanisms Based on Empirical Analysis

- Create a thorough empirical narrative of the case.
- Be careful when working inductively—empirical facts do not speak for themselves.
- Inspired by existing theorization and intuitions drawn from empirical accounts, search for empirical manifestations of potential plausible systematic parts of a mechanism.
- Based on these identified empirical manifestations, formulate a plausible causal mechanism composed of a series of parts (entities engaging in activities).
- Are the parts individually insufficient but necessary parts of the mechanism?
- Are there redundant parts?
- Are all of the identified parts systematic?
- Can the theorized causal mechanism be tested in subsequent empirical research?

A.4. Checklist for Explaining-Outcome Process-Tracing

Case Selection

The purpose of explaining-outcome process-tracing differs from the other two variants. In explaining-outcome process-tracing, we try to establish a minimally sufficient explanation for why an outcome has been produced in a specific case. This type of process-tracing leans more heavily toward being a case-centric case study, interested in the particular case, rather than a theory-centric effort at generalizing to a broader population.

- Choose cases with interesting outcomes—substantively and/or theoretically.

Conceptualization of the Causal Mechanism(s)

Explaining-outcome process-tracing is an iterative research strategy that seeks to trace the complex conglomerate of systematic and case-specific causal mechanisms that produced the outcome in question. The explanation cannot be detached from the particular case. Theorized mechanisms are seen as heuristic instruments whose function is to help build the best possible explanation of a particular outcome.

We disaggregate two alternative paths that can be chosen when building the best possible explanation of an outcome—a deductive and inductive path.

The Deductive Path

- If the deductive path is chosen, follow the guidelines given previously for theory-testing.
- Does the mechanism tested provide a sufficient explanation of the outcome? If not, either repeat the process using a second deductive analysis of alternative competing explanations or engage in an inductive analysis.

The Inductive Path

- Chosen when we are investigating a little-studied phenomenon or when existing explanations are patently unable to account for the outcome.
- Proceeds in a manner more analogous to historical methodology or classic detective work, working backward from the outcome by sifting through the evidence in an attempt to uncover a plausible sufficient causal mechanism that produced the outcome. Often involves the incorporation of nonsystematic mechanisms in the explanation.

- Does the mechanism tested provide a sufficient explanation of the outcome? If not, repeat the process.

Assessing Whether Our Explanation Has Reached "Minimal Sufficiency"

- Have we accounted for the most important facets of the outcome?
- If not, can we build a composite, eclectic theory that can better account for the outcome?
  - If yes, then the composite theory should be tested following the preceding guidelines for theory-testing.
  - If not, do we need to incorporate nonsystematic mechanisms in our explanation? After doing so, the composite explanation should be tested using the preceding guidelines.

Notes

Chapter 2

1. In explaining-outcome process-tracing, we do not use Y to symbolize the outcome, as it is a unique case instead of being a case of a systematic theoretical phenomena (Y).

Chapter 3

1. Brady (2008) distinguishes between four different ontological positions of causality, but only regularity and mechanismic understandings are potentially relevant for small-n methods. Experimental methods, while becoming increasingly used (Morton and Williams 2010), require a relatively large n. Counterfactual explanations, while important as an auxiliary tool for producing compelling explanations, cannot stand alone.

2. These types of relationships can be understood as set-theoretical, where, for example, theorizing that democracy is a sufficient condition to produce peace involves making the claim that democratic country dyads constitute a perfect subset of countries that are at peace with each other (Ragin 2008: 16).

3. It is not process-tracing when causal mechanisms are understood as a set of intervening variables since that approach is based on a probabilistic understanding of causation. Probabilistic ontologies result in theories that can only be assessed at the population level. Mechanisms, if conceptualized as a set of intervening variables, can be analyzed at the population level. However, when mechanisms are conceptualized in this manner, we contend that we are studying not causal mechanisms but instead only patterns of regular association between X and Y.

Chapter 4

1. For good introductions, see, e.g., Adcock and Collier 2001; Goertz 2006; King, Keohane, and Verba 1994.

2. As discussed in chapter 3, there are also variants of these two, such as INUS (individually necessary parts of an unnecessary but sufficient condition) conditions.

3. In qualitative case-study research, the ambition of generalization has clear bounds. Qualitative scholars stress the context-dependent nature of theoretical propositions based on extensive case-specific knowledge and therefore usually make much more limited, context-specific generalizations (Munck 2004). For more on different forms of contexts of political phenomenon, see Goodin and Tilly 2006.

4. We part company with Falleti and Lynch (2009), who argue that mechanisms are probabilistic theories. Instead, we agree with Mahoney (2008), who contends that probabilistic theories in within-case analysis make little logical sense. Either a mechanism is present, or it is not.

5. We selected three top journals that published articles on a wide array of substantive topics and using a variety of methodological approaches and had consistently high rankings for Impact Part in the JCR Citation Rankings. The three journals were the *American Political Science Review, World Politics,* and the *American Journal of Political Science.* The full text of each article in every issue from 2005 to 2010 was searched using the string "mechanism*."

6. Theories about causal relationships between X and Y can be (1) built deductively, using logical reasoning to deduce a theory, or (2) built inductively, drawing on evidence to build a plausible theoretical proposition. The purest variant of deductive theory-building is found in formal methods such as game theory, where mathematical, diagrammatic, and symbolic methods are used to develop theories (Nicholson 2002).

7. There is arguably a third theory-building variant that involves building a theory of the effects of X. However, the first step of this form of theory-building is to trace from X to find an outcome of interest (Y); thereafter, the analysis becomes an X-Y-centric analysis (Rohlfing 2008).

8. Unfortunately, Layne's description of the mechanism is quite vague. Here we have reconstructed the probable mechanism based on the descriptions of the Open Door explanation found throughout his book.

Chapter 5

1. Owen uses the term *causal mechanism* to refer to what can be seen as intervening variables (see Owen 1994, figure 1, p. 102). However, the set of hypotheses for the existence of the mechanism that he develops (102–4) actually describes the workings of the causal mechanism in a series of parts and therefore, in our opinion, can be seen as a proper conceptualization of a causal mechanism.

2. Congruence methods also aim to make within-case inferences, although inferences are being made not about the presence of mechanism but just about causal theories of the relationship between X and Y. For example, Tannenwald's (1999) study of the nuclear taboo involves congruence case studies where she investigates whether traces of X (norms against using atomic weapons) are present in decision-making processes within the U.S. government (Tannenwald 1999). Another example is Khong 1992.

3. Owen could have made clearer his reasoning for attributing different inferential weights to specific observations. By explicitly adopting a Bayesian framework,

the researcher is forced to clearly explicate the reasoning behind differing inferential weights of observations based on prior expectations and the likelihood of evidence.

4. For a critique of the term *causal process observation* from a frequentist position, see Beck 2006.

5. There is considerable debate in comparative methodology about whether the study of necessary and sufficient conditions implies a deterministic understanding (e.g., Mahoney 2007) or whether probabilistic understandings also can be utilized (Goertz 2003; Ragin 2008). A deterministic understanding of causality does not rule out that causality can be analyzed using probability-based inferential tools (such as classic probability theory or Bayesian subjective probability) (e.g., Mahoney 2004).

6. The term *classic* here refers to traditional statistical probability theory, in contrast to Bayesian probability theory (see Chalmers 1999; Howson and Urbach 2006).

7. Truly independent observations are not possible in case study research, resulting in the use of the term *conditional*.

8. See George and Bennett 2005, chapter 9. For an example of a congruence case study, see Tannenwald 1999.

9. Or at least a representative sample of occurrences of Y.

10. More correctly, patterns of invariant relationships between conditions and outcomes.

11. Such as the dog being drugged, which would have required that the perpetrator was able to smuggle a drug into the dog's food without any of the witnesses noticing anything. While this could have happened, it is much less probable than the much simpler explanation that the dog knew the perpetrator.

Chapter 6

1. In most research situations, it makes little sense to define the theoretical priors for each individual part of the mechanism, given that our priors are based on our empirical and theoretical knowledge of causal relationships and mechanisms as a whole.

Chapter 7

1. We use the term *evidence* in the same manner in which many qualitative scholars use the term *causal process observation* (Brady, Collier, and Seawright 2006) or *process-tracing observations* (Bennett 2006).

2. This analogy should, of course, not be taken too far, since there can be different standards of proof (beyond reasonable doubt versus preponderance of evidence) in legal reasoning than in social science and because the nature of the "theories" being tested using legal reasoning.

3. The proof is that $p(h|e)p(h)/p(e) \approx p(e|h \ \& \ {\sim}a)p({\sim}a)p(h)/p(e|h \ \& \ {\sim}a)p({\sim}a) = p(h)$.

4. The continental tradition further distinguishes between primary and secondary sources and what is termed firsthand and secondhand sources. The latter distinction deals with our relation to the source.

Glossary

Abduction: A method or approach that is a dialectic combination of deduction and induction (see Peirce 1955).

Account evidence: A type of evidence in the form of a statement or narrative that gives a description of an event or thing. Common sources of account evidence include participant interviews and documents (e.g., minutes of meetings).

Accuracy of observations: Whether we are measuring what we intended to measure. Inaccurate measures can be the product of either nonsystematic or systematic errors in the measuring instrument we use to collect observations. Nonsystematic (or random) error is commonly termed *reliability,* whereas systematic error is defined as the *bias* in our measuring instrument. Accuracy in Bayesian terms can be represented as the probability or degree of confidence we have that a measure is accurate, depicted as p(a).

Activity: Part of a causal mechanism. Each part of a causal mechanism is composed of entities that engage in activities that transmit causal forces through a causal mechanism. Activities are the producers of change, or what transmits causal forces through a mechanism. Activities are conceptualized as verbs, denoting activity (Machamer 2004; Machamer, Darden, and Craver 2000). Note that nonactivity can also be conceptualized as an activity.

Bayesian logic of inference: A logical formula for estimating the probability that a theory or hypothesis is supported by found evidence based on the researcher's degree of belief about the probability of the theory/hypothesis and the probability of finding given evidence if the theory or hypothesis is valid before gathering the data.

Case-centric research: Research that is more interested in explaining the outcome of a particular case than a generalizing ambition to make theoretical claims beyond the single case. Outcomes are defined in a broader manner, including all of the important aspects of what happened in a case such as the Cuban Missile Crisis. *See also* Systematic mechanisms; Nonsystematic mechanisms.

Causal effect: The difference between the systematic component of observations made when the independent variable takes one value and the systematic component of comparable observations when the independent variable takes on another value (King, Keohane, and Verba 1994: 81–82).

Causal inference: The use of observed empirical material to make conclusions about causation, understood as either patterns of regularity (mean causal effects) or mechanistic relations.

Causal mechanism: Theorized system that produces outcomes through the interaction of a series of parts that transmit causal forces from X to Y. Each part of a mechanism is an individually insufficient but necessary factor in a whole mechanism, which together produces Y. The parts of causal mechanisms are composed of entities engaging in activities.

Causal process observation (CPO): A term used to describe "pieces of data that provide information about context, process, or mechanism and contribute distinctive leverage in causal inference" (Seawright and Collier 2010: 318). The term *CPO* overlaps to some extent with our use of the term *evidence.*

Causality in the mechanismic sense: An ontological understanding where causation is confirmed only when an underlying mechanism can be shown to causally connect X and Y. The mechanismic understanding of causality does not necessarily imply regular association.

Causality as regularity: An ontological understanding of causality where causation is defined as a pattern of constant conjunction between X and Y. For causality to be established, Hume argued that three criteria for the relationship between X and Y needed to be fulfilled: (1) X and Y are contiguous in space and time; (2) X occurs before Y (temporal succession); and (3) there is a regular conjunction between X and Y (Holland 1986).

Certain predictions: Predictions about evidence that are unequivocal, where the prediction must be observed or else the empirical test disconfirms the existence of the part of the mechanism. Also termed *disconfirmatory power.*

Classical statistical methods: Methods that assess the mean causal effects of X on Y in a population. Inferences are made using traditional statistical theory (e.g., Fisher, Pearson) and using tools such as the Central Limit Theorem (termed the *frequentist logic of inference* in this book). The empirical material used is large numbers of data-set observations. Only cross-case inferences to the population of a phenomenon are made. Also termed *large-n statistical methods.*

Comparative cross-case methods: Methods used to assess necessary and/or sufficient conditions that produce Y. Involves using different tools, such as Mill's methods of agreement and disagreement. The methods enable cross-case inferences to be made to for a population of cases, although the scope of populations is usually narrower than in large-*n* statistical methods.

Comparativist logic of elimination: Logic of inference used in comparative, cross-case methods to make causal inferences about necessity and/or sufficiency. Builds on Mill's methods of agreement and disagreement. The method of agreement is used to eliminate potential necessary causes. Here, all of the instances of Y (e.g., social revolutions) are examined, and all potential factors that are not present in all of the cases are eliminated as necessary conditions. The method of difference is used to test for sufficient causation, where two or more cases that have different outcomes are compared. Factors that are present in both types of outcomes are then eliminated as potential sufficient conditions. Enables strong *negative* inferences but weaker *positive* inferences.

Content of observations: When observations are collected, they need to be evaluated for what they tell us in light of our background knowledge about the context of the case. The first phase in turning observations into evidence (o + k → e).

Context: Relevant aspects of a setting where the initial conditions produce an outcome of a defined scope and meaning through the operation of a causal mechanism (Falleti and Lynch 2009: 1152). Scope conditions are used to describe a context in which a theorized mechanism is expected to operate.

Contextual specificity: A theory or concept whose scope is limited based on the temporal or spatial dimension. Usually denoted by introducing adjectives into concepts and theories—for example, a *liberal* democratic peace mechanism.

Crisp-set reasoning: Set-theoretical understanding of concepts where a concept is defined dichotomously as either being a member of the set of the concept or not. For example, a state can be a member of the set of democratic states or not. *See also* Set theory.

Cross-case inferences: Inferences made about causality across the population of a given phenomena. In large-*n* studies, this refers to mean causal effects. *See also* Causal effect.

Data-set observation (DSO): All the scores in a row in a rectangular data set given for a given case to both the dependent and all of the independent variables (Collier, Brady, and Seawright 2010b: 184).

Deductive analysis: In empirical research, a process that starts with the deductive formulation of a theory based on abstract logical reasoning that is then empirically tested. The purest form of deductive analysis is found within formal game theory. In reality, most formulations of theories have an inductive element, being informed by empirical material.

Dependent variable: A variable whose value is dependent on another variable. The independent variable is said to cause an apparent change in or simply to affect the dependent variable. Also termed *outcome variable*. This is what the researcher wants to explain. In our understanding, a dependent variable refers to Y or an outcome, which is a systemized understanding of a concept that can be compared across cases. A particular outcome refers to an outcome or event (for example, the outbreak of World War II) that cannot be compared across cases. *See also* Case-centric analysis; Theory-centric research.

Descriptive inference: The process of reaching descriptive conclusions on the basis of observed data (Seawright and Collier 2010: 325)—that is, what happened in a case.

Deterministic ontology of causation: Qualitative scholars use the term primarily to refer to discussions of necessary and sufficient causes or combinations of these types of conditions (Mahoney 2008: 417). This means that what we are examining is not whether a given X tends to covary with Y in a population but whether X is either a necessary and/or sufficient cause of Y (Collier, Brady, and Seawright 2004a: 216; Mahoney 2008). A factor is necessary if the absence of it prevents an outcome, regardless of the values of other variables, whereas if a sufficient factor is present, the outcome will always take place.

Deviant case: A case "that, by reference to some general understanding of a topic (either a specific theory or common sense), demonstrates a surprising value [outcome]" (Gerring 2007a: 105). In process-tracing, deviant cases are primarily used in the theory-building variant. A deviant case is defined by membership in the outcome (e.g., democracy), and nonmembership in existing potential causes (X). See figure 8.4.

Doubly decisive test: An empirical test that combines high degrees of certainty and uniqueness. The evidence must be found or our confidence in the validity of the hypothesis is reduced; at the same time, the test strongly discriminates between evidence that supports the hypothesis and alternatives (small likelihood ratio).

Eclectic theorization: The combination of different mechanisms in a complex composite to craft a minimally sufficient explanation of a particular outcome (see Sil and Katzenstein 2010).

Empirical predictions: Expectations about what evidence we should expect to see if the hypothesized part of a mechanism exists. Predictions translate the theoretical concepts of a causal mechanism into case-specific observable manifestations for each part of the mechanism. In the Bayesian logic of inference, predictions are related to the likelihood ratio. Empirical predictions include (1) what evidence we should expect to see if a part of a causal mechanism exists, and (2) what counts as evidence for alternative hypotheses, all the while taking into consideration (3) what we can conclude when the predicted evidence is not found—that is, what counts as negative evidence (~e).

Entities: The actors who engage in activities that transmit causal forces through a causal mechanism (i.e., toothed wheels, cogs and wheels). Entities can be individual persons, groups, states, or structural factors, depending on the level of the theory. Entities should be conceptualized as nouns. *See also* Activity; Causal mechanism.

Evidence: Empirical material can be termed *evidence* after it has been assessed for its content and accuracy. Raw empirical observations (o) are assessed for their content and accuracy using our case-specific contextual knowledge (k), after which we term the material *evidence* (o + k → e). There are four different types of evidence: Pattern evidence relates to predictions of statistical patterns in the evidence. Sequence evidence deals with the temporal and spatial chronology of events that is predicted by a hypothesized causal mechanism. Trace evidence is evidence whose mere existence provides proof that a part of a hypothesized mechanism exists. Finally, account evidence deals with the content of empirical material, such as meeting minutes that detail what was discussed at a meeting or an oral account of what took place at a meeting.

Explaining-outcome process-tracing: A single-case study that seeks to find the causes of a particular outcome. The ambition is to craft a minimally sufficient explanation, with sufficiency defined as an explanation that accounts for all of the important aspects of an outcome with no redundant parts being present, marking a significant departure from the two theory-centric variants.

Frequentist logic of inference: Assesses the magnitude of causal effects of X on Y, or the degree to which the presence of X raises the probability of Y in a population. Uses classical statistical theory to make cross-case causal inferences. *See also* Classical statistical methods.

Fuzzy sets: A set-theoretical conceptualization of theoretical concepts where membership in a set of the concept is defined in terms of both differences in kind and degree. A sharp (crisp) qualitative threshold marks the distinction between membership and nonmembership in the set of the concept. Differences in degree range from fully in to more in than out. *See also* Set theory.

Hoop tests: Involve predictions that are certain but not unique; failure of such a test (finding ~e) reduces our confidence in the hypothesis, but finding e does not enable inferences to be made. In practice, hoop tests are often used to exclude alternative hypotheses.

Independent variable: An independent variable is theorized to affect or determine a dependent variable. Also termed *explanatory variable.*

Induction: Observations are made of a particular phenomenon, after which a simplified causal explanation is developed that captures the essence of a more general social phenomenon.

Inference: The process of using data to draw broader conclusions about concepts and hypotheses.

Inferential leap: When we are forced to infer from a small set of empirical observations that a theory was the cause of the phenomenon, we make an inferential leap from what we can observe empirically to infer that an underlying causal explanation exists.

Inferential weight: A function of the probability of evidence ($p(e)$). Not all evidence is created equal. More surprising evidence, if found, results in larger increases in our confidence in a hypothesis than does less surprising evidence.

Intervening variable: A variable that is causally between a given independent variable and the outcome being explained (Seawright and Collier 2010: 334). The distinction between intervening variables and mechanisms is that (1) variables can by definition vary, whereas mechanisms are invariant, and (2) variables have a theorized existence independent of each other, whereas mechanisms are systems where each part has no independent causal impact on Y outside of the operation of the mechanism.

INUS: An "insufficient but necessary part of an unnecessary but sufficient condition" (Mackie 1965).

Least-likely cases: Cases where we should least expect a hypothesized causal mechanism would be present; X and Y are present (but to a lower degree when fuzzy-set scores used, depicted as case 4 in figure 8.3), and the scope conditions lead us to predict that the mechanism would probably only just be present.

Likelihood ratio: The likelihood ratio is comprised of $p(e|\sim h)$ divided by $p(e|h)$. The likelihood ratio is the probability of finding the predicted evidence (e) if the alternative hypothesis (~h) is not true ($p(e|\sim h)$ in comparison to the probability of finding the evidence if the hypothesis is true ($p(e|h)$). The ratio captures the ability of an empirical test to discriminate between predicted evidence that supports h and ~h. If h predicts e, the occurrence of e will raise our confidence in the validity of h depending on the size of the likelihood ratio. When $p(e|h)$ is high and $p(e|\sim h)$ is low, finding e results in a large increase in confidence. While the ratio depicts ~h as a single alternative, it can be defined as any plausible alternative to h. *See also* Bayesian logic of inference; Evidence.

Macrolevel mechanisms: Theories of mechanisms that cannot be reduced to the actions of individuals. Sawyer (2004) captures this with the term *emergence,* which means that macrolevel mechanisms have their own existence and have properties that cannot be reduced to the microlevel. An example of a macrolevel mechanism is the balancing mechanism found in the IR theory of structural realism (Waltz 1979).

Microlevel mechanisms: Relate to how the interests and beliefs of interests of individuals impact their actions and how individuals interact with each other. An example of microlevel theorization is Coleman's (1990) theory of social action.

Minimal sufficiency: Sufficiency is defined as a situation where the presence of mechanism X always produces Y. Minimally sufficient explanations are theories where there are no redundant factors in the explanation (Mackie 1965). Sufficiency is confirmed when it can be substantiated that there are no important aspects of the outcome for which the explanation does not account.

Most-likely cases: Cases where we would most expect that a hypothesized causal mechanism was present given that X and Y have high fuzzy-set scores and the scope conditions that enable the mechanism to function are highly favorable. Using fuzzy-set scores, both X and Y would have high membership scores (case 6 in figure 8.3).

Narrative: A tool used in the congruence method to structure a temporal analysis of correlations between X and Y during a historical process in a single case.

Necessary condition: A factor is necessary if the absence of it prevents an outcome, regardless of the values of other variables.

Nested analysis: When different research methods are combined to analyze the same research question. Nested analysis is often used when we want our case studies to contribute to a broader knowledge of causal relationships.

Nonsystematic mechanisms: Case-specific mechanisms that contribute to explaining Y in a particular case but do not have causal effects across the whole population of cases.

Observations: Raw collected data prior to the evaluation of its content and accuracy (i.e., degree of measurement error). After evaluation for its content and accuracy we refer to observations as *evidence* (o + k → e). *See also* Empirical predictions; Evidence.

Pattern evidence: Predictions of statistical patterns in the evidence—for example, in testing a mechanism of racial discrimination in a case dealing with employment, statistical patterns of employment would be relevant for testing parts of the mechanism.

Population level: The universe of cases to which an inferences refers (Gerring 2007a: 216).

Posterior probability: In the Bayesian logic of inference, defined as our confidence in the validity of a hypothesis after evidence has been collected and evaluated. The posterior is updated in light of new empirical evidence being collected. The ability to update the posterior depends on the values of the likelihood ratio and the probability of evidence. *See also* Bayesian logic of inference.

Prior probability: The researcher's degree of confidence in the validity of a hypothesis prior to gathering evidence based on existing theorization, empirical studies, and other forms of expert knowledge. *See also* Bayesian logic of inference.

Probabilistic ontology of causality: Probabilistic causality means that the researcher believes that we are dealing with a world in which there are random (stochastic) properties, often modeled using error terms (see, e.g., King, Keohane, and Verba 1994: 89 n. 11). This randomness can be the product either of an inherent randomness or of complexity.

Probability of evidence (p(e)): In the Bayesian logic of inference, the more improbable evidence is, the stronger our ability to update our confidence in the posterior probability of the validity of a theorized mechanism. If p(e) is very low, even one piece of evidence can be enough to update significantly our confidence in the validity of a hypothesis.

Regression analysis: An extension of correlation analysis that makes predictions about the value of a dependent variable using data about one or more independent variables. These can be either linear or nonlinear (e.g., logistic) models to describe the form of the relationship between two or more variables—for example, using method of least squares to describe a relationship.

Scope conditions: Parameters within which a given theory is expected to be valid (Falleti and Lynch 2009; H. A. Walker and Cohen 1985). In process-tracing, *scope conditions* refers to the context under which a particular mechanism is theorized as able to be activated.

Sequence evidence: The temporal and spatial chronology of events that is predicted by a hypothesized causal mechanism.

Set theory: Theoretical arguments that deal with set relationships between concepts. Concept X can, for example, be theorized to be a subset of Y: developed states (X) are all democratic (Y). Concepts are defined in terms of membership/nonmembership. Set-theoretical relationships are asymmetrical, meaning that set relationships between two concepts (democracy and peace) are not necessarily related to relationships between nonmembership in the two concepts (nondemocracy and war).

Situational mechanism: Link between the macro- and microlevels. Situational mechanisms describe how social structures constrain individuals' action and how cultural environments shape their desires and beliefs (Hedström and Swedberg 1998). Examples of a macro-micro-level mechanism include constructivist theories of actor compliance with norms that are embedded at the macrolevel.

Smoking gun tests: Test that are highly unique but have low or no certainty in their predictions. Here, passage strongly confirms a hypothesis, but failure does not strongly undermine it. In Bayesian terms, the likelihood ratio is small, with finding e given h highly probable, whereas ~h is highly improbable, thereby greatly increasing our confidence in the validity of h if we find e.

Straw-in-the-wind tests: Empirical predictions that have a low level of uniqueness and a low level of certainty. These test types do little to update our confidence in a hypothesis irrespective of whether we find e or ~e, as both passed and failed tests are of little if any inferential relevance for us.

Sufficient condition: Sufficiency is defined as a situation where the presence of mechanism X always produces Y. In explaining-outcome process-tracing, the aim is to craft a minimally sufficient explanation with no redundant factors (Mackie 1965). *See also* Minimal sufficiency.

Systematic mechanisms: Mechanisms that are theorized to have causal effects in the whole population of the phenomenon instead of being limited to a particular case. Nonsystematic mechanisms, in contrast, are theorized to have only case-specific causal impact.

Theory-building process-tracing: Theory-building process-tracing starts with empirical material and uses a structured analysis of this material to induce a plausible hypothetical causal mechanism whereby X is linked with Y. Utilized in two different research situations: (1) when we know that a correlation exists between X and Y but are in the dark regarding potential mechanisms linking the two (X-Y-centric theory building) as we have no theory to guide us; and (2) when we know an outcome (Y) but are unsure about the causes (X) (Y-centric theory building). In the latter, the analysis first traces backward from Y to undercover a plausible X, turning the study into a X-Y-centric analysis.

Theory-centric research: Aims to find and test theoretical propositions that are applicable to a broader scope of the population of the phenomenon. Includes both theory-building and testing variants of process-tracing.

Theory-testing process-tracing: In theory-testing process-tracing, we know both X and Y and we either have existing conjectures about a plausible mechanism or are able to use logical reasoning. We then formulate a causal mechanism from existing theorization. The goal is to test whether a theorized mechanism is present in a case and whether the mechanism functioned as expected.

Trace evidence: Evidence whose mere existence provides proof that a part of a hypothesized mechanism exists. For example, the existence of the official minutes of a meeting, if authentic, provides strong proof that a meeting took place.

Transformational mechanism: A process whereby individuals, through their actions and interactions, generate various intended and unintended social outcomes at the macrolevel. An example of this type of micro-macro-level mechanism could be socialization processes, whereby actors through their interaction create new norms at the macrolevel.

Typical case: A case where a given causal mechanism hypothetically exists (X and Y are present) but it is neither most nor least likely.

Unique predictions: The formulation of empirical predictions that do not overlap with those of other theories. Uniqueness corresponds to the Bayesian likelihood ratio, where predictions are developed that should maximize the value of $p(e|h)$ over $p(e|\sim h)$. If found, a unique prediction provides strong confirmation of the existence of a hypothesized part of a mechanism, but if not found, it does little to update our confidence.

Variable: Anything whose value changes over a set of units. Variable values can vary, and variables have an existence independent of each other, as each is, in effect, a self-contained analytical unit. Variance implies that a probabilistic understanding of causality is utilized, something that makes little sense when we are engaging in single-case studies. The use of intervening variables usually has the practical consequence that the linkages between the variables are neglected.

Within-case inferences: Causal inferences made, based on observed empirical material, about the presence or absence of the parts and whole of a causal mechanism in a particular case. Within-case inferences can be made using the Bayesian logic of inference.

References

Abbott, Andrew. 1997. Of Time and Space: The Contemporary Relevance of the Chicago School. *Social Forces* 75 (4): 1149–82.

Adcock, Robert, and David Collier. 2001. Measurement Validity: A Shared Standard for Qualitative and Quantitative Research. *American Political Science Review* 95 (3): 529–46.

Allison, Graham. 1971. *Essence of Decision: Explaining the Cuban Missile Crisis.* Boston: Little, Brown.

Allison, Graham, and Phillip Zelikow. 1999. *Essence of Decision: Explaining the Cuban Missile Crisis.* 2nd ed. New York: Longman.

Bates, Robert, Avner Greif, Margaret Levi, Jean-Laurent Rosenthal, and Barry R. Weingast. 1998. *Analytic Narratives.* Princeton: Princeton University Press.

BBC. 1987. *Yes, Prime Minister.* Series 2, Episode 2, "Official Secrets."

Beck, Nathaniel. 2006. Is Causal-Process Observation an Oxymoron? *Political Analysis* 14 (2): 347–52.

Bendor, Jonathan, A. Glazer, and Thomas H. Hammond. 2001. Theories of Delegation. *Annual Review of Political Science* 4:235–69.

Bendor, Jonathan, and Thomas H. Hammond. 1992. Rethinking Allison's Models. *American Political Science Review* 86 (2): 301–22.

Bennett, Andrew. 2004. Case Study Methods: Design Use and Comparative Advantages. In *Models, Numbers, and Cases: Methods for Studying International Relations,* ed. Detlef F. Sprinz and Yael Wolinsky-Nahmias, 19–55. Ann Arbor: University of Michigan Press.

Bennett, Andrew. 2005. The Guns That Didn't Smoke: Ideas and the Soviet Non-Use of Force in 1989. *Journal of Cold War Studies* 7 (2): 81–109.

Bennett, Andrew. 2006. Stirring the Frequentist Pot with a Dash of Bayes. *Political Analysis* 14 (2): 339–44.

Bennett, Andrew. 2008a. Process-Tracing: A Bayesian Perspective. In *The Oxford Handbook of Political Methodology,* ed. Janet M. Box-Steffensmeier, Henry E. Brady, and David Collier, 702–21. Oxford: Oxford University Press.

Bennett, Andrew. 2008b. The Mother of All "Isms": Organizing Political Science around Causal Mechanisms. In *Revitalizing Causality: Realism about Causality in Philosophy and Social Science,* ed. Ruth Groff, 205–19. London: Routledge.

Bennett, Andrew. 2010. Process Tracing and Causal Inference. In *Rethinking Social Inquiry: Diverse Tools, Shared Standards,* 2nd ed., ed. Henry E. Brady and David Collier, 207–20. Lanham, MD: Rowman and Littlefield.

Bennett, Andrew, and Colin Elman. 2006a. Complex Causal Relations and Case Study Methods: The Example of Path Dependency. *Political Analysis* 14 (2): 250–67.

Bennett, Andrew, and Colin Elman. 2006b. Qualitative Research: Recent Developments in Case Study Methods. *Annual Review of Political Science* 9:455–76.

Bhaskar, Roy. 1978. *A Realist Theory of Science.* Brighton: Harvester.

Blatter, Joachim, and Till Blume. 2008. In Search of Co-Variance, Causal Mechanisms, or Congruence? Towards a Plural Understanding of Case Studies. *Swiss Political Science Review* 14 (2): 315–56.

Blatter, Joakim, and Markus Haverland. 2012. *Designing Case Studies: Explanatory Approaches to Small-N Research.* Basingstoke: Palgrave Macmillan.

Bogen, Jim. 2005. Regularities and Causality: Generalizations and Causal Explanations. *Studies in History and Philosophy of Biological and Biomedical Sciences* 36:397–420.

Bouchard, Thomas J., Jr. 2004. Genetic Influence on Human Psychological Traits: A Survey. *Current Directions in Psychological Science* 13 (4): 148–51.

Brady, Henry E. 2008. Causation and Explanation in Social Science. In *The Oxford Handbook of Political Methodology,* ed. Janet M. Box-Steffensmeier, Henry E. Brady, and David Collier, 217–70. Oxford: Oxford University Press.

Brady, Henry E., and David Collier, eds. 2004. *Rethinking Social Inquiry: Diverse Tools, Shared Standards.* 2nd ed. Lanham, MD: Rowman and Littlefield.

Brady, Henry E., David Collier, and Jason Seawright. 2006. Towards a Pluralistic Vision of Methodology. *Political Analysis* 14 (2): 353–68.

Braumoeller, Bear F., and Gary Goertz. 2000. The Methodology of Necessary Conditions. *American Journal of Political Science* 44 (4): 844–58.

Brooks, Stephen G., and William C. Wohlforth. 2000–2001. Power, Globalization, and the End of the Cold War. *International Security* 25 (3): 5–53.

Buckley, Jack. 2004. Simple Bayesian Inference for Qualitative Political Research. *Political Analysis* 12 (4): 386–99.

Bullock, Alan. 1991. *Hitler and Stalin: Parallel Lives.* London: HarperCollins.

Bunge, Mario. 1997. Mechanism and Explanation. *Philosophy of the Social Sciences* 27 (4): 410–65.

Bunge, Mario. 2004. How Does It Work? The Search for Explanatory Mechanisms. *Philosophy of the Social Sciences* 34 (2): 182–210.

Burkhart, Ross E., and Michael S. Lewis-Beck. 1994. Comparative Democracy: The Economic Development Thesis. *American Political Science Review* 88 (4): 903–10.

Büthe, Tim. 2002. Taking Temporality Seriously: Modeling History and the Use of Narratives as Evidence. *American Political Science Review* 96 (3): 481–94.

Caldwell, Dan. 1977. Bureaucratic Foreign Policy-Making. *American Behavioral Scientist* 21 (1): 87–110.

Campbell, John L. 2005. *Institutional Change and Globalization.* Princeton: Princeton University Press.

Carr, Edward Hallett. 1961. *What Is History?* London, Penguin.

Casillas, Christopher J., Peter K. Enns, and Patrick C. Wohlfarth. 2009. How Public Opinion Constrains the U.S. Supreme Court. *American Journal of Political Science* 55 (1): 74–88.

Chalmers, A. F. 1999. *What Is This Thing Called Science?* Buckingham: Open University Press.

Checkel, Jeffrey T. 2005. International Institutions and Socialization in Europe: Introduction and Framework. *International Organization* 59 (4): 801–26.

Checkel, Jeffrey T. 2008. Tracing Causal Mechanisms. *International Studies Review* 8 (2): 362–70.

Checkel, Jeffrey T. 2012. Theoretical Synthesis in IR: Possibilities and Limits. In *Sage Handbook of International Relations,* 2nd ed., ed. Walter Carlsnaes, Thomas Risse, and Beth Simmons. London: Sage.

Christiansen, Thomas, and Knud Erik Jørgensen. 1999. The Amsterdam Process: A Structurationist Perspective on EU Treaty Reform. *European Integration online Papers* (EIoP) 3 (1). http://eiop.or.at/eiop/texte/1999-1a.htm.

Christiansen, Thomas, and Christine Reh. 2009. *Constitutionalizing the European Union.* Basingstoke: Palgrave Macmillan.

Clifford, J. Garry. 1990. Bureaucratic Politics. *Journal of American History* 77 (1): 161–68.

Coleman, James. 1990. *Foundations of Social Theory.* Cambridge: Harvard University Press.

Collier, David. 1993. The Comparative Method. In *Political Science: The State of the Discipline II,* ed. Ada W. Finifter, 105–19. Washington, DC: American Political Science Association.

Collier, David. 1995. Translating Quantitative Methods for Qualitative Researchers: The Case of Selection Bias. *American Political Science Review* 89 (2): 461–66.

Collier, David, Henry E. Brady, and Jason Seawright. 2010a. Critiques, Responses, and Trade-Offs: Drawing Together the Debate. In *Rethinking Social Inquiry: Diverse Tools, Shared Standards,* 2nd ed., ed. Henry E. Brady and David Collier, 135–60. Lanham, MD: Rowman and Littlefield.

Collier, David, Henry E. Brady, and Jason Seawright. 2010b. Sources of Leverage in Causal Inference: Toward an Alternative View of Methodology. In *Rethinking Social Inquiry: Diverse Tools, Shared Standards,* 2nd ed., ed. Henry E. Brady and David Collier, 161–200. Lanham, MD: Rowman and Littlefield.

Collier, David, and Steven Levitsky. 1997. Democracy with Adjectives: Conceptual Innovation in Comparative Research. *World Politics* 49 (3): 430–51.

Collier, David, and James Mahoney. 1996. Research Note: Insights and Pitfalls: Selection Bias in Qualitative Research. *World Politics* 49 (1): 56–91.

Day, Timothy, and Harold Kincaid. 1994. Putting Inference to the Best Explanation in Its Place. *Synthese* 98 (2): 271–95.

Dion, Douglas. 1998. Evidence and Inference in the Comparative Case Study. *Comparative Politics* 30 (1): 127–45.

Doyle, A. Conan. 1892. *The Adventures of Sherlock Holmes.* London: Newnes.

Doyle, A. Conan. 1975. *The Memoirs of Sherlock Holmes.* London: Newnes.

Doyle, A. Conan. 2010. A Study in Scarlet. In *The Complete Sherlock Holmes: All 4 Novels and 56 Short Stories,* 1–51. New York: Doubleday.

Doyle, Michael. 1983. Kant, Liberal Legacies, and Foreign Affairs. *Philosophy and Public Affairs* 12 (3): 205–35.

Doyle, Michael. 1986. Liberalism and World Politics. *American Political Science Review* 80 (4): 1151–69.

Dunleavy, Patrick. 1991. Democracy, Bureaucracy, and Public Choice. London: Harvester Wheatsheaf.

Dyson, Kenneth, and Kevin Featherstone. 1999. *The Road to Maastricht: Negotiating Economic and Monetary Union.* Oxford: Oxford University Press.

Eckstein, Harry. 1975. Case Study and Theory in Political Science. In *Strategies of Inquiry,* ed. Fred I. Greenstein and Nelson W. Polsby, 79–138. Reading, MA: Addison-Wesley.

Elman, Colin. 2004. Extending Offensive Realism: The Louisiana Purchase and America's Rise to Regional Hegemony. *American Political Science Review* 98 (4): 563–76.

Elman, Colin, and Miriam Fendius Elman. 2001. Introduction: Negotiating International History and Politics. In *Bridges and Boundaries: Historians, Political Scientists, and the Study of International Relations,* ed. Colin Elman and Miriam Fendius Elman, 1–36. Cambridge: MIT Press.

Elster, Jon. 1983. *Explaining Technical Change: A Case Study in the Philosophy of Science.* Cambridge: Cambridge University Press.

Elster, Jon. 1998. A Plea for Mechanisms. In *Social Mechanisms,* ed. P. Hedström and R. Swedberg, 45–73. Cambridge: Cambridge University Press.

English, Robert D. 1997. Sources, Methods, and Competing Perspectives on the End of the Cold War. *Diplomatic History* 21 (2): 283–94.

Erslev, K. R. 1963. *Historisk Teknik: Den Historiske Undersøgelse Fremstillet I sine Grundlier.* Copenhagen: Gyldendalske Boghandel.

Epstein, David, and Sharyn O'Halloran. 1994. Administrative Procedures, Information, and Agency Discretion. *American Journal of Political Science* 38 (3): 697–722.

Evans, Peter. 1995. The Role of Theory in Comparative Politics. *World Politics* 48 (1): 3–10.

Falleti, Tulia G., and Julia F. Lynch. 2009. Context and Causal Mechanisms in Political Analysis. *Comparative Political Studies* 42 (9): 1143–66.

Farber, Henry S., and Joanne Gowa. 1997. Common Interests or Common Polities? Reinterpreting the Democratic Peace. *Journal of Politics* 59 (2): 393–417.

Finkel, Steven E., Aníbal S. Pérez-Líñan, and Mitchell A. Seligson. 2007. The Effects of U.S. Foreign Assistance on Democracy Building, 1990–2003. *World Politics* 59 (3): 404–40.

Fischer, David Hackett. 1970. *Historians' Fallacies: Toward a Logic of Historical Thought.* New York: Harper Perennial.

Ford, Harold P. 1998. *CIA and the Vietnam Policymakers: Three Episodes, 1962–1968.* Washington DC: Center for the Study of Intelligence.

Freedman, David A. 1991. Statistical Models and Shoe Leather. *Sociological Methodology* 21:291–313.

Freedman, David A. 2011. On Types of Scientific Inquiry: The Role of Qualitative Reasoning. In *Rethinking Social Inquiry: Diverse Tools, Shared Standards,* 2nd ed., ed. Henry E. Brady and David Collier, 221–36. Lanham, MD: Rowman and Littlefield.

Friedrichs, Jörg, and Friedrich Kratochwill. 2009. On Acting and Knowing: How Pragmatism Can Advance International Relations Theory and Methodology. *International Organization* 63 (4): 701–31.

Gaddis, John Lewis. 1972. *The United States and the Origins of the Cold War.* Ithaca: Cornell University Press.

Gaddis, John Lewis. 1992–93. International Relations Theory and the End of the Cold War. *International Security* 17 (3): 5–58.

George, Alexander L., and Andrew Bennett. 2005. *Case Studies and Theory Development in the Social Sciences.* Cambridge: MIT Press.

Gerring, John. 2005. Causation: A Unified Framework for the Social Sciences. *Journal of Theoretical Politics* 17 (2): 163–98.

Gerring, John. 2006. Single-Outcome Studies: A Methodological Primer. *International Sociology* 21 (5): 707–34.

Gerring, John. 2007a. *Case Study Research.* Cambridge: Cambridge University Press.

Gerring, John. 2007b. The Mechanismic Worldview: Thinking inside the Box. *British Journal of Political Science* 38 (1): 161–79.

Gerring, John. 2010. Causal Mechanisms: Yes But . . . *Comparative Political Studies* 43 (11): 1499–1526.

Gheciu, Alexandra. 2005. Security Institutions as Agents of Socialization? NATO and the "New Europe." *International Organization* 59 (4): 973–1012.

Gill, Christopher, Lora Sabin, and Christopher Schmid. 2005. Why Clinicians Are Natural Bayesians. *British Medical Journal* 330 (7499): 1080–83.

Gill, Jeff, and Lee D. Walker. 2005. Elicited Priors for Bayesian Model Specifications in Political Science Research. *Journal of Politics* 67 (3): 841–72.

Gilpin, Robert. 1981. *War and Change in World Politics.* Cambridge: Cambridge University Press.

Glennan, Stuart S. 1996. Mechanisms and the Nature of Causation. *Erkenntnis* 44 (1): 49–71.

Glennan, Stuart S. 2002. Rethinking Mechanistic Explanation. *Philosophy of Science* 69: 342–53.

Glennan, Stuart S. 2005. Modeling Mechanisms. *Studies in History and Philosophy of Biological and Biomedical Sciences* 36 (2): 443–64.

Goertz, Gary. 2003. The Substantive Importance of Necessary Condition Hypotheses. In *Necessary Conditions: Theory, Methodology, and Applications,* ed. G. Goertz and H. Starr, 65–94. Lanham, MD: Rowman and Littlefield.

Goertz, Gary. 2006. *Social Science Concepts: A User's Guide.* Princeton: Princeton University Press.

Goertz, Gary, and H. Starr, eds. 2003. *Necessary Conditions: Theory, Methodology, and Applications.* Lanham, MD: Rowman and Littlefield.

Good, L. J. 1991. Weight of Evidence and the Bayesian Likelihood Ratio. In *Use of Statistics in Forensic Science,* ed. C. G. Aitken and D. A. Stoney, 85–106. London: CRC.

Goodin, Robert E., and Charles Tilly, eds. 2006. *The Oxford Handbook of Contextual Political Analysis.* Oxford: Oxford University Press.

Gross, Neil. 2009. A Pragmatist Theory of Social Mechanisms. *American Sociological Review* 74 (3): 358–79.

Hall, Peter A. 2003. Aligning Ontology and Methodology in Comparative Politics. In *Comparative Historical Analysis in the Social Sciences,* ed. James Mahoney and Dietrich Rueschemeyer, 373–406. Cambridge: Cambridge University Press.

Hall, Peter A. 2008. Systematic Process Analysis: When and How to Use It. *European Political Science* 7 (3): 304–17.

Haworth, Claire M., M. J. Wright, M. Luciano, N. G. Martin, E. J. de Geus, C. E. van Beijsterveldt, M. Bartels, D. Posthuma, D. I. Boomsma, O. S. Davis, Y. Kovas, R. P. Corley, J. C. DeFries, J. K. Hewitt, R. K. Olson, S. A. Rhea, S. J. Wadsworth, W. G. Iacono, M. McGue, L. A. Thompson, S. A. Hart, S. A. Petrill, D. Lubinski, and R. Plomin. 2010. The Heritability of General Cognitive Ability Increases Linearly from Childhood to Young Adulthood. *Molecular Psychiatry* 15 (11): 1112–20.

Hedström, Peter, and Richard Swedberg, eds. 1998. *Social Mechanisms: An Analytical Approach to Social Theory.* Cambridge: Cambridge University Press.

Hedström, Peter, and Petri Ylikoski. 2010. Causal Mechanisms in the Social Sciences. *Annual Review of Sociology* 36:49–67.

Hermann, Charles F., Janice Gross Stein, Bengt Sundelius, and Stephen G. Walker. 2001. Resolve, Accept, or Avoid: Effects of Group Conflict on Foreign Policy Decisions. *International Studies Review* 3 (2): 133–68.

Hernes, Gudmund. 1998. Real Virtuality. In *Social Mechanisms: An Analytical Approach to Social Theory,* ed. Peter Hedström and Richard Swedberg, 74–101. Cambridge: Cambridge University Press.

Herrnstein, Richard, and Charles Murray. 1994. *The Bell Curve: Intelligence and Class Structure in America.* New York: Free Press.

Hirschman, Albert. 1970. The Search for Paradigms as a Hindrance to Understanding. *World Politics* 22 (3): 329–43.

Holland, Paul W. 1986. Statistics and Causal Inference. *Journal of the American Statistical Association* 81 (396): 945–60.

Howson, Colin, and Peter Urbach. 2006. *Scientific Reasoning: The Bayesian Approach.* 3rd ed. La Salle, IL: Open Court.

Hume, David. 1975 [1777]. *Enquiries Concerning Human Understanding and Concerning the Principles of Morals.* Oxford: Oxford University Press.

Humphreys, Adam R. C. 2010. The Heuristic Explanation of Explanatory Theories in International Relations. *European Journal of International Relations* 17 (2): 257–77.

Jackman, Simon. 2004. Bayesian Analysis for Political Research. *Annual Review of Political Science* 7:483–505.

Jackson, Patrick T. 2011. *The Conduct of Inquiry in International Relations.* London: Routledge.

Jacobs, Alan. 2004. Governing for the Long-Term: Democratic Politics and Policy Investment. Ph.D. diss., Harvard University, 2004.

Janis, Irving L. 1983. *Groupthink: Psychological Studies of Policy Decisions and Fiascoes.* Boston: Houghton Mifflin.

Jervis, Robert. 2010. *Why Intelligence Fails: Lessons from the Iranian Revolution and the Iraq War.* Ithaca: Cornell University Press.

Jones, Christopher. 2008. Bureaucratic Politics and Organization Process Models. Paper presented at the annual meeting of the ISA, San Francisco, March 26.

Kennedy, Paul. 1988. *The Rise and Fall of Great Powers.* London: Fontana.

Khong, Yuen Foong. 1992. *Analogies at War: Korea, Munich, Dien Bien Phu, and the Vietnam Decisions of 1965*. Princeton: Princeton University Press.

Kincaid, Harold. 1996. *Philosophical Foundations of the Social Sciences*. Cambridge: Cambridge University Press.

King, Gary, Robert O. Keohane, and Sidney Verba. 1994. *Designing Social Inquiry: Scientific Inference in Qualitative Research*. Princeton: Princeton University Press.

Kiser, Edgar. 1996. The Revival of Narrative in Historical Sociology: What Rational Choice Theory Can Contribute. *Politics and Society* 24 (3): 249–71.

König, Thomas. 2005. Measuring and Analysing Positions on European Constitution-Building. *European Union Politics* 6 (3): 259–67.

König, Thomas, and Jonathan B. Slapin. 2006. From Unanimity to Consensus: An Analysis of the Negotiations of the EU's Constitutional Convention. *World Politics* 58 (3): 413–45.

Kramer, Mark. 1990. Remembering the Cuban Missile Crisis: Should We Swallow Oral History? *International Security* 15 (1): 212–16.

Kuhn, Thomas. 1962. *The Structure of Scientific Revolutions*. Chicago: University of Chicago Press.

Kurki, Milja. 2008. *Causation in International Relations: Reclaiming Causal Analysis*. Cambridge: Cambridge University Press.

Lakatos, Imre. 1970. Falsification and the Methodology of Scientific Research Programs. In *Criticism and the Growth of Knowledge*, ed. Imre Lakatos and Allan Musgrave, 91–196. Cambridge: Cambridge University Press.

Larson, Deborah Welch. 2001. Sources and Methods in Cold War History: The Need for a New Theory-Based Archival Approach. In *Bridges and Boundaries: Historians, Political Scientists, and the Study of International Relations*, ed. Colin Elman and Miriam Fendius Elman, 327–50. Cambridge: MIT Press.

Layne, Christopher. 1994. Kant or Cant: The Myth of the Democratic Peace. *International Security* 19 (2): 5–49.

Layne, Christopher. 2006. *The Peace of Illusions: American Grand Strategy from 1940 to the Present*. Ithaca: Cornell University Press.

Lebow, Richard Ned. 2000–2001. Contingency, Catalysts, and International System Change. *Political Science Quarterly* 115 (4): 591–616.

Lebow, Richard Ned. 2001. Social Science and History: Ranchers versus Farmers? In *Bridges and Boundaries: Historians, Political Scientists, and the Study of International Relations*, ed. Colin Elman and Miriam Fendius Elman, 111–36. Cambridge: MIT Press.

Lehtonen, Tiia. 2008. Small States—Big Negotiations: Decision-Making Rules and Small State Influence in EU Treaty Negotiations. Ph.D. diss., European University Institute.

Levy, Jack. 2002. Qualitative Methods in International Relations. In *Evaluating Methodology in International Studies*, ed. Frank P. Harvey and Michael Brecher, 131–60. Ann Arbor: University of Michigan Press.

Lewis-Beck, Michael S., and Mary Stegmaier. 2000. Economic Determinants of Electoral Outcomes. *Annual Review of Political Science* 3:183–219.

Lieberman, Evan S. 2005. Nested Analysis as a Mixed-Method Strategy for Comparative Research. *American Political Science Review* 99 (3): 435–51.

Lijphart, Arend. 1968. *The Politics of Accommodation—Pluralism and Democracy in the Netherlands.* Berkeley: University of California Press.

Lijphart, Arend. 1971. Comparative Politics and the Comparative Method. *American Political Science Review* 65 (3): 682–93.

Little, Daniel. 1996. Causal Explanation in the Social Sciences. *Southern Journal of Philosophy* 34 (S1): 31–56.

Lustick, Ian S. 1996. History, Historiography, and Political Science: Multiple Historical Records and the Problem of Selection Bias. *American Political Science Review* 90 (3): 605–18.

Lynch, Scott M. 2005. Bayesian Statistics. In *The Encyclopedia of Social Measurement,* ed. Kimberly Kempf-Leonard, 135–44. London: Academic.

Machamer, Peter. 2004. Activities and Causation: The Metaphysics and Epistemology of Mechanisms. *International Studies in the Philosophy of Science* 18 (1): 27–39.

Machamer, Peter, Lindley Darden, and Carl F. Craver. 2000. Thinking about Mechanisms. *Philosophy of Science* 67 (1): 1–25.

Mackie, J. L. 1965. Causes and Conditions. *American Philosophical Quarterly* 2 (2): 245–64.

Mahoney, James. 2000. Strategies of Causal Inference in Small-N Analysis. *Sociological Methods Research* 28 (4): 387–424.

Mahoney, James. 2001. Beyond Correlational Analysis: Recent Innovations in Theory and Method. *Sociological Forum* 16 (3): 575–93.

Mahoney, James. 2004. Comparative-Historical Methodology. *Annual Review of Sociology* 30:81–101.

Mahoney, James. 2007. Qualitative Methodology and Comparative Politics. *Comparative Political Studies* 40 (2): 122–44.

Mahoney, James. 2008. Toward a Unified Theory of Causality. *Comparative Political Studies* 41(4–5): 412–36.

Mahoney, James, and Dietrich Rueschemeyer, eds. 2003. *Comparative Historical Analysis in the Social Sciences.* Cambridge: Cambridge University Press.

Marini, Margaret Mooney, and Burton Singer. 1988. Causality in the Social Sciences. *Sociological Methodology* 18:347–409.

Marshall, Monty G., and Keith Jaggers. 2002. The POLITY IV Project: Dataset Users Manual. Available at http://www.systemicpeace.org/polity/polity4.htm.

Mayntz, Renate. 2004. Mechanisms in the Analysis of Social Macro-Phenomena. *Philosophy of the Social Sciences* 34 (2): 237–59.

McAdam, Doug, Sidney Tarrow, and Charles Tilly. 2001. *Dynamics of Contention.* New York: Cambridge University Press.

McAdam, Doug, Sidney Tarrow, and Charles Tilly. 2008. Methods for Measuring Mechanisms of Contention. *Qualitative Sociology* 31 (4): 307–31.

McKeown, Timothy J. 2004. Case Studies and the Limits of the Quantitative Worldview. In *Rethinking Social Inquiry: Diverse Tools, Shared Standards,* 2nd ed., ed. Henry E. Brady and David Collier, 139–68. Lanham, MD: Rowman and Littlefield.

Mearsheimer, John J. 2001. *The Tragedy of Great Power Politics.* New York: Norton.

Michaud, Nelson. 2002. Bureaucratic Politics and the Shaping of Policies: Can We Measure Pulling and Hauling Games? *Canadian Journal of Political Science* 35 (2): 269–300.

Miller, Gary, and Norman Schofield. 2008. The Transformation of the Republican and Democratic Party Coalitions in the U.S. *Perspectives on Politics* 6 (3): 433–50.

Milligan, John D. 1979. The Treatment of a Historical Source. *History and Theory* 18 (2): 177–96.

Moravcsik, Andrew. 1993. Preferences and Power in the European Community: A Liberal Intergovernmentalist Approach. *Journal of Common Market Studies* 31 (4): 473–524.

Moravcsik, Andrew. 1998. *The Choice for Europe.* Ithaca: Cornell University Press.

Moravcsik, Andrew. 1999. A New Statecraft? Supranational Entrepreneurs and International Cooperation. *International Organization* 53 (2): 267–306.

Morton, Rebecca B., and Kenneth C. Williams. 2010. *Experimental Political Science and the Study of Causality: From Nature to the Lab.* Cambridge: Cambridge University Press.

Munck, Gerardo L. 2004. Tools for Qualitative Research. In *Rethinking Social Inquiry: Diverse Tools, Shared Standards,* 2nd ed., ed. Henry E. Brady and David Collier, 105–22. Lanham, MD: Rowman and Littlefield.

Nagel, Ernest. 1961. *The Structure of Science: Problems in the Logic of Scientific Explanation.* New York: Harcourt, Brace, and World.

Nicholson, Michael. 2002. Formal Methods in International Relations. In *Evaluating Methodology in International Studies,* ed. Frank P. Harvey and Michael Brecher, 23–42. Ann Arbor: University of Michigan Press.

Oneal, John R. 1988. The Rationality of Decision Making during International Crises. *Polity* 20 (4): 598–622.

Oneal, John R., Bruce Russett, and Michael L. Berbaum. 2004. Causes of Peace: Democracy Interdependence and International Organizations, 1885–1992. *International Studies Quarterly* 47 (3): 371–93.

Owen, John M. 1994. How Liberalism Produces Democratic Peace. *International Security* 19 (2): 87–125.

Owen, John M. 1997. *Liberal Peace, Liberal War: American Politics and International Security.* Ithaca: Cornell University Press.

Parsons, Craig. 2007. *How to Map Arguments in Political Science.* Oxford: Oxford University Press.

Peceny, Mark, Caroline C. Beer, and Shannon Sanchez-Terry. 2002. Dictatorial Peace? *American Political Science Review* 96 (1): 15–26.

Peirce, C. S. 1955. *Philosophical Writings of Peirce.* Ed. J. Buchler. New York: Dover.

Peters, B. Guy. 1995. *The Politics of Bureaucracy.* 4th ed. White Plains, NY: Longman.

Peters, B. Guy. 1998. Managing Horizontal Government: The Politics of Co-Ordination. *Public Administration* 76 (2): 295–311.

Pierson, Paul. 2003. Big, Slow-Moving, and . . . Invisible: Macrosocial Processes in the Study of Comparative Politics. In *Comparative Historical Analysis in the Social Sciences,* ed. James Mahoney and D. Rueschemayer, 177–207. Cambridge: Cambridge University Press.

Pierson, Paul. 2004. *Politics in Time: History Institutions and Social Analysis.* Princeton: Princeton University Press.

Pollack, Mark. 2003. *The Engines of European Integration.* Oxford: Oxford University Press.

Preston, Thomas, and Paul t'Hart. 1999. Understanding and Evaluating Bureaucratic Politics: The Nexus between Political Leaders and Advisory Systems. *Political Psychology* 20 (1): 49–98.

Przeworski, Adam, and Henry Teune. 1970. *The Logic of Comparative Social Inquiry.* New York: Wiley.

Ragin, Charles C. 1988. The Comparative Method: Moving beyond Qualitative and Quantitative Strategies. Berkeley: University of California Press.

Ragin, Charles C. 2000. *Fuzzy-Set Social Science.* Chicago: University of Chicago Press.

Ragin, Charles C. 2008. *Redesigning Social Inquiry: Fuzzy Sets and Beyond.* Chicago: University of Chicago Press.

Reskin, Barbara F. 2003. Including Mechanisms in Our Models of Ascriptive Inequality. *American Sociological Review* 68 (1): 1–21.

Rihoux, Benoît. 2006. Qualitative Comparative Analysis (QCA) and Related Systematic Comparative Methods. *International Sociology* 21 (5): 679–706.

Roberts, Clayton. 1996. *The Logic of Historical Explanation.* University Park: Pennsylvania State University Press.

Rohlfing, Ingo. 2008. What You See and What You Get: Pitfalls and Principles of Nested Analysis in Comparative Research. *Comparative Political Studies* 41 (11): 1492–1514.

Rosati, Jerel A. 1981. Developing a Systematic Decision-Making Perspective: Bureaucratic Politics in Perspective. *World Politics* 33 (2): 234–52.

Rosato, Sebastian. 2003. The Flawed Logic of Democratic Peace Theory. *American Political Science Review* 97 (4): 585–602.

Rubach, Timothy J. 2010. "Let Me Tell the Story Straight On": *Middlemarch,* Process-Tracing Methods, and the Politics of the Narrative. *British Journal of Politics and International Relations* 12 (4): 477–97.

Rueschemeyer, Dietrich. 2003. Can One or a Few Cases Yield Theoretical Gains? In *Comparative Historical Analysis in the Social Sciences,* ed. James Mahoney and D. Rueschemeyer, 305–37. Cambridge: Cambridge University Press.

Russett, Bruce, and Steve Oneal. 2001. *Triangulating Peace: Democracy, Interdependence, and International Organizations.* New York: Norton.

Salmon, Wesley. 1998. *Causality and Explanation.* Oxford: Oxford University Press.

Sanday, Peggy Reeves. 1981. *Female Power and Male Dominance: On the Origins of Sexual Inequality.* Cambridge: Cambridge University Press.

Sartori, Giovanni. 1970. Concept Misformation in Comparative Politics. *American Political Science Review* 64 (4): 1033–53.

Sawyer, R. Keith. 2004. The Mechanisms of Emergence. *Philosophy of the Social Sciences* 34 (2): 260–82.

Schimmelfennig, Frank. 2001. The Community Trap: Liberal Norms, Rhetorical Action, and the Eastern Enlargement of the European Union. *International Organization* 55 (1): 47–80.

Schroeder, Paul. 1994. Historical Reality vs. Neo-Realist Theory. *International Security* 19 (1): 108–48.

Schultz, Kenneth A. 2001. *Democracy and Coercive Diplomacy.* Cambridge: Cambridge University Press.

Seawright, Jason. 2002. Testing for Necessary and/or Sufficient Causation: Which Cases Are Relevant? *Political Analysis* 10 (2): 178–93.

Seawright, Jason, and David Collier. 2010. Glossary. In *Rethinking Social Inquiry: Diverse Tools, Shared Standards,* 2nd ed., ed. Henry E. Brady and David Collier, 313–60. Lanham, MD: Rowman and Littlefield.

Sil, Rudra, and Peter J. Katzenstein. 2010. *Beyond Paradigms: Analytical Eclecticism in the Study of World Politics.* Basingstoke: Palgrave Macmillan.

Skocpol, Theda. 1979. *States and Social Revolutions: A Comparative Analysis of France, Russia, and China.* Cambridge: Cambridge University Press.

Steel, Daniel. 2004. Social Mechanisms and Causal Inference. *Philosophy of the Social Sciences* 34 (1): 55–78.

Stinchcombe, Arthur L. 1991. The Conditions of Fruitfulness of Theorizing about Mechanisms in Social Science. *Philosophy of the Social Sciences* 21 (3): 367–88.

Streek, Wolfgang, and Kathleen Thelen, eds. 2005. *Beyond Continuity: Institutional Change in Advanced Political Economies.* Oxford: Oxford University Press.

Strøm, Kaare. 2000. Delegation and Accountability in Parliamentary Democracies. *European Journal of Political Research* 37 (3): 261–89.

Tallberg, Jonas. 2006. *Leadership and Negotiation in the European Union: The Power of the Presidency.* Cambridge: Cambridge University Press.

Tannenwald, Nina. 1999. The Nuclear Taboo: The United States and the Normative Basis of Nuclear Non-Use. *International Organization* 53 (3): 433–68.

Tannenwald, Nina. 2005. Ideas and Explanations: Advancing the Theoretical Agenda. *Journal of Cold War Studies* 7 (2): 13–42.

Tansey, Oisin. 2007. Process Tracing and Elite Interviewing: A Case for Non-Probability Sampling. *PS: Political Science and Politics* 40 (4): 765–72.

Thies, Cameron G. 2002. A Pragmatic Guide to Qualitative Historical Analysis and the Study of International Relations. *International Studies Perspectives* 3 (4): 351–72.

Tilly, Charles. 1995. To Explain Political Processes. *American Journal of Sociology* 100 (6): 1594–1610.

Tilly, Charles. 2004. Social Boundary Mechanisms. *Philosophy of the Social Sciences* 34 (2): 211–36.

Trachtenberg, Marc. 2006. *The Craft of International History.* Princeton: Princeton University Press.

Waldner, David. 1999. *State Building and Late Development.* Ithaca: Cornell University Press.

Waldner, David. 2007. Transforming Inferences into Explanations: Lessons from the Study of Mass Extinctions. In *Theory and Evidence in Comparative Politics and International Relations,* ed. Richard Ned Lebow and Mark Lichbach, 145–76. New York: Palgrave Macmillan.

Waldner, David. 2010. What Are Mechanisms and What Are They Good For? *QMMR Newsletter* 8 (2): 30–34.

Waldner, David. 2012. Process Tracing and Causal Mechanisms. In *The Oxford Handbook of the Philosophy of Social Science,* ed. H. Kincaid, 65–84. Oxford: Oxford University Press.

Walker, Henry A., and Bernard P. Cohen. 1985. Scope Statements: Imperatives for Evaluating Theory. *American Sociological Review* 50 (3): 288–301.

Walker, Vern. 2007. Discovering the Logic of Legal Reasoning. *Hofstra Law Review* 35: 1687–1708.

Waltz, Kenneth N. 1979. *Theory of International Politics.* New York: McGraw-Hill.

Wendt, Alexander. 1999. *Social Theory of International Politics.* Cambridge: Cambridge University Press.

Western, Bruce. 1999. Bayesian Analysis for Sociologists: An Introduction. *Sociological Methods Research* 28 (7): 7–34.

Western, Bruce, and Simon Jackman. 1994. Bayesian Inference for Comparative Research. *American Political Science Review* 88 (2): 412–23.

White, Timothy J. 2000. Cold War Historiography: New Evidence behind Traditional Typologies. *International Social Science Review* 75 (3–4): 35–46.

Wight, Colin. 2004. Theorizing the Mechanisms of Conceptual and Semiotic Space. *Philosophy of the Social Sciences* 34 (2): 283–99.

Wight, Colin. 2006. *Agents, Structures, and International Relations.* Cambridge: Cambridge University Press.

Williams, William Appleman. 1962. *The Tragedy of American Diplomacy.* New York: Delta.

Wohlforth, William C. 1997. New Evidence on Moscow's Cold War: Ambiguity in Search of Theory. *Diplomatic History* 21 (2): 229–42.

Wood, Elisabeth Jean. 2003. *Insurgent Collective Action and Civil War in El Salvador.* Cambridge: Cambridge University Press.

Van Evera, Stephen. 1997. *Guide to Methods for Students of Political Science.* Ithaca: Cornell University Press.

Yin, Robert K. 2003. *Case Study Research Design and Methods.* Thousand Oaks, CA: Sage.

Ziblatt, Daniel. 2009. Shaping Democratic Practice and the Causes of Electoral Fraud: The Case of Nineteenth-Century Germany. *American Political Science Review* 103 (1): 1–21.

Index